AF378899

READING FAITHFULLY

A volume in the NIU Series in

Slavic, East European, and Eurasian Studies

Edited by Christine D. Worobec

For a list of books in the series, visit our website at cornellpress.cornell.edu.

READING FAITHFULLY

RUSSIAN MODERNIST CRITICISM AND THE MAKING OF DOSTOEVSKY, 1881–1917

LINDSAY CEBALLOS

NORTHERN ILLINOIS UNIVERSITY PRESS
AN IMPRINT OF CORNELL UNIVERSITY PRESS
Ithaca and London

First published 2025 by Cornell University Press

Library of Congress Cataloging-in-Publication Data

Names: Ceballos, Lindsay. author.
Title: Reading faithfully : Russian modernist criticism and the making of Dostoevsky, 1881–1917 / Lindsay Ceballos.
Description: Ithaca : Northern Illinois University Press, an imprint of Cornell University Press, 2025. | Series: Slavic, East European, and Eurasian studies | Includes bibliographical references and index.
Identifiers: LCCN 2024059876 (print) | LCCN 2024059877 (ebook) | ISBN 9781501782756 (hardcover) | ISBN 9781501782763 (epub) | ISBN 9781501782770 (pdf)
Subjects: LCSH: Dostoyevsky, Fyodor, 1821–1881—Criticism and interpretation. | Criticism—Russia. | Russian literature—History and criticism—Theory, etc. | LCGFT: Literary criticism.
Classification: LCC PG3328.Z6 C34 2025 (print) | LCC PG3328.Z6 (ebook) | DDC 891.73/3—dc23
/eng/20250106
LC record available at https://lccn.loc.gov/2024059876
LC ebook record available at https://lccn.loc.gov
/2024059877

CONTENTS

Illustrations

Acknowledgments

I completed this book with support from a grant awarded by the American Council of Learned Societies, a postdoctoral fellowship from the Davis Center at Harvard University, and two grants provided by the Summer Research Laboratory at the University of Illinois Urbana-Champaign. I would also like to thank Lafayette College for awarding me two faculty research grants in 2018, a grant for publishing expenses, and an Excel scholarship that funded my work with Julia Jin-Wolfson.

Versions of two chapters in this book were first published as articles. Chapter 2 is based on "Aryan or Semitic? On the Racial Origins of 'Tolstoy vs. Dostoevsky,'" *Russian Review* 81, no. 2 (April 2022): 247–64. Chapter 5 is based on "The Politics of Dostoevsky's Religion: Nemirovich-Danchenko's 1913 Nikolai Stavrogin," *Slavic and East European Journal* 65, no. 1 (Spring 2021): 21–40. I want to thank the *Russian Review* and *SEEJ* for permission to publish revised versions in this book.

I would like to thank the staff and librarians at the St. Petersburg Theater Library and the Museum of the Moscow Art Theater for their assistance with materials referenced in this book.

Many people helped me write this book. I want to thank my editor, Amy Farranto at NIU-Cornell University Press, for her enthusiasm about my project and help navigating the publishing process. I'm grateful to my colleague and collaborator at Lafayette College, Joshua Sanborn, for his steady mentorship and support of my career. I thank the members of my reading group—Jinyi Chu, D. Brian Kim, Alisa Lin, and Emily Wang—who read every chapter at its roughest and who offered unceasing encouragement. Special thanks go to Emily, who pushed me to apply for grants I thought I could not get, saw the value of my work, and has been the best doctor-sister a person could hope for. Thank you to those who offered encouraging feedback and support over years of drafting and revision, especially Chloë Kitzinger, Paul Contino, and Helen Stuhr-Rommereim. As a doctoral student, I had the good fortune of studying under Caryl Emerson, Olga Peters Hasty, Ellen Chances, Ksana Blank, and Serguei Oushakine. I'm constantly aware of how they shaped my scholarly path. My interest in the Russian language began at Wesleyan University, where I was inspired by the passion of my teachers, Priscilla Meyer, Irina Aleshkovskaya, Duffield White, and Sergei Bunaev. I also studied intellectual history at Wesleyan, where I developed as a writer and thinker thanks to the inspiring teaching of Bruce Masters, Ethan Kleinberg, and Cecilia Miller. I want to express the deepest gratitude to my mentors, Susanne Fusso and Michael Wachtel. Susanne has been my model of a teacher and scholar since I took her course on Russian literature as a sophomore at Wesleyan. Susanne's humanity and brilliance has been a gift to me and so many others fortunate to have studied with her. At Princeton, I was so lucky to work with Michael, whose seminars in Russian poetry taught me to balance analysis with wonder. I'm grateful for his dedicated mentorship throughout graduate school and beyond. He has empowered me to develop as a writer and trust my own ideas. I feel honored to be his student.

My final thanks are for those closest to me. To my parents, Danna Ramquist and Javier Ceballos, and my sister Angel—thank you for supporting what I do. To John Teoli IV—thank you for the love and happiness I needed to finish this book. To my dearest friends, especially Deanne Dworski-Riggs, George Diep, Lyu Azbel', Evan Winter Morse, Rebecca Chávez, and Saara Ratilainen—thank you for believing in me and lifting me up in dark times. This book is dedicated to the memory of my grandmother, Patricia Ramquist.

Abbreviations

Muzei MKhAT Muzei "Moskovskii khudozhestvennyi akademicheskii teatr" (Museum of the Moscow Artistic and Academic Theater)

N.S. New Style (Gregorian calendar)

O.S. Old Style (Julian calendar, used in Russia until 1918). Some dates are given with the abbreviation O.S., or dates are given in both Old and New Styles with Old Style listed first, i.e., November 6/18, 1899. For newspaper citations, assume that the date is O.S. unless otherwise indicated.

Pss *Polnoe sobranie sochinenii* (Complete collected works)

SPbGTB, ORiRK Sankt-peterburgskaia gosudarstvennaia teatral'naia biblioteka (Saint Petersburg State Theater Library); Otdel redkoi knigi, rukopisnykh, arkhivnykh i izobrazitel'nykh materialov (Department of rare books, manuscript, archival and visual materials)

Ss *Sobranie sochinenii* (Collected works)

Note on Transliteration

I use the Library of Congress transliteration system. For frequently referenced first and last names, I use the spelling that is most common in Anglophone contexts, for instance, Dmitry Merezhkovsky instead of Dmitrii Merezhkovskii.

READING FAITHFULLY

Introduction

The Origins of "Two Dostoevskys" and Faithful Reading

In 1906, Russia's intelligentsia found itself commemorating the twenty-fifth anniversary of Fyodor Dostoevsky's death amid revolution. The events of Bloody Sunday, when a priest led a group of workers to the Winter Palace to announce their grievances to the Tsar, only to be fired upon by the imperial guard, had taken place just a year earlier. Workers' strikes and protests were breaking out across Russia. Divided camps of liberals lobbied for a constitutional government while the autocracy crushed dissent and remained resistant to reform. For writers and intellectuals of the so-called Silver Age of Russian culture (1890–1917), characterized by innovation and experiment across the arts and in social and religious thought, the empire's violent display against democratic assembly and faith-based protest assaulted their utopian vision of political transformation through artistic and religious reawakening.

Dostoevsky's religious ideas, especially their more complex representations in novels such as *The Idiot* and *Devils*, had inspired these thinkers, poets, and critics. But it was, plainly, a terrible time to commemorate the death of a writer who had once defended the sacred bonds between the people (*narod*) and the autocrat, whose proclamations that Russia would lead the world to a universal Christian church rang hollow amid an unfolding political crisis, calls for socialist reform, and outrage directed toward the repression of free speech and assembly. But in a time of state violence against the people, some critics still remembered Dostoevsky as the youthful radical who once faced a firing squad before his sentence was commuted. It was about this Dostoevsky that the critic Yurii Aikhenval'd wrote in 1907: "Often when today's all too regular news about capital punishment arrives, one involuntarily recalls what a terrifying moment in [Dostoevsky's] inner world it constituted and how relentlessly he returned to it in his works. . . . He was the only writer to create anything after seeing the world and listening to the soul from the heights of the scaffold."[1] Despite the incompatibility of Dostoevsky's political views and the events of 1905–1906, his insight into human experience, insistence on the necessity of religious faith, and utopian visions continued to hold value.

Indeed, since 1899 Silver Age critics such as Dmitry Merezhkovsky had already begun renegotiating Dostoevsky's politics, preparing the ground for his authoritative role as a religious figure of not reactionary, but revolutionary or at least reformist, potential. By 1906, critics like Sergei Bulgakov, Nikolai Berdiaev, and the Symbolist poet and theoretician Viacheslav Ivanov had helped to transform Dostoevsky into a religious thinker who could rival the still-living, internationally celebrated progressive Lev Tolstoy. These readings were some of the first nuanced, systematic attempts to understand the religious ideas of Dostoevsky's novelistic world, which they understood to be the pathway to understanding his verbal art. They believed that Dostoevsky's religious worldview was Christian, woven from Russian Orthodox culture, but not necessarily subservient to its dogma and the autocratic state that directed its activity. Many of them were once the young readers whom Dostoevsky, toward the end of his life, had hoped to divert from radical politics and to enlist in his call for Christian ecumenicity.

The debate that unfolded during Dostoevsky's 1906 death jubilee was one moment in the history of the "two Dostoevskys" phenomenon, a problem that would persist into the next century of criticism on the writer. This perception assumes that Dostoevsky's fiction was qualitatively different in style and content from his mixed-genre publication, *A Writer's Diary*, in which his support of state power, xenophobia, and imperialist religious commentary are perceived to be most concentrated.[2] This bifurcation of his literary activity into separate categories began the moment obituaries commemorating his death appeared in newspapers, as one from January 1881 evidences: "As in Gogol we see the creator of *The Inspector General* and *Dead Souls*, but not *Correspondence with Friends*;

so also in Dostoevsky we will see only the author of *Poor Folk* and *Notes from the House of the Dead*, having committed to oblivion his activity in the reactionary sphere."[3] In a similar but more ecstatic vein, the most popular poet of the Symbolist era, Konstantin Bal'mont, wrote that, among the best writers, "There are even writers whose souls do not coincide with their poetic image [*oblik*], not for lack of talent or some other affliction, but because they have two faces, and both are sincere. . . . Such, perhaps, is our best writer, the one who sees our hearts [*nash sertseved*], our prophet, Dostoevsky."[4] In later periods, critics would develop more nuanced approaches to unsettling the division of the writer into two writers, which became less obvious the more Dostoevsky's complex and contradictory narrative strategies were better understood.

Reading Faithfully is the story of how the "two Dostoevskys" problem came to a head in the Silver Age, when critics and thinkers began recovering his religious ideas and renegotiating their relationship to his art and politics. Investigating their critical method, I draw on what Eve Kosofsky Sedgwick called "reparative reading" and argue that their reception of Dostoevsky took a special form, which I term "faithful reading." By faithful reading, I describe a hermeneutics that privileges the critic's creative relationship toward the text, which seeks answers outside of the author's biography and resists the critical impulse to reject the text by diagnosing its ideological sins. The term "faith" functions in two ways. In the first place, it describes the actual religious positionality of the critics and thinkers examined in this book, which had a genealogical relationship to Dostoevsky's religious ideas, but that departed from them in generally liberal or even antistatist stances. In the second meaning, "faith" signifies the critics' belief in the constructive, transcendent potential of Dostoevsky's moral-religious worldview toward social change—a fundamentally different critical relationship toward the text based on cocreation and theoretical speculation rather than suspicion.

This reading of Silver Age critics as faithful readers aligns with calls from recent scholars in literary studies, such as Rita Felski and Bruno Latour, who have encouraged their intellectual communities to imagine a future beyond critical suspicion and negation—criticism's methodological arsenal—toward a new postcritical relationship between critic and text.[5] This new relationship would reflect, as one response to Felski's *Limits of Critique* (2015) phrases it, "what [the text] creates in readers, not what it conceals from them."[6] A forum hosted in 2017 by the *PMLA* on responses to *The Limits of Critique* produced a nearly unanimous call to reevaluate the role of negation in critique, "the explicit act of rebuttal, refusal, or rejection" that has come to dominate the mood of critical thinking and discourse.[7] Scholars advocated for different critical moods to counter the impulse to negation, ranging from a focus on constructive and generative potentials, the privileging of "experiences of making to acts of interpretation," and the insistence on nurturing existing "positive affect" in critique.[8] In her book, Felski relates this last critical mood to "a broader 'eudaimonic turn' in literary studies: a disenchantment with disenchantment and a new willingness to embrace such themes as joy, hope, love, optimism, and inspiration."[9] I argue that these reparative affective modes align closely with the religious experience of faith and help to deepen our understanding of the prevailing moods and modes of Silver Age critics.

Most trace the origins of the suspicious mode of criticism to the philosopher Paul Ricoeur's *Freud and Philosophy: An Essay on Interpretation* (1965), in which he argues that Freud, Marx, and Nietzsche "clear the horizon for a more authentic word, for a new reign of Truth, not only by means of a 'destructive' critique, but by the invention of an art of *interpreting*."[10] Indeed, Ricoeur had framed the school of suspicion as a reaction to an earlier critical mood, a "hermeneutics as a restoration of meaning," which expressed not the "first faith of the simple soul, but rather the second faith of one who has engaged in hermeneutics, faith that has undergone criticism, postcritical faith."[11]

This book examines the path to faithful reading in the work of the most prominent critics of the time and particularly of Dostoevsky's work. Such figures included Akim Volynsky, once an influential editor and critic at the *Northern Herald* (Severnyi vestnik); Vasily Rozanov, the eccentric, staunchly conservative cultural commentator and advocate for reform of the Orthodox Church; Dmitry Merezhkovsky, a leading Symbolist poet, internationally acclaimed author of historical novels, and cofounder of the St. Petersburg Religious-Philosophical Society; Sergei Bulgakov, a political economist and former Marxist, who infused Soloviev and Dostoevsky's thought into his journalist attacks on historical materialism and promotion of his movement for Christian socialism; and Viacheslav Ivanov, the eminent poet and Symbolist theoretician, whose ecstatic interpretations of Dostoevsky were less accessible but essential to an understanding of the critical mood of the early twentieth century. In the more public-facing sphere of theater, this was also a time of the first adaptations of Dostoevsky's novels to the stage, all of which had to circumvent the narrative form of the novels and adjust the political and religious themes of the plots to appease the strictest censorial demands of the empire. Russian adaptations of Dostoevsky, as well as critics such as Rozanov, Merezhkovsky, Ivanov, and Bulgakov, each had their own Dostoevskys, in the same way that Dostoevsky himself and subsequent Russian writers had their own Pushkin.

At its most productive, reading faithfully can construct an engaged response to a text; at its worst, it can turn into apology. In the chapters that follow, I provide examples of how faithful reading can serve various political ends, some of them disturbing corruptions of fact and decency. By claiming that Silver Age critics engaged in faithful reading, I seek to understand what their approach to reading a complex, contradictory writer like Dostoevsky says about interpretation that moves beyond skepticism and seeks to generate usable values and paths forward. Interpretation and remaking always create distortions, but they are creative distortions that offer insight into how we think about Dostoevsky's work today and how we could think about it in the future. To quote Sedgwick at the conclusion of her landmark essay on reparative reading, "What we can best learn from such practices are, perhaps, the many ways selves and communities succeed in extracting sustenance from the objects of a culture—even of a culture whose avowed desire has often been not to sustain them."[12] This sentiment fits astonishingly well the experience of Silver Age critics, many of whom turned to Dostoevsky's work as a framework for resisting the very political order that he had once openly defended. I believe a case can be made for why the postcritical turn in literary studies is such a useful lens for revisiting Silver Age critics' faithful reading of Dostoevsky. More broadly, what can historians of Russian criticism, which saw the "birth and death of literary theory," according to Galin Tihanov, learn from the framework of reparative reading?[13]

Finding Religion in the "Two Dostoevskys" Problem

In "The Death of the Author" (1968), when Roland Barthes characterized biographical criticism as the search for the author in "the more or less transparent allegory of the fiction," he was assuming the author is a single, stable person, of whom biographical facts could be collected (or excavated), analyzed, and applied to the interpretation of her work.[14] "When the Author has been found, the text is 'explained'—victory to the critic," wrote Barthes.[15] Felski has termed this approach to reading "digging down"—the critic is a hero, a "valiant archaeologist," and the text is "an object to be plundered, a puzzle to be solved, a hieroglyph to be deciphered."[16] But just after his death, Dostoevsky's biography seemed to reveal not one author but two. His bifurcated self remained a puzzle despite the critical desire to "discover" him, to catch him out. It was the inability to find a single Dostoevsky that helped faithful reading come into existence.

It is unsurprising that biography offered certain challenges to reconciling the author's selves. The eminent biographer of Dostoevsky, Joseph Frank, confessed in the preface to the fifth and final volume of his monumental book, "I found highly unsatisfactory the general notion that, since Dostoevsky's involvement with the ideologies of his time seemed so unsympathetic, it was best either to forget about them or to expatiate on the vast difference between literary creativity and social-political sobriety."[17] Frank's intention was to fuse the literary and the social-political in the writer's work, but other scholars insisted that Frank had not gone far enough in his handling of *A Writer's Diary*, in particular.[18] Prior to the publication of volume five of Frank's *Dostoevsky*, Gary Saul Morson called Frank a "guilty apologist" in response to his unconvincing explanations for Dostoevsky's antisemitism.[19] Morson's book *The Boundaries of Genre: Dostoevsky's* Diary of a Writer *and the Traditions of Literary Utopia* (1981) subverted the recurring scholarly bifurcation of Dostoevsky's art and politics by proposing that the *Diary* was a kind of hybrid literary genre and thus should be viewed as a heterogenous creation with deep roots in his fictional endeavors. This book was a crucial step toward debunking the myth of "two Dostoevskys," but the problem continues to shape recent work, particularly the scholarship dedicated to Dostoevsky's religion.

Leaving aside biography, Dostoevsky's novels alone have caused no shortage of wonder at his politics, however clear they may seem to some. Everything about his prose and plot dynamics suggests two paths at once, an idea Ksana Blank has traced back to Vasily Rozanov, who called him "the best example of a dialectical thinker in our country, and perhaps in all of world literature."[20] Decades later, in his landmark *Problems of Dostoevsky's Poetics* (1929), Mikhail Bakhtin distilled an even more comprehensive theory out of Rozanov's observation of such dynamics: Dostoevsky had discovered the "polyphonic novel," in which the author gives way to the autonomous voices of his characters and thus calls his own authority over the meaning of the work into question. This theory has provided generations of scholars with a rich approach to understanding Dostoevsky's poetics, but Bakhtin's theory has encouraged some to connect the phenomenon of multivoicedness (heteroglossia) in the novels to Dostoevsky's ambivalent politics. Stephen Carter, who has written on Dostoevsky's political and social thought in the context of the polemical antisocialist novel *Devils*, has noted the tendency to accept too readily Bakhtin's "polyphony" as "politically indeterminate," writing that "Dostoevsky draws his characters and their interrelationships as embodiments of, and dialectic between, ideas," quoting Bakhtin in *Problems*: "It is futile to seek in it (Dostoevsky's world-outlook -SC) a systematic monological finalisedness, even of a dialectical nature, not because the author failed to achieve it, but because it was not part of his intention."[21] This assumption—that Dostoevsky's poetics are not integrated with his political ideology or guiding moral idea by design—drove a bigger wedge between readers' perceptions of two authorial personas: "the artist" and "the idealogue."

Since the "two Dostoevskys" problem has mostly corresponded to the "artist vs. reactionary" bifurcation, the writer's religious views are occasionally left in an ambivalent position. To which of the Dostoevskys should we assign his religious ideas? In his important review article, Morson's phrasing assumes, as many Silver Age critics did and I would argue most scholars now do, that the artistic category encompasses the religious ideas in Dostoevsky's work. This assumption is clear when Morson refers to the problem as an issue of reconciling "the subtle, compassionate novelist and the neurotic, chauvinist idealogue."[22] This view of the artist as "compassionate" (i.e., moral) and the reactionary as unsociable, even shameful, aligns with a broader tendency in scholarship to locate Dostoevsky outside the establishment of state Orthodoxy, either folk tradition or the system of eldership (*starchestvo*), exemplified by his portrayal of Father Zosima in *The Brothers Karamazov*.[23] It is commonly accepted that Dostoevsky's Christianity was personal, culturally rooted to Orthodoxy and the *demos*, but extremely heterodox and at times reliant on folk or pagan belief—all features of his faith that to some scholars have demonstrated his overcoming of state Orthodoxy toward an ecumenical Christian idea. Such a reading has also made him appealing to secular readers around the world. Indeed, the Russian people (*narod*) practiced an "unofficial" Orthodoxy, marked by such phenomena as double faith (*dvoeverie*), but this fact should not confirm a view of Dostoevsky's Christian heterodoxy as exhibiting a latent antiauthoritarian tendency.[24] In a different essay, Morson points out that Dostoevsky's preferred version of the Holy Trinity was antihierarchical and prone to emphasize the lateral position of Christ the Son vis-à-vis human beings: "The God who foreknows all—God the Father—has little, and grudging, place in Dostoevsky's Christianity. Rather, he stresses the Son, who participated in history and suffered with us, and, in *The Brothers Karamazov*, the Holy Spirit, which does indeed intervene in the world. Dostoevsky's is a strange heresy, which to my knowledge never developed a name: stressing both the second and third persons of the Trinity at the expense of the first."[25] It may have been the case that Dostoevsky's faith was personal and antiestablishment, but such a conclusion does not negate the possibility that Dostoevsky could be simultaneously an unorthodox believer *and* supportive of the autocratic state. As we will see, this question of Dostoevsky's relationship to the official church and the autocracy was an ongoing anxiety for Silver Age critics, but it fueled their creative criticism about him.

Finally, it should be noted that the Formalist claim to scientific rigor in analyzing literary works helped drive the two Dostoevskys further apart. Formalists and associated groups, like the Dostoevsky seminar led by the eminent scholar A. L. Bem in Prague in the 1920s and 1930s, focused only on the literary-historical genesis and technical aspects of the writer's artistic (*khudozhestvennyi*) texts. While in 1935 Bem insisted that his group's method "[did] not mean that the personality of the great writer and the ideological side of his work has been completely ignored," he nevertheless framed his group's concentration on "artistic" texts as a departure from Silver Age critics such as Merezhkovsky, Bulgakov, Rozanov, and Ivanov, among others, who had attempted to create a new author from the text.[26]

These scholarly approaches placed religion in an unsettled position with regard to Dostoevsky's fictional practice and political beliefs. In a way, the "strange heresy" that Morson identifies in Dostoevsky's understanding of the Trinity parallels the scholarly problem of fully reconciling the three dimensions of Dostoevsky's unified body of work: art, politics, and religion. Since the collapse of the Soviet Union, Russophone and Anglophone scholars have become more interested in Dostoevsky's religion, and it is common to encounter a conflation of his art and moral-religious views, with both considered separate from his political worldview.[27] In other words, his religious ideas have become absorbed into "Dostoevsky the artist."[28] Due to their unique confessional identity, it was Silver Age thinkers and critics who first truly grappled with the unsettled position of religion with regard to political and artistic considerations of the author's work.[29] Faithful reading arose in response to the sterile methods of interpreting Dostoevsky that began appearing right after his death, when literary compilations and edited volumes by and on the author began reaching the public. I will now turn to this scholarly landscape just prior to Silver Age critical work.

From Biographical Criticism to Faithful Reading

Recollections of Dostoevsky and commentaries about his life and work began appearing almost immediately after his death. The author's closest friends and literary associates, Nikolai Strakhov, and O. F. Miller, the writer's first biographer and a mentor of sorts to a young Dmitry Merezhkovsky, were chief among such contributions. Their efforts produced *Biography, Letters, and Remarks from the Notebook of F. M. Dostoevsky* (1883), which warned its reader that "it goes without saying that one can use Dostoevsky's novels as sources for his biography only with the greatest of caution," a statement intended as a response to literary historians and critics such as N. N. Bulich.[30] In 1881, Bulich had argued that future scholars should read characters in Dostoevsky's works as emblematic of their times but also "with regard to the circumstances of the writer's life and his inner world, with regard to his soul, which was burdened and fractured by the impressions of contemporary life."[31] Rather than advocating for this biographical approach, Miller and Strakhov produced materials of an encyclopedic, informational nature. Both men were close personal friends of Dostoevsky, which perhaps helped them resist the allure of finding answers to the texts in the author's biography or reading the novels as biographical fact. Thus, Strakhov wrote in his own reminiscences, "In these and in the following notes, the reader should not see an attempt to portray in full the deceased writer; I directly and decidedly refuse to do this."[32] In the 1890s, journal publications such as the *Russian Review* (Russkoe obozrenie) aligned with his rather archival approach, printing materials relevant to the biography of the deceased writer. There seemed to be a desire to know more about Dostoevsky's life without directly assuming that knowledge so gleaned would ensure the ability to explain his texts.[33]

It is natural to question whether Strakhov's own ideological commitments and personal feelings for Dostoevsky compelled him to eschew criticism in favor of simple documentation. Many years later, the critic Viktor Shklovsky would accuse Strakhov and Miller of turning Dostoevsky into a mouthpiece for their own conservative views, setting readers back decades in grappling with the writer's complex work. "It is time to understand Dostoevsky: to break the chain fettering the living Dostoevsky to repudiated corpses," Shklovsky wrote, with reference to the long-dead architects of the writer's legacy.[34] But going into the 1890s, the writer's friends could not forestall the suspicious tendencies of biographical criticism, which was coming under the influence of the emerging field of psychopathology.[35]

The year 1885 saw the appearance of Vasily Zelinskii's *Historical Critical Commentary to the Works of F. M. Dostoevsky*, an early attempt to create a chronological record of the most notable criticism on Dostoevsky's work toward "an objective comparison of different critical reviews on him."[36] The first of three volumes (the last was published in 1886), each major section was devoted to a novel, with footnotes on publication history and excerpts from reviews published since its debut, spanning the decades up to contemporary criticism. A unique feature of this publication is a list of characters from each of the major novels—such as *Devils* and *The Brothers Karamazov*—who are described using excerpts from some of the same critics. The organization of this section creates the illusion of scholarly attention to the artistic work rather than the writer's life. However, one of the most well-known contemporary commentators included in Zelinskii's publication was Dr. Vladimir Chizh, author of *Dostoevsky as a Psychopathologist* (Dostoevskii kak psikhopatolog). Chizh had little interest in the artistic merit of the novels and contributed nothing to the dominant critical conversation initiated by Vladimir Soloviev, a philosopher and close friend of Dostoevsky, about the core religious "social ideal" in Dostoevsky's textual afterlife. James Rice once confirmed Chizh's limited psychopathological lens when he noted that *Devils*, which was later hailed as Dostoevsky's most religious novel by the religious-philosophical and Symbolist critics, "remained the most resistant to [Chizh's] medical understanding."[37] Indeed, Chizh had insisted that a single lens would dominate his approach. "I will mainly look at Dostoevsky not as a novelist," he wrote, "but as a first-hand witness [*neposredstvennyi opisatel'*] of reality."[38] In his book, Chizh attended to how psychological types reflected real trends in psychopathological study, often speculating about the role of Dostoevsky's own psychology and medical struggle with epilepsy in his fiction. Of course, this sort of approach to biographical criticism was exactly what the editors of *Biography, Letters, and Remarks* had cautioned against. Chizh's approach was quintessentially suspicious in nature, aimed at unearthing the author's real-life medical conditions in the fictional works.

These earliest attempts to systematically understand Dostoevsky's complete work as a straightforward corpus that spoke primarily to psychological patterns of human experience more broadly did not resonate with the generation of critics writing in the Silver Age. Their intellectual antecedent was Soloviev, who, years previously, had inaugurated an expansive reading of Dostoevsky's religious ideas. Soloviev declared him a prophet of the "social ideal of brotherhood or universal solidarity," as he put it in his *Three Speeches in Dostoevsky's Memory* (1881–1883), a role that for him overcame the writer's nationalism and allegiance to the autocrat.[39] The two men had been quite close; Soloviev is believed to have been the inspiration behind Alyosha Karamazov, the angelic hero of *The Brothers Karamazov*. In his *Three Speeches*, Soloviev insisted that Dostoevsky's religion was universal in its ambitions in a way that ultimately made state authority subject to the higher power of a unified future church. Soloviev insisted that Dostoevsky had acknowledged the "religious-moral, and not national significance" of the unifying brotherhood that the church would bring to all peoples.[40] In Soloviev's utopian vision, Dostoevsky's art, which had been spiritualized by its search for a binding religious idea, superseded his malignant nationalist politics and fidelity to the autocratic state.

Drawn to this rosier characterization of Dostoevsky's messianism via Soloviev, Silver Age critics rejected encyclopedic, biographical, and psychopathological approaches to his work, generating critical moods that resonate with more recent scholarly speculation about postcritical futures. Eve Kosofsky Sedgwick's classic essay "Paranoid Reading and Reparative Reading, or, You're So Paranoid, You Probably Think This Essay Is about You" teases out affective fields of reparative reading that resonate with those available to religious believers such as those among Silver Age critics. Following Ricoeur, Sedgwick addressed the fear out of which suspicious, or what she called "paranoid," reading arose, prompting her to advocate for an alternative, "reparative" hermeneutics. It will be seen that Silver Age critics were regularly drawn to the gnarled psychological and religious themes of Dostoevsky's work. Their aversion to seeking clarity in the illuminating potential of the suspicious gaze and preference for grasping at transcendent possibilities in the darkness of self-annihilation and violence parallels what Sedgwick observed in the work of psychoanalyst Melanie Klein (1882–1960). Based on observations of human subjects, Klein isolated two fundamental "positions": a paranoid one and a depressive one. The paranoid position is characterized by a "terrible alertness" to "part-objects that one defensively projects into . . . from the world around one."[41] This position is a good corollary to the critic's vigilance over the dubious critical object. The depressive position, however, which we can compare with Silver Age criticism's faithful reading and which illustrates Sedgwick's reparative reading, is one "from which it is possible in turn to use one's own resources to assemble or 'repair' the murderous part-objects into something like a whole—though, I would emphasize, *not necessarily like any preexisting whole.* Once assembled to one's own specifications, the more satisfying object is available both to be identified with and to offer one nourishment and comfort in turn. Among Klein's names for the reparative process is love."[42] The paranoid position builds a feedback loop of alienation and anxiety, whereas the depressive one constructs a world that can be lived in out of part-objects that once harmed but that now can potentially heal. But as Sedgwick specifies, the wholeness of the created world is "not necessarily like any preexisting whole." In the same way, the Dostoevsky created in the Silver Age was a compilation, a technically unfaithful rendering of an original crafted by faithful reading.

The contemporary critic who comes closest to a postcritical reading of Dostoevsky is Carol Apollonio, whose *Dostoevsky's Secrets* launches an "apophatic approach to interpretation." Drawing on the core idea of negative theology, which proposes that we can know God only by cataloguing what and where He is *not*, Apollonio proposes that readers of Dostoevsky "look beyond the primitive logic of external appearances" and "move beyond deconstructive approaches that dismantle the text to reveal only disorder, chaos, oppression, and the death of the author."[43] The meaning of the text, she writes, can be located in the *"literary* facts" and rhetorical "sins of language"—the swirling falsehoods and self-contradictory monologues of his garrulous characters—not in real-world antecedents or the biography of the author who created them.[44] She poses a provocative question and provides a discomfiting answer, but the question is in line with her insistence on the primacy of the literary text: "How did this anti-Semitic, warmongering, male supremacist Russian imperialist happen to produce these powerful works? It doesn't seem fair, it doesn't make sense, and it doesn't matter."[45] Drawing on Sedgwick's critique of paranoid reading, we might respond that the recovery of deeper truths in Dostoevsky's fiction and his participation in oppressive systems are not mutually exclusive but the necessary "crucible" of reparative reading: they are the "murderous part-objects" that must be wrangled into a new whole. A reparative reading aims to find an integral reading, one that Sedgwick noted is not "like any preexisting whole."[46] This abstract description of the process of reparative reading is not the critic's cynical cherry-picking of evidence from texts and amalgamating of them into an integrated fallacy. Because the critic builds this whole with devotion—what Sedgwick called "love" and what I label "faith"—it becomes more than simple apologia and alien to the moods of suspicion and negation. By this process, critics of the Silver Age evolved Dostoevsky into their comparably more progressive era—it is the same challenge facing us today as we teach and write about Dostoevsky in the aftermath of Russia's prolonged war in Ukraine and the warranted connections that Ukrainian intellectuals have made between Dostoevsky's writings and the deeds of the current Russian state.[47]

Sedgwick early on addressed concerns that paranoid reading, associated with a politics of struggle and a healthy, critical gaze, would make reparative reading by comparison "seem naïve, pious, or complaisant."[48] Indeed, this characterization of "suspicious/paranoid" and "restorative/reparative" reading as occupying respective "left" or "right" political positions remains a concern among scholars of the postcritical turn. In their book *Critique and Postcritique*, Elizabeth Anker and Felski explain that there is a risk that calls for postcritique represent a variety of political apathy or even "an ominous sign of defeatism, exemplifying a failure of nerve on the part of intellectuals who are no longer prepared to embrace the role of gadflies and oppositional figures."[49] But they insist, as did Sedgwick, that postcritique is neither apathetic nor apolitical. Rather, postcritique is "more willing to avow the creative, innovative, world-making aspects of literature and criticism."[50] Concluding his seminal essay "Why Has Critique Run Out of Steam" (2004), Bruno Latour accordingly redefined the critic's aspirations: "The critic is not the one who debunks, but the one who assembles. The critic is not the one who lifts the rugs from under the naïve believers, but the one who offers the participants arenas in which to gather."[51] Silver Age critics sought to create such an arena.

These thinkers and critics related to their objects from a reparative stance, a position enabled by their own investments in Russian religious culture and personal spirituality: an author with conservative political views and a complex religious background was approached not with suspicion but with an eye to creating a new constituted whole of ideas and futures. Their criticism—of literary-scientific value but also deeply entrenched in social, religious, and political questions—modeled a complex field of knowing and being that could not be reduced to systems ("Christian" or "anarchist") or empirically evaluated. However, in replotting Dostoevsky's world of ideas and integrating his texts into a social-religious project, their thinking conjured utopias rather than constructed assemblies, to borrow terms from Latour's postcritical argument. Among the many questions explored hereafter, a few predominate: Are the faithful worlds read into being by Silver Age critics still with us, and, if so, do they constitute more than naïve belief? Are they instructive for today's readers of Dostoevsky and those who produce critical work on writers with abhorrent political associations or views? Is there a critical path beyond unmasking and beyond blind faith?

The Structure of This Book

The chapters of this book offer a historical narrative sketching the emergence of faithful reading of Dostoevsky that began in the wake of his death and coincided with the unraveling of the Russian Empire, whose acceleration into collapse was its entry into the First World War. Providing context for the key interventions of Silver Age criticism in Dostoevsky's cultural reception, chapter 1, "Adapting *The Idiot* and *Crime and Punishment*, 1890–1900," reviews the state of the writer's symbolic value in the decade just after his death and through the 1890s, before critics began taking an interest in the author's religious ideas. This chapter introduces one of the main hermeneutical approaches of this period, the *peredelka* (literally, "remaking"), or theatrical adaptation. To call a play version of a novel a "remaking" implies the coexistence of primary and secondary authorship. The term also signifies a new perspective or frame of mind, making room for the power of interpretation to transform ideological, cultural, or artistic style into a renegotiated version of its previous self. A remaking thus exists in a curious temporal zone, reflecting the past original and the present form it acquires, which permits it a measure of creative autonomy. Accounting for archival playscripts of the earliest adaptations of *Crime and Punishment* and *The Idiot*, many of which did not pass the censor and were never staged, this chapter shows how the censorship regime and the conservative reading of Dostoevsky as a supporter of the autocracy dominated stage adaptations of his works and guided his public reception. Even in doing so, the theatrical "remakings" of 1890s adapters show how the acutely modern process of adaptation as an alternative form of criticism served to destabilize not only Dostoevsky's conservative image but also the relationship of author to text.

Chapter 2, "Rozanov, Merezhkovsky, and the Conjuring of Authorial Fictions, 1899–1903," takes a close look at polemics between two major critics of Dostoevsky in the Silver Age, Vasily Rozanov and Dmitry Merezhkovsky, the undisputed leaders of the Russian religious renaissance. Rozanov's essays on culture and literature and Merezhkovsky's groundbreaking book *L. Tolstoy and Dostoevsky* (1902) staged a debate about the essential cultural identity of Dostoevsky, the figurehead of their arguments for religious renewal. These critics sought to establish Dostoevsky's authority over their own religious projects and, as such, exemplify the creative spirit of faithful reading while also calling its political utility into question. Each sought to prove Dostoevsky's radical spirituality but in opposite ways. Merezhkovsky presented him as the prophet of a new stage in Christianity, while Rozanov believed he was the harbinger of its necessary destruction. This chapter reconstructs an undiscovered polemic between the two critics over Dostoevsky's identity. The diverse currents of antisemitism in late-century Russian culture are an important backdrop to their dispute. While Rozanov claimed Dostoevsky had a "Semitic worldview," Merezhkovsky argued that he was neither Aryan nor Semitic; rather, Dostoevsky's universal genius as a "seer of the spirit" exempted him from both cultural and racial categories. The effect of Rozanov and Merezhkovsky's criticism of Dostoevsky was to remake him into either an Old Testament or a New Testament prophet, a retrograde or a spiritual revolutionary. This latter fiction of his authorial person as a "revolutionary of the spirit" was taken up by a new group of idealist critics, who were eager to revise Dostoevsky's religion into their own liberationist politics.

In chapter 3, "Idealist Critics and the Reign of Character over Author, 1901–1905," our story turns to the liberal thinkers and philosophical idealists who made Dostoevsky a spokesman for their anti-Marxist political projects. This chapter returns to a central debate of Marxist revisionism, in which some critics turned to philosophical idealism to transcend the ethical morass they viewed in the Marxist theory of the inevitable destruction of capitalism (known as the *Zusammenbruchstheorie*), an outcome necessitated by the historical materialist method. The liberal activists and former Marxists Sergei Bulgakov and Nikolai Berdiaev received this theory as morally suspect, as it seemingly justified sacrifices in the present toward some future good obtained by communism. As part of their rejection of this theory, they relied on an unusual reading of Ivan Karamazov's theodicy; his rebellion against God in *The Brothers Karamazov*, to them, debunked Marxist justifications of present suffering for future happiness. This unorthodox appropriation of Ivan, who has been received predominantly as a nihilist atheist, was refashioned into the voice of Dostoevsky in the liberal movement's ideological sparring with the Marxists. The idealist critics pulled off a major reframing of Dostoevsky that placed Ivan at the center of his religious vision, rather than Alyosha and Father Zosima, whose religious faith the author had intended to defeat Ivan's rebellion.

Chapter 4, "Symbolist Critics and the Death of the Author, 1905–1910," contextualizes the twenty-fifth anniversary of Dostoevsky's death as a turning point in the writer's cultural and critical reception. The 1905 revolution had intensified the ongoing conflict between Dostoevsky's religious views and his political affiliations. Whether they renounced him or clung tighter to his image, different generations of the Symbolist school, including Merezhkovsky, Andrei Belyi, and Viacheslav Ivanov, attempted to take Dostoevsky into an uncertain future at a time when his ideas were breaking away from the biographical persona that for some had previously anchored them. This shift occurred out of the need to salvage Dostoevsky's work from the limitations of his biography, which had become synonymous with the political contingencies of his lifetime. The image of Dostoevsky as a "revolutionary" (Merezhkovsky) and the view of his work as channeling prototypical energies of creative freedom (Ivanov) arose alongside the abandonment of the author. This chapter shows how, for these Symbolist critics, the artistic text became the authentic testament of his religion, which they legitimized by extracting its spiritual insights from biographical contingency. Their embrace of text over author was not the Formalist rejection of biography as a mode of analysis; it arose instead from the demands of their own radical ideologies, personal religious convictions, spiritual eclecticism, and creative activity (they were poets, after all). Looking in particular at the radical shift in Merezhkovsky's reading of Dostoevsky's cultural value and the unrecognized centrality of Dostoevsky to Ivanov's collaboration with the controversial "mystical anarchist" movement, this chapter is about the beginning of the end of Dostoevsky as author and the inception of his autonomous textual existence. The critical ambivalence of Merezhkovsky and the about-face of second-wave Symbolists such as Andrei Belyi coincided and should even be seen as precipitated by the influence of Dostoevsky on mystical anarchism and in Ivanov's inspired scholarly writings on Dionysian religion. Along the way the text emerges as a transmuted object capable of stimulating new faith in their version of Dostoevsky.

Symbolist and religious-philosophical figures of the Silver Age had by 1910 created a critical tradition of reading Dostoevsky by faithful renderings of his ideas into their religious, political, and artistic projects. Chapter 5, "The Moscow Art Theater's Rewriting of *Devils*, 1910–1914," returns to the stage, namely to the Moscow Art Theater's production of *Nikolai Stavrogin*, an adaptation of *Devils* (1871) written by the company's cofounder, Vladimir Nemirovich-Danchenko. While the theater had already adapted *The Brothers Karamazov* in 1910, it was *Stavrogin* that incarnated the religious-philosophical reading of Dostoevsky in the bodies of actors, representing the next phase in making him a religious thinker. Published letters and surviving archival scripts of *Stavrogin* reveal that Nemirovich demonstrated a keen interest in revamping the religious idea of *Devils*, which even now is often read as merely a takedown of socialist revolutionaries. On the contrary, Nemirovich considered far more significant the nationalist vision articulated in one of the novel's key dialogues, in which Ivan Shatov and Stavrogin debate the identity of the Russian nation as a "bearer of God" (*bogonosets*). This chapter shows how religious-philosophical critics had made the "god-bearer" a central idea of Dostoevsky's religion, to the extent that the concept made its way onto the stage of the popular theater. Nemirovich's rendering of the dialogue between Shatov and Stavrogin adds no new language to the exchange and avoids paraphrase, but it recycles and omits portions of the novel's text to yield a restorative vision of Shatov as the god-bearer's righteous theoretician. Nemirovich purged the "god-bearer" theory of its Orthodox messianism and refurbished it for an ambivalent political moment on the brink of Russia's entry into the First World War.

The problem of Dostoevsky's reception at the beginning of the twentieth century was the first indication that a unified and complete portrait of the writer was impossible alongside the religious insight and artistic promise evident in his textual corpus. The rejection of the suspicious bent of biographical criticism and the uncritical documentary approaches to Dostoevsky's work led Silver Age critics to read faithfully and locate meaning in Dostoevsky's texts—especially the speech of his vibrant, gregarious characters—since the traces of his authorial self in the narrative and extranarrative biographical contexts were often compromised by political views that directly undercut what they perceived as the moral and political potential of his religious ideas. The synthesized critical object resulting from such critical work could be termed the "textualized author," an idea that parallels the theological concept central to many of their beliefs and aesthetics: "the Word made Flesh." This metaphor reflects how the text's dominance in the Silver Age reading of Dostoevsky did not lead to the author's death; I argue that it instead enabled a kind of resurrection or merging of the transformed, remade author into a newly conceived, but usable, text—one that the faithful reader could *believe in*.

As a whole, this book seeks to move beyond generations of negative evaluations of Silver Age critics, which have predominated in scholarly discourse since the 1917 revolution. Those critics associated with Russian Formalism accused this generation of relying on biographical criticism (the author explains the text) or subjective criticism (the critic explains the text). I hope to show that the religious-philosophical and Symbolist critics examined in this book were actually staunch textualists; the phenomenon of "two Dostoevskys" made it impossible for them to read faithfully *and* treat the author's biography as the key to understanding his religious views and thus his artworks. About the latter, I aim to show that, as faithful readers, Silver Age critics consciously wrote about Dostoevsky's texts with an eye to disrupting the critically distant and more suspicious "realist" (socialist or "democratic") critics of their time.

Silver Age critics were utopianists—a mix of reactionaries, reformers, and revolutionaries—whose interpretations of Dostoevsky show us the collision of fin-de-siècle desired futures and the possibilities of criticism as cocreation. Their readings also show us new approaches to reading difficult and divisive writers, who elude understanding both underneath and on the textual surface. Rather than viewing them as "before their time," we might receive their work as one moment in the flow of modern critical inquiry, which oscillates dialectically between periods of suspicion and reparative reading. New critical moods and perspectives made available in fictocriticism—what strict Formalists may have dismissed as too subjective—are part of imagining a postcritical future beyond negation and suspicion.

CHAPTER 1

Adapting *The Idiot* and *Crime and Punishment*, 1890–1900

On January 25, 1881, near the very end of Dostoevsky's life, his wife remembers returning home from the theater where she and their children had attended a performance of Charles Dickens's *Pickwick Papers*.[1] It is thus possible that one of Dostoevsky's last conversations was about a theatrical adaptation of a novel by "one of his favorite writers."[2] In his lifetime, he was approached with requests to oversee adaptations—or *peredelki* ("remakings")—of his own novels, most often of his most popular work, *Crime and Punishment*. As early as 1867—just a year after that novel was finished—an enthusiastic bookseller named Ushakov wrote to ask for permission to adapt it to the stage. While Dostoevsky approved of the effort and sent along suggestions (which have not survived), the theater censor forbade the script's performance for the reason that Raskolnikov had not been portrayed as repentant enough of his crime.[3] Over the course of fifteen years, Ushakov remained unsuccessful in his petitions to the censor to stage revisions of his script.

It would continue to be difficult to stage Dostoevsky until the close of the 1890s, when well-connected playwrights managed to get their adaptations staged for the first time.[4] These altered texts and reformulations of their original ideological contexts aroused certain anxieties about the permeable boundary between the author and the text commonly accepted among critics in that decade. Any distortion to the text of novels was perceived by the majority of critics as a violation of the author, a view that makes understanding the problem of adaptation during this period a prerequisite for grasping Silver Age critical innovations in destabilizing the author's close hold over the text through faithful reading.

This chapter looks at the first adaptations of Dostoevsky's novels to reach the imperial and commercial theaters in St. Petersburg and Moscow in 1899. On October 4, an adaptation of *Crime and Punishment* by Ia. A. Del'er, the pseudonym of Iakov Alekseevich Pliushchevskii-Pliushchik (1845–1916, hereafter Del'er), was produced at Aleksei Suvorin's theater in St. Petersburg. A few days later, on October 11, *The Idiot* premiered at the Malyi theater in Moscow and was a month or so later staged at the Aleksandrinka theater in St. Petersburg. The authors of this adaptation were the prolific playwright Viktor Krylov (who also wrote under the pseudonym V. Aleksandrov), whose plays dominated the repertoire of both imperial theaters between 1882 and 1897, and Sergei Sutugin (the pseudonym of Osip Ettinger).[5] Contemporary and later Soviet critics did much to canonize Krylov's inferiority; he is remembered as little more than a hack writer of superficial comedies and vaudevilles.[6] The staging of these plays was quite a shift from Ushakov's hopeful attempts in earlier years. All of a sudden, at the end of the century, an adaptation of Dostoevsky was running at a new commercial theater in Petersburg and at an imperial theater in Moscow at the same time. In the following sections, the special case of *The Idiot* will receive more attention, because it sparked additional anxiety in the press about adapting Dostoevsky's novels.

There are two words for "adaptation" in Russian. One is *instsenirovka* ("scenic staging") and the other is *peredelka* ("remaking"). The first gets at the visual aspect of bringing a novel or story to the stage while also addressing its potentially fragmentary rendition of the original (i.e., "Scenes from *The Idiot*" is different from *The Idiot*). The second invites richer theoretical speculation. To call something a "remaking" implies the coexistence of an original and a secondary creator. The term also promises a new perspective or frame of mind, making room for the power of interpretation to transform ideological, cultural, or artistic style into something not quite new but that points to an original thing and the product of the remaking at the same time. In this way, remaking is a creative act that relates to the text without suspicion and thus aligns with reparative modes of interpretation.

In his book on the cultural history of Charles Dickens's *A Christmas Carol*, Paul Davis has described the interaction of the original text and the resultant "culture-text" as "a concretization of the process W. H.

Auden described as 'the words of a dead man [being] modified in the guts of the living.' For the meaning of the *Carol* is not determined by the words of the author. Its meaning is created anew by each generation of readers."[7] The work is never complete, in other words. Remaking is part of the process by which the work continues to be created, realized in different media, and interpreted. This process does not negate the author but redefines him in relation to the work and provides the interpreter (the adapter, or even the critic) a stake in the creation and its afterlife. A reenvisioning of the author in this way resonates with Latour's actor-network theory, which helps critics reenvision authors as just one of the actors in a network of relationships charged with creation, interpretation, consumption—and remaking.[8]

Del'er's *Crime and Punishment* and the Krylov/Sutugin *Idiot* offer interpretations of the novels in which Dostoevsky's ideological goals—decrying nihilism or atheism in favor of an ecstatic vision of Christian sacrifice and forgiveness—are expunged and significantly modified for a bourgeois audience. In other spheres, too, there was value in rearranging and reframing the author's texts for new readers. Theatrical adaptations coincided with a broader trend of excerpting in the republication of his work. In 1898, *Dostoevsky for Children of High-School Age* appeared and claimed in its introduction that the author's "fragmentariness" made such a book both possible (because violent or distressing portions could be excised), and, when read with other authors, pedagogically useful and "not harmful."[9] Adapters had similar hopes of cutting up and remaking Dostoevsky's novels into ideologically correct—and commercially viable—plays. But what interpretive decisions about the novel's moral-religious message did adapters make when offering the plays to popular audiences? What were the political stakes of remaking a writer like Dostoevsky during an era of conservative resurgence? As I will argue, evidence shows that Dostoevsky's first adapters were not merely tools of imperial ideology; they also engaged with the religious ideas of the novels in ways that rendered their meaning more accessible to an increasingly secular and socioeconomically diverse modern public.

All of this is not to say that adapters challenged the conservative aesthetic and political demands of their age—they successfully brought Dostoevsky to the stage because they offered versions of the novels that censors deemed ideologically acceptable. Staging Dostoevsky was an opportunity for official spheres of culture to claim ownership over the writer's perceived moral authority and sympathy for the regime. The imperial court was still the most significant patron of the performing arts in the 1890s, and it did not hurt that Dostoevsky had been one of Alexander III's favorite authors.[10]

Adapters were likely comfortable with some aspect of cocreation implied in adaptation, but the majority of traditional critics of the time were not. To them, adaptation posed a challenge to biographical criticism, the reigning interpretive method of the time. *Peredelki* foiled the critical approach of locating the writer in the text because it was so closely connected to the author herself and rearranging the text meant destabilizing, even doing violence to, its relationship to the author. Critics feared that the author was being cut loose from the text, which would shift the core ideas of the original and confirm the author's death and irrelevance. A scholar of Shakespeare's reception, Howard Marchitello, recounts how early nineteenth-century critics labeled free editions and loose theatrical adaptations of his works as corruptions, reflecting the critic's desire for "unmediated access" to the bard strictly through the veneration of unchanged, original texts. One British critic wrote in 1822, writes Marchitello, that "the ideal (and only) appropriate *textual* relationship to Shakespeare is that of the properly 'just and reasonable' *commentator* who 'should be in some sort of love with his author.' "[11] While the authority of interpretation still resided with the critic in the 1890s, numerous adaptations of Dostoevsky during the same decade suggest that other ways of envisioning the author's relationship to the text were emerging and that altering the text could produce a "new," synthetic Dostoevsky.

The fact that Dostoevsky's novels were being adapted in the 1890s—never mind the artistic and ideological failings of those separate adaptations themselves—prepared the ground for faithful reading among Silver Age critics in two ways. First, the rearrangement of texts by adapters fostered discussion in reviews and journals about the relationship between the author and the text that made speculation and imaginative interpretations possible in Silver Age critical work. Second, the popularization of Dostoevsky signaled by adaptations offered a provocation to critics invested in the social value of Dostoevsky's novels' artistically formulated religious ideas. It translated to their mission to imagine their own creative interpretations of Dostoevsky in criticism.

Adaptations and the Russian Repertoire in the 1880s and 1890s

One of the earliest adaptations of Dostoevsky's work was perhaps not coincidentally by a man who would become world famous for his contribution to theater and who would put on a critically acclaimed production of *The Brothers Karamazov* in 1910. In 1888, a young Konstantin Stanislavsky adapted Dostoevsky's *Village of Stepanchikovo* but struggled to get it to the stage.[12] It was finally performed in 1891 for the Society of Art and Literature, with the title *Foma: Scenes of the past in three acts* (Foma. Kartiny proshlogo v trekh deistviiakh). Stanislavsky altered the characters' names and omitted Dostoevsky's name entirely to get it past the censors, but at the same time he offered a play so faithful to the original text that some criticized it for its length and the outmodedness of its language.[13] "If this is so, then one must transfer this rebuke to Dostoevsky and not to the author of the adaptation, because their language is one and the same."[14] The reviewer's accusation of "outmodedness" must have referred to the story's setting and social types, which belonged to the era before the abolition of serfdom. The considerable tenacity Stanislavsky demonstrated staging his play and the lackluster result indicate the real challenges of working in the theater in an era of great changes in the industry.

In 1882, an official decree abolished the imperial monopoly on performances, providing greater opportunities for the founding and funding of private, commercial theaters.[15] As Louise McReynolds notes in her book *Russia at Play*, the era of the commercialization of the theaters made the stage "the first such organized, spectacular, mass-oriented medium that sought financing from the ticket-buying public."[16] But the theater historian Murray Frame has observed that although the end of this monopoly appeared to hail a liberal period in the most censored art form of imperial Russia, Alexander viewed it as a means of social control. The decree would facilitate the cultural extension of his nationalist policies, which sought to protect "indigenous Russian theatre art by removing the authority of the Western-influenced Directorate over non-state theatrical affairs in the capitals."[17] In the long run, the decree had the opposite effect of creating more spaces for experimental theater work, but its core ideological goal bears on any study of adaptations of Dostoevsky in the 1890s. Since the commercialization of the theaters coincided with the popular theater movement and its impulse to enlighten bourgeois and working-class audiences, adaptations of major novels were often seen as socially appropriate and commercially viable options.[18]

In the same era, critics in Russia's few theater journals almost universally observed the poor state of repertoires. With few exceptions, second-rate playwrights dominated the contemporary offering of dramatic works, creating a "yearning for a 'literary theater.'"[19] Akim Volynsky, a leading critic active in the Symbolist literary scene, was similarly shocked at the low quality of plays that were staged in the 1890s. In addition to serving as editor-in-chief of the *Northern Herald*, Volynsky also contributed major studies of Dostoevsky's work. In his essay "The Old and New Repertoire" (1901), Volynsky rebuked leading playwrights such as Krylov, Petr Boborykin, Petr Gnedich, and Ignaty Potapenko, commenting scornfully, "As a whole this repertoire is a real nightmare of a sort of pathetic tastelessness."[20] The playwrights who were earning critical praise or catching the attention of audiences were foreign: this was the era of Strindberg, Ibsen, Maeterlinck, and Hauptmann. Amid a dearth of high-quality plays, dramatists turned to the Russian classics and to Dostoevsky in particular, who soon emerged as a clear Russian analogue to these European playwrights. The same themes of individualism, spiritual and physical degeneration, and social alienation ran through his works.

In this way, the Petersburg staging of *The Idiot* in 1899 was perceived as a deliberate attempt to "enrich the repertoire" and it attracted audiences "as much by the name of the novel's author as the performance."[21] Despite Volynsky's general dislike of the Krylov/Sutugin *Idiot*, he admitted that "Dostoevsky, even in fragments and sputters, can ignite the entire theater."[22] In this assessment, just staging Dostoevsky was a healthy direction for a theater culture in crisis. He continued, "Strange as it is to say, given the completely moribund contemporary repertoire, works—in principle, even ridiculous performances—are in their own way a rejuvenating school for developing scenic powers and talent."[23]

Interest in adapting Dostoevsky's novels to the stage thus coincided with contemporary anxiety about the seeming absence of new drama in the national dramatic catalog. Still, the assumption would persist that theatrical adaptations were by their very nature inferior artistic works catering solely to popular audiences. As one theater critic noted in 1895, speaking about a recent production of a prose work by Gogol, bringing artistic prose to the stage led many to keep bracing for the latest "act of literary vandalism."[24] One scholar of Victorian adaptations of Dickens and Robert Louis Stevenson has noted that the art of performance was at the time considered "unfixed, impermanent, and potentially unstable, in contrast to the immutable, enduring printed text."[25] A theatrical adaptation of a novel would always call attention to its source text and thus announce its own inferiority.

Alongside contemporary complaints about the lack of good plays, those in the state bureaucracy who held influence over theater censorship had interests of their own to consider. Taking an active role in censoring new plays was Dostoevsky's friend, Ober-Prokuror of the Holy Synod, Konstantin Pobedonostsev, who assumed the post in 1880 (he left it in 1905 and died in 1907).[26] His biographer Robert Byrnes noted that "from 1883 until 1900, the main official responsible for censorship in Russia was a nominee and collaborator of Pobedonostsev."[27] If during their friendship Pobedonostsev claimed to have had considerable influence over some of Dostoevsky's creative choices (the depiction of Zosima, for instance), it is likely that after his friend's death he—and his successors in the censorship regime—carefully followed plans to stage his novels.

Even though the greatest novelist at the time, Lev Tolstoy, was still alive and writing socially engaged plays, there are indications that Pobedonostsev, who famously hated Tolstoy, believed that Dostoevsky's novels were better suited to what he saw as the moral demands of public performance. Writing directly to Alexander III, who did not object as strongly to Tolstoy's tragedy of peasant life, *The Power of Darkness*, Pobedonostsev expressed horror at the thought of such a work reaching Russian stages, referring significantly to *Crime and Punishment*. Unlike Tolstoy's play, Dostoevsky's novel dealt with murder and the problem of moral guilt, in which "not for a minute does the ideal disappear from the action."[28]

Not only the broader governmental regulation of the theater but also the personal ownership and administration of commercial theaters played a role in the staging of these adaptations. The spheres that hosted theatrical events had connections to the powerful imperial and conservative establishment. Aleksei Suvorin's theater, which staged Del'er's *Crime and Punishment*, was founded in 1895. Suvorin is best known as the editor of *Novoe vremia* (the *New Times*), which he purchased in 1876, and which became synonymous with reaction and blatant antisemitism. While other private theaters in Moscow, Petersburg, and the provinces were proliferating at this time, his theater was in a unique position. Suvorin could lean on *Novoe vremia* to promote the theater, positively review its plays, and guide its repertoire.[29] Such heavy-handed influence on Russian culture was infamous and ridiculed by his critics.[30] The production of *Crime and Punishment* at his theater was only the first novel of Dostoevsky's to appear on their stage; in 1908, Suvorin's son worked with the publicist and parodist Viktor Burenin on a highly tendentious adaptation of *Besy* (Devils), a work that I will discuss in chapter 5.

Like Pobedonostsev, Suvorin had a personal connection to Dostoevsky and to his posthumous literary reception, reflecting the extent to which he saw himself as part of the writer's "unfinished" literary legacy.[31] Joseph Frank summarizes Suvorin's account of an 1881 discussion with Dostoevsky, just ten days before his death, which touched on his political ambitions for the next phase of his *Writer's Diary* and his interest in dramatizing certain scenes from the recently completed *Brothers Karamazov*.[32] One cannot know for sure, but the prospect of staging Dostoevsky's novels must have interested Suvorin from a combination of literary, personal, and financial perspectives. As his theater was preparing *Crime and Punishment* in 1899, Suvorin decided to read *The Idiot* for the first time.[33] His comments reveal a tension between the dramatic power of the novel ("there are many amusing pages, many truly dramatic scenes") and his concern about the unflattering way that certain characters in the novel reflected Russian culture ("What criminal, dark, and mysterious souls he depicts. Is this really the Russian soul?").[34] If Suvorin had doubts about some of Dostoevsky's characters, he seemed convinced of the clear moral religious message of the works. In a brief 1898 recollection of an adaptation of *Crime and Punishment* that he attended in Venice with Anton Chekhov, Suvorin wrote of how the audience seemed pleased with the play, "but when Dunia began saying that Raskolnikov could be reborn in the labor camp, the public started whistling and burst into laughter. Here is the difference between the cultured West and our Fatherland. There they already don't believe in repentance and lop off the heads of criminals with a firm conviction in the usefulness of the axe. We have pity and doubt. A majority of Russian educated society are Hamlets in their soul."[35] Despite his own views, Suvorin did not have total control over the adaptation of *Crime and Punishment*, even if it did premiere at his theater: Del'er's adaptation would in fact oversimplify Raskolnikov's spiritual anguish. Whether Suvorin's interpretation of Dostoevsky won out or not, it is telling that the first staged adaptation of *Crime and Punishment* was at the theater of a man with such pervasive influence on the culture and press of his time.

But why was it that these novels were the first to captivate adapters and, with many exceptions, earn the censors' approval? There was some precedent for successful readings of *Crime and Punishment*. In 1884, the beloved actor V. N. Andreev-Burlak (1843–1888) performed a dramatic reading (*monospektakl'*) of Marmeladov's confession to Raskolnikov, which takes place early in the novel.[36] According to the recollection of an attendee of that reading, this was purportedly the first scenic adaptation of any of Dostoevsky's works.[37] It is hard to ignore the deeper significance of the popularity of this dramatic reading, tethered as it was to the precise language of the author's literary text and evoking the author's widely acknowledged talent as a reader of his own work.[38]

After all, it was this chapter that Dostoevsky selected for his first public reading from the novel in its publication year of 1866.[39] It was also one of Dostoevsky's best known and most read novels. The performance of "Marmeladov's Story" (Rasskaz Marmeladova) apparently "positively enthralled the public—it took their breath away!"[40]

There are other explanations for why Raskolnikov's story and *The Idiot* would have been selected for adaptation. In the climate of the 1880s and 1890s, the revolutionary struggle had stalled under Alexander III's quelling of dissent and many young radicals succumbed to disease and a veritable epidemic of suicide.[41] Though the ideological and political views of Raskolnikov and Myshkin did not directly align with the radical communities of the late century, young audience members could have identified with the social position of the former and the passionate empathy of the latter. In *The Idiot*, Myshkin is even accused of being one of the "new men" when he awkwardly breaks a Chinese vase, as it seemed to some of those present, as if in nihilist "defiance of social conventions."[42] For the young Maximilian Voloshin, who would later become a prominent Symbolist poet and critic, Myshkin offered a certain model of humanity that one scholar has claimed he emulated in real life.[43] There had already been a long tradition of so-called Don Quixote characters in Russian literature—idealistic youths eager for political change with no practical or legal landscape to realize their social ideals. Dostoevsky of course consciously modeled Myshkin on the Don Quixote archetype. To stage *The Idiot* in the 1890s made his idealism and its feeble utility for Russian reality resonate in the decline of revolutionary populism and the younger generation's search for purpose. Krylov and Sutugin also took the opportunity to reassess Myshkin's character, who had drawn more recent critical attention because of his epilepsy, social awkwardness, and lack of sexual motivation, all of which resonated in the contemporary interest in psychopathology and decadence.

But the artistic irregularities of *The Idiot* and its author's struggle to create a "truly beautiful" hero have always marked the novel as especially difficult. In commentary prescient of Robin Feuer Miller's landmark book on the chronicler-narrator of *The Idiot*, one critic in an essay on *The Brothers Karamazov* noted, "Everyone familiar with all of Dostoevsky's novels knows that usually the best part of all is the beginning. The first chapter of *The Idiot*, the entire first third of *Crime and Punishment*—are as if written by a different person."[44] Its original public found the novel perplexing, a trend that continued when the Krylov/Sutugin version was staged at the Aleksandrinka. Reviewers noted poor attendance and audience disinterest and doubted that any of those present were familiar with the novel's plot at all.[45] Comic verses published after the Malyi premiere of the play read

> And the spectators in the theater
> Lost the thread of meaning . . .
> Afterwards I had to take some *natri* [i.e., smelling salts]
> To strengthen my nerves . . .
> Who hasn't read the novel,
> Will not understand the play,
> And will ask sooner or later:
> "So, which one is the 'idiot'?"[46]

Del'er's *Crime and Punishment* was better received, partly because the novel itself was simply better known to the public. A reviewer of Del'er's adaptation noted favorably, "The reason for its success is the fact that everybody knows the novel *Crime and Punishment*. Raskolnikov's psychology is understood by everyone and appears as an addendum to his speeches and acts. Here it follows that there can be no talk of a lack of clarity or incompleteness. Before us plays out a sequence of illustrations from a work long familiar to us."[47] Finally, the plot of *The Idiot* is more pessimistic than *Crime and Punishment*, which could have influenced audience's preferences for the latter. Michael Holquist has noted the tension between the overarching problem of resurrection in *Crime and Punishment* and the dark apocalyptic destruction that pervades *The Idiot*, a novel that professed "not a sudden beginning of life but rather its too abrupt *end*."[48]

Crime and Punishment without the Politics: Del'er's Adaptation

Del'er was a lifelong civil servant based at the Ministry of Internal Affairs who found time to translate a number of foreign plays for the stage. With such a position, Del'er was connected to the governing body that determined the censorship of theatrical works, as well as to the influential owners and artists of the private theaters of the 1890s. An obituary noted Del'er's lasting impact on the theater of his time, claiming that it was due to his influence that performances were finally permitted on Saturdays and during Lent.[49] *The Idiot* (1868-69), which followed *Crime and Punishment* (1865-66), offers major contrasts in composition and theme. The religious problems at the heart of *The Idiot*, which dealt explicitly with atheism, capital punishment, and the Book of Revelation, also made it more difficult to stage without major revisions and distortions, given the reality of censorship.

This first Russian production of *Crime and Punishment*, forty-three years after its initial publication, would run at Suvorin's theater over fifty times.[50] Del'er's script and its relatively well-received performance sparked thoughtful debate about adapting Dostoevsky, most notably from the writer, playwright, and critic Osip Dymov (the pen name of Osip Isidorovich Perelman). In his pioneering 1900 essay on adaptations of Dostoevsky, Dymov held that in Dostoevsky's characters, "the drama is not outside of them, but in them. It is not the plot that makes the drama, but the plot flows out of their 'dramaticness.'"[51] He continued, "In the drama's plot there is nothing to develop and nothing to uncover: what is hidden at the beginning of the action will remain hidden from the spectator until the end; what is clear is clear already during the course of the action."[52] Dymov claimed that it is more accurate to speak not of the "*personalities* of the people" in Dostoevsky's novels, who interact in a recognizably realistic world, but of them as "symbols of the passions," figurations of spiritual concerns that have no business being portrayed realistically.[53] This view of the nature of drama in Dostoevsky's novels as emanating from internal, rather than external, circumstances is indebted to the influence of Symbolist aesthetics on the theater. But Dymov's thinking also bears traces of the related and growing interest in the intangible, unrepresentable religious dimension of the writer's characters, what he called in the essay's final installment an "invisible tragedy," likely drawing on Maeterlinck.[54] "All of this in Dostoevsky's works we do not understand; we feel it, become aware of it," Dymov wrote.[55] "How can you express on the stage that eternal vacillation of thought, that passionate search for truth [*istina*], that *relative* sincerity, that self-analysis, digging still deeper and deeper and hoping to find the foundation of foundations?"[56] This task would be immense. It was not the goal of Del'er's adaptation.

Del'er began his *peredelka* with the famous tavern scene featuring Marmeladov and Raskolnikov. None of the drunkard's long speech about his lies and deceptions against his family is excised from the script (perhaps because the censor had already approved the performance of this speech back in 1884). His statement of piety at the end of his long speech, full of an elevated lexicon observable in the word "*rutsi*" (the Old Church Slavonic word for *ruki,* or "hands") in a direct address to the Savior, is the ultimate statement of humility before the will of God and Christ the miracle-worker. While the play does not write off Marmeladov as a failed moral agent in the life of Raskolnikov, in Del′er's scenario a far greater authority than Marmeladov's drunken religion is Porfiry Petrovich's stewardship of the law and the power of the state that it signifies. If au courant audience members expected to see contemporary references to the Übermensch in Raskolnikov, this play would have been a disappointment.

Other gross amendments to the religious theme of the plot reflect a few possible motivations at once. Such changes might reflect the censor's demands, Del′er's own (likely) conservative politics, or some combination of the two. One of the most egregious revisions was to the setting of the story. Detailed descriptions of makeup and costume suggestions for the dramatis personae indicate that the dress of many characters should reflect "the style of the '50s" or of "the end of the '50s," meaning that the action takes place in the years just before the abolition of serfdom in 1861. Of course, Dostoevsky set the novel *after* emancipation, in the reform era. Del′er's Raskolnikov is not driven to crime by the "new ideas" (i.e., nihilism)—which in the play's new time setting had not yet been coined in Russian discourse—nor are his noble qualities developed before the spectator's eyes. This shift back in time circumvents the nihilist motivations of Raskolnikov's crime; in the play, he murders in order to rescue his sister, Dunia, from "selling herself" in marriage to the cynical liberal, Mr. Luzhin. Luzhin is barely mentioned in the adapted version, and his young companion Lebeziatnikov, the author's parodic take on the nihilist generation, is notably absent.

In the final act, when Raskolnikov and Sonia appear in the prison camp, the religious commandment against murder and the state's pursuit of justice emerge as the primary drivers of the plot's moral universe. While in the script, Raskolnikov and the investigator Porfiry Petrovich still spar over his article "On Crime," without the nihilist setting the argument about the right of extraordinary men to overstep the bounds of morality turns Raskolnikov into merely an arrogant youth rather than a tortured victim of the atheist nihilism of those days. Del′er's decision to avoid any contingent political debates about radical ideas is also balanced with the noticeably positive role of the novel's chief investigator, Porfiry Petrovich, who represents state order.

Porfiry Petrovich is treated with palpable irony in the novel, but in Del′er's interpretation acquires serious ideological authority with a completely invented monologue inserted into the scene devoted to Raskolnikov's provocative article:

> Porfiry Petrovich *alone*. There is no double. . . . Raskolnikov is implicated in the murder. . . . And what a pity. . . . A smart guy . . . and a man of a sort of special spiritual beauty. If only to bring him to voluntary awareness . . . if only to lessen the punishment some-what. Tomorrow here's what I'll try: I'll question Nikolai [one of the suspects] in front of him and I'll say that he will be accused. . . . He won't be able to stand it . . . that he won't be able to stand. . . . His soul is too elevated . . . He'll give himself up. . . . (*Sinks into a chair and becomes pensive*) A murder because of an idea . . . and so young . . . just a boy. . . . What did he ruin himself for? A pity, a tormenting pity![57]

This entirely invented aside converts Raskolnikov's subsequent interrogations with Porfiry Petrovich into a moral struggle, with the investigator emerging as the superior authority figure. Porfiry Petrovich is even able to sense the "spiritual" essence of the prodigal student, linking his authority with compassion for those straying from the law. Gone is the darkly absurd battle between Porfiry Petrovich's blunt psychology and Raskolnikov's delusional nihilistic egoism that takes shape in the novel's long denouement after the murders. Del'er's changes seek to retain a moralizing and legalistic message—"thou shalt not kill"—without its broader religious premise: that atheistic pride, rather than momentary delusion—or even a compassionate concern for his sister—is what prompted Raskolnikov to kill.

Though Del'er portrayed Raskolnikov as a repentant criminal, with none of the internal spiritual dynamic observed by the theater critic Dymov, he proved to some that a *peredelka* of Dostoevsky could be achieved with well-chosen novelistic material.[58] But his decision to end the play with a triumphant portrayal of Raskolnikov's spiritual renewal in Siberia was a flagrant denial of the unresolvable internal drama unfolding in the souls of Dostoevsky's characters.[59] Subsequent scholars and casual readers alike have criticized the Epilogue as deus ex machina: out of nowhere, Raskolnikov experiences a sudden thirst for salvation and redemption that is hard to square with his long resistance to Sonia's numerous pleas that he show humility to God and repent of his crimes.

In his review of the production, Alexander Kugel', the influential theater critic and editor of *Teatr i iskusstvo* (Theater and Art), read Raskolnikov as a Nietzschean hero and found fault in Del'er's too simplistic interpretation of the Epilogue. Kugel' believed that if the Epilogue is read as plain evidence of Raskolnikov's spiritual redemption, both characters end up as mediocrities: if before Raskolnikov was a "plus," the representative of a "will to power," and Sonia was always a "minus," the Epilogue leaves the reader with two minuses.[60] Dymov, who was Kugel''s right-hand man and colleague at the journal, also found fault with Del'er's emphasis on Raskolnikov's hasty arrival at spiritual rebirth, noting that it "diametrically departs from the entire structure, the foundation of the creative genius of Dostoevsky."[61] If Dymov had such reservations about the interpretation of *Crime and Punishment* offered by Del'er, the Krylov/Sutugin *Idiot* would raise even more alarms.

The Krylov/Sutugin *Idiot*: Pastiche and Adaptation as Authoricide

This section will examine the 1899 production of the Krylov/Sutugin script of *The Idiot* in brief comparison with numerous adaptations of the novel that did not pass the censor.[62] In the small body of existing scholarship on early scenic adaptations of Dostoevsky's novels, there has been little to no attention paid to the scripts that have survived but were never staged.[63] The Saint Petersburg Theater Library behind the Aleksandrinka theater holds several manuscripts of scenic adaptations of *The Idiot* in the 1890s in its censors' archive of dramatic works.[64] The censors deemed most of these "unsuitable for the stage," and there is no evidence that they were ever staged at a later time. Ranging in quality and dramatic feasibility, the scripts collectively provide a sense of how adapters' rearrangements of the plot reflect their interpretations of the originals. They will be considered alongside a closer reading of the script of the Krylov/Sutugin *Idiot*.

The premiere in Moscow took place at the Malyi theater, home to the bulk of talented actors of the day and, despite being an imperial theater, a place known informally as "Moscow's second university." Mariia Ermolova, the star of their troupe, often played "radical" characters, to the delight of progressive young audience members.[65] Some years later, prominent critics (who were then writing during the Soviet regime) credited the Malyi's performances of Ostrovsky with bridging gaps in the political education of its audiences.[66] The long-standing reputation of the Malyi as friendly to critiques of class inequality matched the tenor of the Krylov/Sutugin adaptation. Its script prominently featured the exploited heroine Nastasya Filippovna, whose abuse by wealthy men contrasts with the devotion of the Christlike Myshkin.

In a survey of the earliest *peredelki* of Dostoevsky's novels, the scholars Ornatskaia and Stepanova report that the censors had both artistic and ideological reasons for rejecting the many versions of *The Idiot* submitted to them in the 1890s. One censor's comments are exemplary: "The extreme realism of Dostoevsky's creations renders them almost entirely inappropriate for the stage. One of the most inappropriate of the deceased novelist's works, to this end, is *The Idiot*."[67] A reviewer of the Krylov/Sutugin *Idiot* phrased this problem slightly differently, noting the difficulty of translating characters' psychological and spiritual complexity to the stage: "Only the corporeal image of the external form of the idea is strengthened, but from the stage we don't get its soul."[68] Though theater critics in the 1890s were often skeptical of theatrical adaptations of literary classics, they seemed especially anxious about how such works evacuated the psychological and religious intricacies of Dostoevsky's work, even if they held so much dramatic potential. Such a collective position contributed to a view of Dostoevsky's work as particularly unsuitable for the kind of desecration of adaptation, since critics had long acknowledged that his novels were ideological abstractions from real life and not mere representations of life itself. The adapter thus held the potential to become either a criminal or a penitent worshipper at the altar of the author's masterpiece, as one critic had noted in a review of Del'er's *Crime and Punishment*: "If the dramatist has actually distorted and misrepresented [*izvratil i izkazil*] a classical work, then punish and execute him. . . . But if he has taken to his work with prayerful trembling, if he has guarded and preserved, like a pearl, every word uttered by the great author, if he has resolved to neither add nor clarify anything, if, 'like an industrious bee,' he has tried only to gather what is brightest and most important in the novel—then why crucify him?"[69] The religious language employed in this review—at one point lapsing into Old Church Slavonic patristic commentary on the Gospel—demonstrates the valance of sacrality and its potential violation that overlays the problem of adaptation during this time. That this particular concern would lead to mounting criticism of adaptations' handling of the religious content of Dostoevsky's works was no surprise.

There were of course more practical concerns about adapting *The Idiot* in particular, which had more to do with the complex structure of the original. The novel's narrative system, numerous, often meandering monologues (many of which deal with religious themes like the "Russian God" or the apocalypse), and uneven dramatic tempos did indeed make it an especially challenging candidate for adaptation. To be sure, the critical history of the novel leading up to Miller's book on *The Idiot*, which made a case for its formal arrangement and artistic integrity, tended to follow Dostoevsky's own self-evaluation of it as a failure.[70] To adapt *The Idiot* meant replotting a story that the novelist himself had considered artistically flawed. Working on the script for *Nikolai Stavrogin* in 1913, the Moscow Art Theater's second adaptation of Dostoevsky, Vladimir Nemirovich-Danchenko wrote in a letter, "*Devils* is a very weak thing. *The Adolescent* is, too. It is impossible to represent [*illiustrirovat'*] *The Idiot* in images, since all of the remarkable places turn into recitation and become boring."[71] The censors seem to have shared Nemirovich's later concerns about the "*stsenichnost'*" and dramatic potential of Dostoevsky's novel, as one censor reported about a *peredelka* of admittedly dubious quality: "I will permit myself to note that the best guarantee of the complete failure of a staging of this play is its frustrating monotony and preposterous interminability, since one quick read through takes four hours, and at an imaginable performance, taking into account the necessary changes in decoration, make-up and so on, the show would take not less than six hours, and no artist or entrepreneur would risk venturing on such an endeavor."[72]

But at the forefront of these technical problems of adaptation was how to portray the strange hero, Prince Myshkin. Krylov and Sutugin offered a version of Prince Myshkin stripped of the socially disruptive Christian passion of Dostoevsky's original. Myshkin was received as just another impotent, moralizing hero—a Hamlet of the fin de siècle. This outcome undercut the religious symbolism of Myshkin's original characterization. In one glaring addition to the novel's dialogue, Myshkin is permitted a certain self-consciousness about his own irrelevance, which displays the adapters' preference for melodramatic social commentary over Symbolism's hints and spiritual moods. Myshkin proclaims, "I know that I have been offended by nature. . . . I do not know how to make things turn out well; I don't even know how to express what I feel and because of that I am superfluous to society."[73] These attempts by the adapters to make Myshkin's core motivations explicit led one reviewer to admit, "The moral image of the Prince has disappeared in the adaptation and only his apparent mental impotence remains."[74]

In reviews of the Krylov/Sutugin play, Myshkin was repeatedly likened to a recent portrayal of Tsar Fedor in Aleksei Tolstoy's play *Tsar Fedor Ioannovich*. Just the year before in 1898, two productions of this long-banned play had premiered—one at Suvorin's theater and the other at the newly incorporated Moscow Art Theater. If even the sixteenth-century Fedor Ioannovich was portrayed as a contemporary neurasthenic, it was no wonder that such an archetype would also appear in depictions of the epileptic Myshkin in the same years. In his appraisal of *The Idiot*, Dymov insinuated that Krylov's insertion of moralizing language absent in the novel's text sounded like an imitation of the sort of pale virtue displayed by Tsar Fedor in the earlier play.[75] Writing about the same production, the poet and critic Zinaida Gippius was pessimistic about how "the crowd" would perceive any treatment of religious or spiritual themes in the theater. "Weakened aestheticism, languishing depravity—in a negative sense—and weakened love, ecstasy, and the thoughtless sincerity of the holy fool—in a positive one: this is what they consider signs of our time, what they see and want to see in every new work of art."[76] Her views were echoed by another reviewer, who was critical of the actor Pavel Orlenev's rendition of Tsar Fedor in Suvorin's production, writing that "paying homage in this way to the newest fashion, finding symptoms of contemporary nervous illnesses in historical figures, the actor deprives his creation of a well-known share of charm and attractiveness."[77] But at least one commentator rather liked the resonance between Myshkin and Tsar Fedor, suggesting that Orlenev might have made a better Prince Myshkin in the Krylov/Sutugin production at the Aleksandrinka.[78]

Glancing at unstaged and censored adaptations proves that Krylov and Sutugin were not alone in their struggle to effectively rearrange the plot's dramatic structure and represent Myshkin. Some plot elements were discarded by necessity: any mention of capital punishment, sustained attention on the novel's treatment of epilepsy, and the foregrounded philosophical conversations about atheism were disallowed by the censor. This was the reason that at least one script did not pass the censor. Most of the scripts marginalize Prince Myshkin's role, which circumvents any serious treatment of the religious symbolism and the apocalyptic theme that some believe provides one of the only structural foundations for the plot.[79] Dramatic action becomes concentrated on the self-destructive plight of the "emancipated" Nastasya Filippovna, driven by pride and revenge against her would-be suitors, Ganya and Rogozhin. To sum up, the play looks to the social drama of *The Idiot* and crafts its moral dimension from the secularized value of "pity." In most of the unrealized scenarios, Rogozhin speaks in extended dialogue exchanges only in the second part of Act III. In photographs taken from the Petersburg production of the Krylov/Sutugin adaptation, it is clear that costume and set design contributed to this play's commentary on class conflict in the depiction of Rogozhin and Nastasya Filippovna. In one photograph of the design for Nastasya Filippovna's birthday,

FIGURE 1.1.   Set for Nastasya Filippovna's birthday party in *The Idiot*, adapted by Viktor Krylov and Sergei Sutugin

she wears an elegant dress, whereas Rogozhin appears in stereotypical merchant attire (see figure 1.1).

Krylov and Sutugin gave Myshkin a prominent role as the play's powerless *raisonneur* and moralist; however, they discard the prince's famous diatribe against Catholicism and passionate defense of Russian Orthodoxy. For a newspaper reviewer of the production at the Malyi theater, this disregard for the religious role of Myshkin in the play was unacceptable. He caught on to the fact that the invented final speech in the play was acting as a kind of placeholder for the actual key sermon that Myshkin delivers earlier in the novel in a salon setting, in which he attacks Catholicism and expounds on the renewal of the Russian people through "the Russian idea, the Russian God." "*The Russian God. . . .* Prophetic words," the reviewer wrote, noting that in the novel Myshkin alone serves such a God: "The Prince is the incarnation of pity, the immense passive force of the soul."[80] Myshkin's speech about the Russian God was the first time Dostoevsky had articulated this idea in his fiction and it became a central theme in his succeeding novels; however, due to its direct commentary on religious subjects it might have been a target for censorship. It also would have distracted from the social drama that Krylov and Sutugin were aiming to distill into a new play.

In the end, their scenario spends 60 percent of the play's action on part 1 alone, which deals with Myshkin's introduction to the Epanchin family and his first encounters with Nastasya Filippovna, Ganya, and Rogozhin. They compressed most of parts 2–4 of the novel into two acts in order to develop the love plot between the prince and Aglaia, but the nihilist subplot is discarded. Just as Del'er had avoided placing Raskolnikov in the nihilist context of the 1860s, Krylov and Sutugin avoid the atheist theme, and its tragic youth, Ippolit Terent'ev, vanishes from the action. Their scenario is thus completely stripped of the political and religious material that the author packaged carefully in the social drama. The result is a morality play told in melodramatic form.

In adaptations such as these, dialogue can serve as material for avoiding traces of ideological commentary provided by the author in the narration. There are some indications that the adapters still wished to leverage the authority of the author in their script. One of the features of Krylov's adaptation style, the theater historian Aleksandr Chepurov has explained, involved the incorporation of narration into dialogue, which is observable at times in his adaptation of *The Idiot*.[81] The Aleksandrinka had been offering adaptations of Tolstoy, Turgenev, and Dostoevsky, and it had been crafting new strategies for synthesizing plot structure and "nonplot" (*vnesiuzhetnyi*) elements, such as narration. The significance of this technique lies in its exploitation of the assumption many made at the time that the narrator of a work and its author were the same. In this way, Krylov's conversion of narrative elements into dialogue can be read as an attempt to channel and remobilize hints of the author into characters' direct speech. An example of this approach can be seen in the play's reconstructed exchange between Myshkin and Rogozhin. Krylov borrowed narrative material from third-person free indirect discourse about Myshkin's state of mind following Ippolit's powerful speech justifying his planned suicide, an episode that was of course removed from the reworked plot of the scenario. The shift of this narrative material into dialogue transposes narration to first-person dialogue, which by the audience is experienced as Myshkin's self-conscious reflection: "I remember that in Switzerland, on a clear sunny day, I was walking in the mountains: a sparkling sky, below me a lake, and all around a limitless horizon. . . . I thought to myself: what is this great constant celebration that is always pulling me towards it and I cannot adhere to it . . . every blade of grass grows and is happy, and everything has its own path; I alone know nothing, I don't understand anything, neither people, nor sounds."[82] The original narration actually functions to convey Myshkin's compassion for Ippolit, who has been plunged into loneliness in the God-created world—the sort of alienation that would drive a young man to plan his own suicide. But in the play, the atheist subtext with Ippolit is expunged and Myshkin's language reflects merely his impotence and expresses a generalized alienation from social life. In the end, the trademark passion of Dostoevsky could be repurposed toward fleshing out emotional topics more accessible to theater audiences.

Evidence from Sutugin's writings on theater suggests that Krylov's technical approach to adapting the novel was combined with a new interpretation of its central idea. In "Thoughts on the Theater," a three-part essay published after the production, Sutugin distinguished between his own "two Dostoevskys": "Dostoevsky the moralist" and "Dostoevsky the novelist." The moralist advocates forgiveness of the offense; the novelist never portrays an offended heroine forgiving her offender. Instead, the offended character is entirely consumed by the offense done to them, which manifests in their self-destruction and their abuse of others. He then asks a question that invites doubt as to whether he acknowledged the religious dimension of the offended, humiliated person in Dostoevsky's work at all, using an example from *The Idiot*—an older man's humiliating predation of the young heroine: "Wouldn't it have been better if Nastasya Filippovna had responded to Totsky's offense in kind—if only even in the most cruel way—than to torment herself and Rogozhin and Prince Myshkin, who were not guilty before her of anything, with the evil and suffering that has accumulated from an unavenged offense?"[83] This question is astonishingly oblivious of the novel's central religious themes of humility and forgiveness. Sutugin frames Nastasya Filippovna as responsible for her own demise, thus transforming her murderer, Rogozhin, from victimizer into victim.

As a result of Krylov's formal changes and Sutugin's rather bizarre misunderstanding of Christian humility in the novel, in their adaptation, Myshkin becomes an eccentric aristocrat whose pleas for pity and compassion have no place in a world of pride and unavenged humiliation. But perhaps the most striking shift in the Krylov/Sutugin scenario is the way they handle the aftermath of Nastasya Filippovna's murder. Most of the other unrealized scenarios exploit the explosive argument between Aglaia and Nastasya Filippovna toward the end of the story, making it the motivating event that directly precedes and perhaps causes Nastasya Filippovna's stabbing by Rogozhin. Krylov and Sutugin follow more closely the novel's sequence of events with some revealing differences.

Their fifth act follows the novel's basic denouement. Myshkin appears at Rogozhin's house. Once inside, he discovers the already deceased Nastasya Filippovna, who is behind a curtain. Once Myshkin understands what has happened there is a knock at the door and suddenly the minor characters General Epanchin, Kolya, and Ptitsyn appear. In the novel, the corpse of the heroine serves as the setting for a private vigil between Myshkin and Rogozhin. In the play, this moment of mourning and strangely mystical bonding between sinner and saint becomes a public event. Epanchin inquires about Rogozhin's whereabouts. Myshkin responds:

> *Prince*: He's over there . . . there (*Pointing to the curtain*). Don't touch it . . . no one . . . never . . . you know, I saw a quick death . . . in Switzerland. When you shoot a goat, it jumps for the last time and . . . it's done. What a lot of light there is! Trees, green . . . the sun's beams shine with joy . . . why suffer, why be sick at heart? . . . the heart . . . (*He is very pale. Begins to speak again, first with a quiet voice, then gradually becoming more animated*). All are unhappy and suffering . . . the heart is being torn apart from torment . . . (*With great force*). People are alone on earth, what misfortune . . . "is anyone alive in this field?" cries the Russian hero—thus I also cry—and there is no answer. Everything is dead and there are corpses everywhere . . . (*Pointing to the curtain*). There, there it's terrible . . . she was not at fault . . . (*Almost screaming*). Why did it happen like this? . . . why? (*Sobs on Epanchin's chest*).[84]

This speech melodramatizes one of the most somber moments in the novel, but I want to focus not on its dramatic failure but on the meaning of the text and how it affects Myshkin's social and moral position. After Myshkin speaks these lines, Epanchin tries to comfort him while Kolya walks over to the curtain to discover Nastasya Filippovna's body. Rogozhin is curled up unresponsive at her feet.[85] The stage direction calls for a general commotion and Myshkin delivers these lines just before the final curtain:

> *Prince*: Don't go over there, don't. . . . I won't let you. . . . Beauty is a terrible force. There God fights with the devil and the field of battle is the hearts of men. Leave them, they are good . . . pure of heart—children. . . . Hey, gentlemen, will you agree to be children? (*Looks inquisitively at all of them*). Why aren't you answering me?
>
> *Ptitsyn* (in Epanchin's ear): He has gone completely mad. We need to take him to Switzerland to see the doctor again.
>
> *Prince*: We need to have pity, we need to pity everyone, pity the blade of grass . . . the tree, the little branch . . . the little flower. . . . Everything is born, blooms, and dies. . . . We need to have pity . . .[86]

Myshkin is not quite rendered an "idiot" in this final scene; he does not even suffer an epileptic attack as he does in the novel. More significantly, some of his final words are not part of the original text—or from any of Dostoevsky's other works for that matter—but borrowed from Alexander Herzen's 1846 novel, *Who Is to Blame?* (Kto vinovat?), additionally quoted in Dostoevsky's short story "Meek One" (*Krotkaia*, 1876). Also included in Myshkin's final speech is amalgamated text from *The Brothers Karamazov*: Dmitry's line about the cosmic struggle for good and evil in the hearts of men, Zosima's exhortations about divine power in the natural world, and Alyosha's faith in children amid sin.[87] Myshkin pleads for the childlike innocence of the murderer, who lies at the feet of his victim, a clear instance of Sutugin's interpretation of the perpetrator as worthy of pity. In sum, Krylov and Sutugin offer a mash-up of a total of four other distinct characters from Dostoevsky's novels in Myshkin's culminating remarks. Myshkin thus channels the "brand" of Dostoevsky's morality—secularized for the stage—and somehow the adapters' creative rearrangement of the *text* and careful expunging of ideological material helps their preferred version of the *author* speak again. The resulting pastiche of Dostoevsky's works in Myshkin's speech evidences how effective *The Brothers Karamazov* had been at articulating a broad notion of Dostoevsky's core religious idea of brotherly love. Amusingly, one critic noticed that Myshkin's speech at the end was odd, but got the key source text wrong: "In the fifth act, instead of Dostoevsky's humane final, the most respected author, Mr. Krylov, has Prince Myshkin speak some sort of monologue cobbled from various German plays, which he has awkwardly cribbed from others his entire life."[88]

The Krylov/Sutugin *Idiot* had obviously missed the mark, but these artistic failures merely exacerbated anxieties about adaptation held by most critics of the time. Since adaptations of the classics received greater scrutiny because of the intimate relationship critics assumed existed between text and author, one reviewer of *The Idiot* posed a question about the ethics of adaptation without the author's direct participation, "Is it possible to remake a novel by a deceased [*umershii*] writer into a dramatic work?"[89] Another reviewer of the same production expressed similar concerns about any adaptation, but especially one of Dostoevsky, outside of the validating existence of the authorial body: "The whole essence, the depth of the late [*pokoinyi*] writer's works, the traces of the excised descriptive portion, where the sense and meaning of the characters' actions are illuminated by the author, have evaporated somewhere."[90] This commentary may be read as more than mere reverence for the author—it is proof that critics were seeing the text begin to have a different life beyond and independent of its author, a process which was necessary to producing *one* (or one's own) Dostoevsky, instead of two Dostoevskys.

As the death of the author seemed imminent after adaptations like the Krylov/Sutugin *Idiot*, some reviews looked to dark humor to express their discomfort. One such appraisal that appeared in the newspaper *The Citizen* concluded a review of the Krylov/Sutugin *Idiot* with a comic exchange between an upstart actor and a seasoned veteran of the theater:

> The youth poses and declaims, but he is awfully bad and the old
>   artist shakes his head hopelessly.
> -Do I have a chance in the theater?—asks the young man.
> -Only one chance.
> -What is it?
> -You can die.
> -?! . . .
> -Yes, die and you might end up in the theater . . . the anatomical
>   one.[91]

The reviewer signals both the morbidity of the contemporary theater, as well as the larger anxiety about the threats posed to the author by the proliferation of adaptations: in the same way that the aspiring actor has a chance only at playing a corpse in the anatomical theater, a remaking of Dostoevsky will lead to the death of the author and the meaninglessness of the text. In this light, the conclusion of the Krylov/Sutugin scenario, with an ensemble encircling the corpse of Nastasya Filippovna, appears as an ironically fitting visualization of how many reviewers understood the adapters' violation and "murder" of Dostoevsky's "corpus." Yet another reviewer took up the metaphor of the adaptation rendering the living novel a lifeless corpse, while also offering a comparatively more positive review of the production: "Mr. Sutugin and Mr. Krylov have shown not a little mastery; however, the soul of Dostoevsky has departed [*otletela*] these characters."[92]

One particularly nasty lampoon of the production published in *Russkii listok* carried the title "The Idiot. An Outrageous Crime in Five Acts by V. Krylov and S. Sutugin." The inept adapters and frivolous members of the Theatrical-Literary Committee provide the bulk of the dialogue in this parodic playlet, in which Sutugin's caricatured accented speech markedly reveals both his incompetence as a dramatist and the lampoonist's antisemitic attack on his Jewish heritage. The parody ends in a reimagining of the fifth act of the Krylov/Sutugin *Idiot*, with one of General Ivolgin's comic monologues spiraling into chaos and metacommentary on the adaptation itself. Ivolgin muses about a tax on common sense before noting that it would be more lucrative to tax the more widespread behaviors of "insolence or audacity":

> Ivolgin [*Maksheev*]: Krylov and Sutugin would never have to pay because, you must agree, extreme supplies of audacity are necessary in order to encroach on [*pokusit'sia na* can also mean "to assassinate"] Dostoevsky. So, you see, we will soon reach the point when they'll turn Pushkin's *Boris Godunov* into an operetta. We'll sing a fashionable little tune; we'll do the cancan . . .
> *Rogozhin* (runs up): I'll kill you! I'll kill all of you. . . . Stand in a line!
> *Everyone* (in unison): Kill us, darling, kill us; be merciful. It's better to die than disgrace the pride and glory of Russian literature.
> *Dostoevsky's ghost*: Shame on you, gentlemen!
> Curtain.[93]

In probably the most extreme response to the adapters, albeit mitigated by its comic tone, the author of this lampoon goes far enough to liken the remaking of Dostoevsky's novel to the author's assassination. The character-actors themselves rebel against the scenario, breaking the fourth wall, and demanding their release from the sham adaptation. These critical responses to *The Idiot* reflect a phobia of adaptation and the assumption that the author enjoys exclusive ownership and posthumous identification with the text, which is framed as a *living* object: "Let the works of famous novelists *live*, let tens and hundreds of thousands of old and young readers read them for many years; but we will not try to revamp them into dramas, even if the novels of this famous writer abounded with almost ready-made dramatic scenes [my emphasis]."[94]

As we have seen, 1890s theatrical adaptations of Dostoevsky's novels reworked the ideological content and context of the originals, offering dramatic versions that favored secularized versions of their religious preoccupations. The plays were moralistic melodramas for mass audiences. Del'er, Krylov, and Sutugin had the support of the overwhelmingly politically conservative and bureaucratic theater boards. Combined with the limiting and dulling effects of censorship on religious language and themes on the stage, the adapters' conservative bona fides produced a streamlined version of Dostoevsky's religious worldview, which critics panned, but that may have appealed to audiences. However, if adapters' political conservatism rendered the novels' religious foundations digestible to theatergoers, their actual methods of theatrical adaptation were for the time quite radical to critics, who generally regarded remakings of the text as violations to authorial integrity. Though their artistic achievements have gone unrecognized, fin de siècle theatrical adaptations proclaim the fact of textual rearrangement and selective quotation as forms of creative interpretation. Adaptations such as these posed the question of who had authority over the creative reimagining of the moral-religious content of the originals, which, in the Silver Age, would become the basis for new critical work on Dostoevsky. What unites these adaptations and Silver Age criticism is their reparative orientation toward interpretation and critical work. These adapters, though their projects were far less ambitious than the utopian faithful readers of subsequent chapters, did not relate to their object with suspicion. On the contrary, it was the prevailing methodology of biographical criticism—as the survey of reviewers of these productions has demonstrated—that did, and with a great deal of paranoia, at that. It was slowly becoming possible to read the novels independent of Dostoevsky's authorship. Toward realizing a new interpretive field, adaptations had the additional advantage of excising the narrator and thus dispensing with traces of the author within the fictional text.

Despite the ruthless reviews they received, Krylov and Sutugin had managed to give audiences a synthetic work, at times cribbed from fragments of other texts by the author, but one that proclaimed a new relationship between author and text than the one permitted in biographical readings. Although their moralizing version of Dostoevsky was roundly panned, they and their colleagues in theatrical adaptation should be credited with participating in the liberation of the text from the author and the search for conveying new forms of the moral-religious idea in Dostoevsky's body of work. A radical shift was occurring in theater and criticism of the time, despite the fact that these spheres were often separated by their publics and social functions. The author was backstage—still there—but was being remade by new readings of textual material activated by urgent political and social questions arising out of the doldrums of the 1890s. In the next chapter, two of the most influential Silver Age commentators on Dostoevsky—Rozanov, the eccentric feuilletonist, and Merezhkovsky, the poet and self-styled prophet of a new religious synthesis—would go head-to-head with their own creations of Dostoevsky as the figurehead of their religious projects.

CHAPTER 2

Rozanov, Merezhkovsky, and the Conjuring of Authorial Fictions, 1899–1903

In 1899, the literary critic Akim Volynsky responded to the recent wave of interest in Dostoevsky that he perceived was just beginning. Noting the recent theatrical adaptations of his work, he wrote, "One can say almost with certainty that many are now once again rereading his works and, while rereading, understanding them differently than they did before—more deeply, with great personal, psychological interest. It is precisely Dostoevsky—and not Tolstoy—who has been summoned to bring to wholeness that fracturing of old intellectual foundations and principles, where new paths for life and art are opened."[1] Dmitry Filosofov, the critic and literary ally of Dmitry Merezhkovsky, made a similar observation; however, he drew attention to the "fatal" outcome of a writer's popularization. In the same way that Nietzsche had been made "generally more accessible" in recent years, "the very same destructive process of dumbing down (*nivellirovka*) was carried out for us with Dostoevsky and Tolstoy. In the first, people saw some sort of criminal psychologist; in the second, a protesting liberal. Only in the most recent years has a more serious regard for these great Russian wisemen started to permeate our society."[2]

If Russian critics and readers were becoming more enthralled by Dostoevsky's work, non-Russians seemed to be increasingly baffled by it. In the February 1903 edition of the literary and religious-philosophical journal the *New Path* (Novyi put'), a summary of a review appeared that originally ran in the *New York Times* of the translation of Merezhkovsky's landmark book on Tolstoy and Dostoevsky. The reviewer admits, "We vaguely accept Pushkin as a considerable author. We can understand Turgenev, mainly because he was not representative of Russia, but the product, rather, of European civilization. Tolstoi is a more difficult task. Dostoievski is frankly impossible."[3]

As the intelligentsia was increasingly drawn to Dostoevsky's religious thought, Tolstoy had steadily become a pariah. The publication of his provocative novel *Resurrection* (1899), which was critical of the Russian Orthodox Church, assisted in his excommunication in 1901. Famously abandoning the spiritual questions of literature for social activism and moral philosophy, Tolstoy was viewed by the younger generation of writers with a mixture of admiration and disappointment. Many now believed, as Volynsky had written, that only Dostoevsky could respond to the problems that Tolstoy "awakened but did not satisfy."[4] His sober Christianity, based on a philosophy of nonresistance to evil that entailed an utter rejection of aesthetic beauty, appeared to some of their generation as a new kind of abject asceticism at odds with their understanding of art, religion, and society. Tolstoy's excommunication seemed symbolic of the tragic rift between culture and religion in Russian society and ensured that the questions posed by critics sympathetic to the religious reawakening of Russia retained a contemporary relevance.

As Dmitry Merezhkovsky (1865–1941) would say in response to his critics at the time, the question of whether Tolstoy's religion was or was not Christianity was "a question beyond measure, not only of religious, but also of world historical, cultural, and social importance."[5] Answering that question would, for him, clarify the contributions of Dostoevsky. Thus, the Russian origins of the now clichéd pairing of Tolstoy and Dostoevsky, which Vladimir Nabokov famously ridiculed in the portmanteau "Tolstoevsky," stems from the perceived religious-philosophical divide between the two novelists. Tolstoy often appears in the undignified position of a mere foil or scapegoat; his "rational" and moralizing Christianity, as it was received in the 1890s, seemed moribund compared to the perceived riches of the unfinished but compelling potential of Dostoevsky's religious ideas.

There seemed to be a common sentiment among this generation of critics at the turn of the century. Tolstoy was out, Dostoevsky was in, and discussions of their work began to unfold in the space opened at the nexus of both writers' religion and art. The reason for the critical fixation on Dostoevsky in particular was a religious renewal that was taking place in circles of poets and critics associated with the Symbolist movement. A collective rejection of so-called utilitarian literature and positivism, the apocalyptic mood ushered into Russian letters at the fin de siècle, and a new fascination with the occult and world religions fueled new critical readings of Tolstoy and Dostoevsky that used their religious worldviews as a lens for interpreting their art. Positioning themselves against demands by old guard "democratic" critics like N. K. Mikhailovsky that literature's primary function was to hold up a critical mirror to Russian reality, other critics soon overtook Volynsky and sought to understand the artistic and spiritual dimensions of Russia's two most prominent novelists. Foremost among these critics were Vasily Rozanov (1856–1919) and Merezhkovsky, who were initially close friends and partners but eventually ideological opponents.

Beyond advocating for a Russian religious renaissance, as Nikolai Berdiaev would eventually name it, both Rozanov and Merezhkovsky had personal reasons for becoming the primary Dostoevsky interpreters of their era. Both had a degree of direct contact with him. Not only had Rozanov met Dostoevsky, he had also razed the boundary between critic and critical object when he married his idol's former lover, the writer and emancipated woman Apollinaria Suslova, who had served as the inspiration for the tragic heroine of *The Idiot*, Nastasya Filippovna. Merezhkovsky's personal relationship with Dostoevsky was not nearly as complex, but the two had met briefly when he was a teenager. In 1880, Merezhkovsky's father took his son to meet the novelist at his St. Petersburg apartment. Merezhkovsky recalled the experience in what is now a well-known anecdote. As he makes clear in his recollection, the visit played out like an intrusion: "Blushing, growing pale and stuttering, I read him my childish, pitiful little verses (*zhalkie stishonki*). He listened silently with impatient annoyance. We must have disturbed him. 'Weak, poor, these aren't any good,' he said, finally. 'In order to write well, you need to suffer!' 'No, it's better that he doesn't write so he doesn't suffer!' father objected."[6]

Merezhkovsky's later role as Dostoevsky's critical champion, convinced of his prophetic import to Russian culture, is loud and clear in the reminiscence. The writer's intense visage, which many of his contemporaries remarked on in their memoirs, comes across vividly in the account: "I remember the translucent and piercing gaze of pale blue eyes."[7] Not only that, the image of Dostoevsky, toiling over corrections as he is interrupted by the boy and his father—amid the disarray of many copies of his latest and last novel, *The Brothers Karamazov*—conjures a feverishly productive writer in the year just before his death. In the eyes of the young Merezhkovsky, Dostoevsky's work was unfinished.

Rozanov and Merezhkovsky supplied many of the topics for the first real public venue for debating religious questions in Russian history at the Religious-Philosophical Meetings (1901–1903), which provided a forum for the intelligentsia and members of the Russian Orthodox clergy to discuss the role of the church in modern society. The proceedings of these discussions were published in the journal the *New Path*, which was edited by Merezhkovsky's close friend Petr Petrovich Pertsov. Merezhkovsky's spouse, Zinaida Gippius, and Filosofov, their companion, were deeply involved in the meetings. Also making a regular appearance at these gatherings was Rozanov, who—at the time—sought to rejuvenate the Russian Orthodox Church by returning it to what he believed were the life-affirming Jewish roots of Christianity, which had gone into decline. He was an especially passionate advocate for reforming the Church's policy on divorce, which he felt went against the procreative and family-centered daily life and rituals of Judaism, whose directive he emulated as the father of many children. In a stark contrast, the childless Merezhkovsky and Gippius used the meetings to establish the foundation of their so-called Third Testament, a reformation of Christianity that would end the historical conflict they perceived between "flesh" and "spirit." The new era of religious renewal, they believed, would lead to so-called consecrated flesh, the transformed state of being exemplified by Christ's miraculous divine body, which would reveal a new religious consciousness.

Beginning a bit before their historic participation at the meetings, from 1890 until the revolutionary years of 1905–1907, Rozanov and Merezhkovsky were publishing the most influential writing on Dostoevsky. With their *F. M. Dostoevsky's "Legend of the Grand Inquisitor"* (1890) and *L. Tolstoy and Dostoevsky* (1900–1901), Rozanov and Merezhkovsky proclaimed the author's prophetic import. Merezhkovsky's book on Tolstoy and Dostoevsky inaugurated the long "rivalry" between the two great novelists.[8] *L. Tolstoy and Dostoevsky* identified Tolstoy as a "seer (*tainovidets*) of the flesh" and Dostoevsky as a "seer of the spirit" and proclaimed that finally reconciling the writers' contrasting religious worldviews would bring about a Russian spiritual renewal.[9] This desired synthesis was elaborated in his Third Testament; however, it is in his literary essays that Merezhkovsky first worked out this binary and his dream of synthesizing its poles. Much of Merezhkovsky's portrait of Dostoevsky hinged on a comparison with the differing artistic qualities and religious values that he identified in Tolstoy.

Both Rozanov and Merezhkovsky adopted an approach to faithful reading that challenged the dominant critical methods of their day. In a reversal of biographical criticism, which purported to use the author to understand the text, they used the text as inspiration for creating their ideal author. In a similar way, they refuted the other mode of critique that had surged to prominence in the nineteenth century—civic and democratic criticism—by using Christianity as their motivational ideology rather than a form of socialism or agrarian populism (*narodnichestvo*). They employed their eclectic knowledge and interpretations about key events and cultures of the ancient world and early religious frameworks, reenvisioning Dostoevsky as a prophetic figure and presenting his texts as gateways to religious truth. Rozanov is famous for his selective use of quotations and invented, conversational dialogues between critic and invented critical object, while Merezhkovsky employed poetic, associational logic in his interpretations of authors and their texts. One of his most influential works of criticism that preceded *L. Tolstoy and Dostoevsky* was *Eternal Companions: Portraits from World Literature* (Vechnye sputniki. Portrety iz vsemirnoi literatury, 1897), which collected sermon-like analyses of major writers and their contributions to pressing religious topics such as faith, earthly temptation, and his hopes for a cultural synthesis of pagan and Christian worldviews. Rozanov and Merezhkovsky read literature as skilled interpreters of its forms and contexts, but, like other critics of the nineteenth century, they were deeply enmeshed in their own ideological projects and the social and political climate of their times. Aiming to repair what they perceived as the mistakes of suspicious "democratic" critics, who rejected Dostoevsky's religious obscurantism, their faithful reading was intended to restore him to a newly articulated intellectual trajectory that culminated in *their* work and the pressing need for religion, as they saw it.

Their readings had broader, nationalist aims, even as they critiqued the major state and cultural institutions of their day. In their separate interpretations of his cultural significance, they understood Dostoevsky in terms of his relationship to Russianness, which is seen as a gateway to a future religious renewal. Rozanov drew on the novels—especially *Crime and Punishment*—to challenge Dostoevsky's ties to Russian identity and Orthodoxy, making the daring argument that his artistic representations of spiritual turmoil had a latent connection to ancient Jewish culture and ritual. Merezhkovsky, on the other hand, understood Dostoevsky in terms of the chauvinist universalism proclaimed by the writer himself in his famous Pushkin speech: the pinnacle of Russianness was its ability to incorporate within its boundaries all nations and peoples. For Merezhkovsky, Dostoevsky was culturally European and the religious insight of his work turned back to ancient rites of Greek civilization rather than the Byzantine periphery of the Russian Orthodox Church. While Dostoevsky transcended national and ethnic boundaries, Tolstoy emerges in his book as a remnant of the Jewish past. By offering a glimpse into this little-known polemic between two famous commentators on Dostoevsky, this chapter seeks to highlight a peculiar case of reading faithfully. If in the previous chapter, the rearrangement and performance of Dostoevsky's text permitted a new relationship to the author and to his religious idea, Merezhkovsky and Rozanov relied on a reinvention of the author's cultural and historical position in order to establish greater control over his religious authority and link themselves to it. The efforts of Merezhkovsky and Rozanov reveal a troubling facet of the desire to eradicate the "two Dostoevskys" problem within utopian nationalist and racializing frameworks. Their era was a time of establishing who Dostoevsky was by determining what he was not.

While both Rozanov and Merezhkovsky agreed that something had gone wrong in the historical development of Christianity, they disagreed about the source of the ascetic (life-denying) forces that had come to direct it. Although Merezhkovsky was already an established poet and novelist, his *L. Tolstoy and Dostoevsky* is in large part a working out of his answer to this problem. This work began its publication in the journal *World of Art* (Mir iskusstva) in the first issue of 1900.[10] His book was in line with other nineteenth-century investigations into the origins of Christianity, which often relied on racial typologies like "Semitic" and "Aryan" to distinguish between the two societies whose collision, it was argued, gave rise to early Christianity. Following this approach, Merezhkovsky claimed that the ascetic turn in Christianity had "Semitic" origins, strong traces of which he identified in Tolstoy's religion. Dostoevsky's promising religious vision, by comparison, indicated the future of Christianity a third path—that could resolve the damage wrought by Semitic forces on contemporary Christian culture.

Meanwhile, Rozanov, in numerous essays on religious ritual and Russian literature dating from the same period, believed the Church's asceticism was merely the modern culmination of Christian dogma. Christianity itself was at fault and could potentially renew itself through reconnecting with the life-affirming rituals of Judaism and Semitic culture. Dostoevsky, Rozanov argued at the time, seemed to embody an essentialized notion of the spirit of Semitic proximity to divine revelation and mystical ritualism.[11] In other words, while Merezhkovsky sought to rejuvenate modern Christianity with an infusion of earthbound mysticism from Greek and Roman ("Aryan") paganism, Rozanov looked even more deeply into the past, to ancient Semitic and Egyptian cultures, which were perhaps less known and thus more pliable to his imagination. Merezhkovsky's "Semitic" Tolstoy directly contradicted Rozanov's "Semitic" Dostoevsky; both strove to underscore their own fundamental superiority, albeit by opposing interpretations of Semitism's role in world history and of Dostoevsky's texts themselves.

Finally, the fact that these debates about which races—Semitic or Aryan—held the key to Christianity's renewal were unfolding in the context of adjudicating Tolstoy and Dostoevsky as religious thinkers and artists shows how common new "scientific" notions of race had become in the discourse of their time.[12] The way Rozanov and Merezhkovsky used these terms—and the way they thought about what today we would call "race"—were quite individual, on the one hand, and on the other, conditioned by their historical moment. In their usage, the terms "Semitic" or "Semitism" (*semitstvo*) indicated a more general cultural field relating to belief, doctrine, or rituals of Judaism; at other times, semantic, tonal, and metaphorical indicators make clear that the term "Semitic" voiced an antisemitic worldview rooted in racial prejudice and belief in the biological and intellectual inferiority of Jews. Both employments of the term "Semitic" are inextricable from the semantic valance of the other.

"Semitism as a Point of View": Rozanov's Dostoevsky

Scholars often characterize Rozanov's earlier writings examined in this chapter as "philo-Semitic" in order to contrast them with his later virulent antisemitic writings. While the positive valance of his philo-Semitism is dubious, in that period, Rozanov had applied racial typologies to an admiring treatment of Jewish history and ritual. After 1908, Rozanov's understanding of Semitic culture had degraded into a more sophisticated racist worldview and the concurrent intensification of his antisemitic journalistic activity led to his ostracism by the liberal intelligentsia, who had once tolerated his "eccentric" attraction to Jewish culture.[13] Despite the evolution of Rozanov's views about Jews and Judaism over the course of his career, he consistently essentialized Jewishness and relied on stereotypes, even when he intended to elevate their race and culture. For this and other reasons, his reading of Dostoevsky as a Semitic figure deserves closer scrutiny.

Even when ostensibly employed to signify basic linguistic and cultural differences, the terms "Semitic" and "Aryan" had always implied the racial superiority of the latter category and its heirs: white, Western European society. By the turn of the century, these notions of cultural superiority acquired a veneer of scientific legitimacy. In the context of late-imperial Russia, where reactionary policies of the autocracy had stoked antisemitic rhetoric and violence, race and ethnicity were emerging as far more salient categories to classify and discipline the empire's diverse population.[14] In the second half of the nineteenth century, antisemitism was an acute social problem throughout Europe; however, frequent instances of ethnic violence (pogroms) against Jews in the late-tsarist period made Russia an especially volatile setting for the discursive application of Western European racial typologies. That being said, ethnic Russian and white Western European prejudice toward Jews and other groups was not restricted to reactionary circles. Merezhkovsky was a liberal Westernizer who denigrated Jews, Judaism, and "Semitic" cultural legacies, after all, and Rozanov was a conservative Slavophile, at the time, who held what appears to be the opposite view. But while the terms "Semitic" and "Aryan" were approaching a kind of biological fixity and bureaucratic utility, their persistent abstract philosophical signification made them highly mobile concepts, especially when they were employed by essayistic critics and religious thinkers such as Merezhkovsky and Rozanov. For this reason, not only the emergent role of race science and racial thinking should bear on a reading of the debates examined in this chapter but also should these critics' ample reliance on metaphor and analogy.[15]

Today, Rozanov is often remembered for his antisemitic articles in Aleksei Suvorin's newspaper, the *New Times* (Novoe vremia). The writings covered in this chapter deal with Rozanov's earlier period, between 1890 and 1903, before what some scholars identify as the "political" turn in his writings about Jewish identity and Judaism from "philo-Semitism" to antisemitism.[16] His criticism on Dostoevsky's writing and views on the evolution of Jews and Jewish culture align in this earlier period. Henrietta Mondry has expertly related the story of Rozanov's Semitization of Dostoevsky as a paradoxical form of his extreme idolization of the writer, whose own antisemitism would seem to disallow such associations.[17] But the broader implications of Rozanov's Semitic Dostoevsky are to be found in his relationship with Merezhkovsky and their disagreements about Christianity. Some background about Rozanov's intellectual trajectory is necessary before turning to their complex relationship.

When he was still virtually unknown and teaching history and geography at a high school in Elets (the philosopher Sergei Bulgakov was one of his students), Rozanov published an essay entitled *The Place of Christianity in History* (Mesto khristianstva v istorii, 1890). Its goal was to chart the development of Christianity as a reconciliation between Semitism's divine revelation and Aryan culture's gift for abstract thought and artistic talent.[18] Vladimir Soloviev, who reviewed it, commended Rozanov on the narrative of reconciliation in his portrait of the two groups. Rozanov's solution at the time had been to suggest a rapprochement of Semitic and Aryan cultures in world historical development, which Soloviev placed in contrast to "savage theories, [which] directly or indirectly deny the solidarity of races and cultural-historical types in joint historical work."[19] Soloviev's review shows that the fashionable terms "Semitic" and "Aryan" were seen at the time as both helpful descriptors and potential incitements to racial division.[20]

Racial typologies appear in Rozanov's influential book *F. M. Dostoevsky's "Legend of the Grand Inquisitor,"* but its pioneering examination of Dostoevsky's religion expends greater effort distinguishing the Christian superiority of the "Slavic" (Orthodox) race from "Germanic" (Protestant) and "Latin" (Roman Catholic) ones.[21] Rozanov was still a devoted Slavophile at this time and felt that Dostoevsky had failed to leverage the already superior culture of Orthodoxy. (We can compare Rozanov's tragic Dostoevsky to Merezhkovsky's view of Tolstoy as an earnest thinker desperate for but incapable of joyful faith.) In that book, Rozanov famously argued that "The Grand Inquisitor"—Ivan Karamazov's nightmare tale of a Roman Catholic hegemony over the cowed masses—was so artistically perfect and expertly argued that Dostoevsky had to have believed in its pessimistic vision. Dostoevsky seemed better able to understand the Latin passion for universality and the Germanic passion for particularity, Rozanov reasoned, than to articulate a victorious vision of the Slavic race (*rasa*), whose Orthodox beliefs could synthesize and overcome the two. After he broke with the St. Petersburg Slavophile circle and began writing more about Dostoevsky at the end of the 1890s, Rozanov abandoned his joyful vision of a triumphant Orthodoxy.[22] He began to extend his reading of Dostoevsky's gloomy regard for Western Christianity to an even broader critical stance on the Russian Orthodox Church and Christianity as a whole.

In one decade, Rozanov drifted from hopes for reconciliation between Aryan and Semitic races—and the related Slavophile impulse toward religious synthesis articulated during the same period—toward a growing critique of Christianity. This shift coincided with a new fascination that for many came out of left field: ancient Egypt.[23] He considered ancient Egyptian culture a product of Semitic civilization and brought what he claimed was its previously undiscovered survival into his contemporary cultural iconography and discourse. While his critical stance evokes the suspicious textual excavation of the "valiant archeologist," his prose style and conclusions foreshadowed the postmodern genre of "fictocriticism." His criticism was closer to the spirit of the *peredelka* examined in chapter 1, discovering unexamined details in the text that could be crafted into new, often shocking, interpretations of their originals. This was reading faithfully that hinged on a particular cultural-historical vision of Christianity's erasure of ancient religious ritual and worldviews. What on earth could ancient Egyptian culture tell us about Dostoevsky's religion?

Rozanov's articles on ancient Egyptian culture began appearing in *World of Art* and the *New Times*, where he had signed on as a regular columnist in 1899. In a particularly dense essay published in *World of Art*, "On Ancient Egyptian Beauty" (1899), Rozanov offered his own interpretation of ancient Egyptian hieroglyphics, claiming that burial rituals in ancient Egypt (which he saw reflected in Jewish practices) prove their belief in a *bodily* resurrection after death. Christian theology, of course, denies such a posthumous outcome (the body is left behind; the spirit is immortal).[24] More and more, Semitism's ancient roots had become the solution to the ascetic dogmatism he identified in the Russian Orthodox Church, which he saw in its strict divorce policies and rejection of sexuality. In keeping with his new embrace of Semitic culture, well into his philo-Semitic turn, Rozanov in these years revised some of his previous arguments in *The Place of Christianity in History* and regarded more favorably the role of Jewish ritual and culture in religion, both of which were instrumental to his Semitization of Dostoevsky.

Rozanov's gradual incorporation of Dostoevsky into his vision of life-affirming Semitism coincided with his turn away from Christianity and toward ancient Egypt and Judea. His contemporaries found this interpretation bizarre, but in 1906, Andrei Belyi considered Rozanov's observation that "Dostoevsky turns out to be Egyptian" a spark of genius.[25] In a rarely commented upon portion of "On Ancient Egyptian Beauty," Rozanov argues that Dostoevsky, like the Egyptians, understood immortality in a bodily, as well as spiritual, dimension. Halfway through this essay, Svidrigailov, the sensualist villain of *Crime and Punishment*, emerges as an inheritor of this fleshy afterlife.[26] In the novel, Svidrigailov and Raskolnikov have a rather theological discussion about life after death, in which Svidrigailov reveals that he believes in an immortality that few would desire: "Imagine if there's just a little room, like a village bathhouse blackened with soot with spiders in every corner; and that's all eternity is."[27] Rozanov takes this confession as a sign of his insightful mysticism, which is even more profound given the criminal proportions of his lust (he has perpetrated spousal murder and child rape). At the novel's conclusion, when a Jewish fireman becomes the last person to converse with Svidrigailov before his death by suicide,[28] Rozanov has all the evidence he needs of a connection between Svidrigailov's spirituality and ancient Egyptian (Semitic) death cults: "Why, having portrayed in his entire work no more than two or three Jewish figures, does [Dostoevsky] put one of them *there*, leading Svidrigailov before his end face to face with a Jew?" Just as Rozanov had read the Grand Inquisitor as Dostoevsky's mouthpiece in *The Brothers Karamazov*, he claims that Svidrigailov's self-inflicted death in the presence of a Jewish fireman demonstrates the author's attraction to Jewish death rituals (which, for Rozanov, derive from ancient Egyptian ones). Svidrigailov goes from being a man lost to Christian redemption to one mystically connected to ancient Jewish rites. Just as he had once claimed that Dostoevsky had sided with the Grand Inquisitor, Rozanov was now offering a reading of the villain Svidrigailov that endowed him with mystical significance. By the essay's final installment, the Jewishness of Svidrigailov comes to signify *Dostoevsky's* Semitism:

> Dostoevsky is a figure of our history—and an enormous one at that. It doesn't matter what that hanger-on babbled to Ivan (*The Brothers Karamazov*) [a reference to Ivan's conversation with the Devil in that novel], or what Svidrigailov personally feared; what matters is the person who drew *these characters* and thousands of

others, and, with insatiable energy, spoke "about the mysteries of eternity and the grave" [a verse from Pushkin's drafts]. This person is by now an ineradicable point of our historic course, an ineradicable feature also of general European development, even Aryan development. We know Semites as a *race*, but there is also *Semitism* as a point of view, as a tendency, and Dostoevsky has assumed this position. In his face we suddenly observe the characteristic head of a Jew, not of our own time, but of an ancient Jew.[29]

In Rozanov's writings of these years, there are other examples of this kind of associative logic that ties Dostoevsky's mysticism to Semitic, rather than Christian, origins, but this is the most explicit. Crucially, Rozanov's critical authority is based on his own peculiar analysis of characterization, which permits him to make surprising conclusions about Dostoevsky's intended meaning and even his ethnicity. The critic reaches an authoritative position vis-à-vis the author by using the text to explain the author, rather than the route of biographical criticism, which used the author to explain the text. Rozanov attributes more weight to the text, since the biography could turn up nothing definitive about a single author for the excavating critic. In the end, Rozanov discards biographical criticism in favor of his own biological criticism.

Rozanov's Semitization of Dostoevsky developed first from metaphysical similarities (Svidrigailov and ancient Egyptian beliefs about the afterlife) to more concrete cultural, social, and ritualistic ones. For instance, two years later in the essay "Stars" ("*Zvezdy*," 1901), Rozanov reads "tender and nervous Raskolnikov" as a recent manifestation of traditional sacrifices of doves made by Jewish women to "Jehovah."[30] Having committed a murder, Raskolnikov becomes initiated into a ritualistic connection to blood's sacrality, which Rozanov locates in an imagined Semitic "Orient"—from Babylon to "tender" China—and contrasts with the "bloodless sacrifice" of Christianity's Eucharist.[31] Framing the act of murder as ritual sacrifice, Rozanov's is an extremely unusual reading of the development of Raskolnikov's spirituality, which usually looks to the character of Sonia. In other words, his reading reorients the significance of the murder that Raskolnikov commits toward Jewish ritual and away from the more typical Christian narrative of sin and salvation. These attempts to attach themes of spirituality and ritualism to Dostoevsky's fictional universe is expanded upon a few years later in the essay "Ends and Beginnings" (1902), where Rozanov associated Jewish forms of kinship with the utopian society depicted in Dostoevsky's short story "Dream of a Ridiculous Man" (1877).[32]

Rozanov's persistent critique of Christianity and the rosy view of ancient Semitic culture that accompanied it both amused and frustrated those in his circle. Gippius considered his shifting religious allegiances a delusional quest, which was especially worsened by his erroneous elevation of the Old Testament God (the Jewish God): "He throws himself from one god to another, from Egyptian divinity to Zeus, from Zeus to the Biblical God, whom he calls God the Father totally in vain. He becomes a Father when the Son is born."[33] His religious search, she wrote elsewhere, was a kind of religious atavism: Rozanov seemed to think that "we'll come to, return to the succulent Biblical truth, we'll start living like the old days so we can descend into the grave, 'taking succor in the days' and having solid immortality in numerous descendants. A Biblical life [*byt*]—that's what we need to aim for!"[34]

Merezhkovsky, too, worried frequently about the early stages of Rozanov's eccentric views, but in an 1897 letter to Pertsov, it was clear he wished to avoid conflict: "[Rozanov] alone is the only person in Petersburg with whom we can unburden our hearts."[35] Rozanov, Gippius, and Merezhkovsky, for better or worse, were allies in their joint work of injecting literary and cultural criticism into the new spiritual searching of the first decade of the twentieth century. But their disagreements about the future of Christianity led them to diametrically opposed interpretations of Dostoevsky's place within it. Their critical work embodied the new direction of criticism toward poetic, associative interpretations of the text in order to reinvent the author as a figurehead of their religious searching—either toward or away from Christ.

Interlude: Dostoevsky's Jewish Critics

Merezhkovsky's concern about the influence of "Semitism" in Rozanov's writings was not unrelated to his own petty rivalries with Jewish colleagues who were responsible for some of the most popular writing on Tolstoy and Dostoevsky appearing in contemporary journals. Merezhkovsky's reflections on the work of the philosopher Lev Shestov and Akim Volynsky seemed to ask this question: Is it possible to be Jewish and write criticism about Dostoevsky? Occasionally these literary rivalries, as in the case of Shestov, were brought into sharp relief in journalistic venues. For example, the final installment of Merezhkovsky's serialized publication of *L. Tolstoy and Dostoevsky* and the beginning of Shestov's book-length examination of Dostoevsky and Nietzsche appeared in the same issue of *World of Art*.[36]

Volynsky, who was more proximate to Merezhkovsky's literary career and private life, may have posed a greater threat than Shestov.[37] Around the time Merezhkovsky was writing his novel about Leonardo da Vinci, *Resurrected Gods*, Volynsky was doing his own research on the artist. Volynsky had also written extensively on sensuality and religious impulses in Dostoevsky's novels (for instance, his *Karamazov Kingdom* [Tsarstvo Karamazovykh], 1901; and *The Book of Great Wrath* [Kniga velikogo gneva], 1903). A brief discussion of some key observations in those works helps unpack the racist motivations behind Merezhkovsky's attacks on him.

Volynsky produced his first extended critical essays on Dostoevsky (*Karamazov Kingdom*) while Merezhkovsky was finishing *L. Tolstoy and Dostoevsky*. In the same way that Merezhkovsky isolated two dominant tendencies in the work of both writers—flesh and spirit—Volynsky treated Dostoevsky's final novel as the pinnacle of the metaphysical dynamics of his whole corpus, all of which reflected either what he called "bogofiliia" or "bogofobiia" (love of God or rejection of God). "He shows us out of which native principles the human soul is constituted and how these native principles—rejection of God and love of God—constantly struggle among themselves, strengthening or weakening, depending on where human consciousness is directed. . . . Dostoevsky looks at the human being through the religious idea, which appears like a lens, deepening his vision and opening up the possibility for the sharpest artistic perceptions."[38] Volynsky's primary interest in Dostoevsky was the artistic potential of his religious idea rather than the religious idea itself. As he made clear in his volume of collected essays, *The Struggle for Idealism* (Bor'ba za idealizm, 1900), authentic art had always emerged from metaphysical searching—the Symbolist school of his time was such a moment. Symbolists were seeing the world through an idealist lens, which he considered synonymous with "the perception of life in ideas of the spirit, in the ideas of the divine and religion."[39] Out of the depths of psychological experience, Volynsky argued in an 1899 essay, new threads woven from the difficult contradictions of life would form. "From delicate, multicolored threads will be woven a new transparent and noble cloth, which lets in the sun's light; from transformed impressions will be woven a new higher art, which will emanate through itself the light of metaphysical truth."[40] For Volynsky, religion and spiritual awakening created good art; for Merezhkovsky, however, art was like divination, a method used by prophetic seers to communicate religious truths. Scholars of the early modernist period in Russian literature and criticism might recognize this debate as central to its time: Was spirituality just a means of generating art, or was art a means of spiritual communion?

Volynsky observed that Dostoevsky's own struggle to reconcile the material world with spiritual truth was reflected in the madness, or "holy-foolishness," of his religious idea and the novels that communicated it. While Kant had managed to expose the split between empirical and metaphysical realities, Russians (including Dostoevsky) could only sense this rift through madness.[41] However, in his "mad and disordered novels" the peculiar insight of Russian metaphysics into the formation of the modern psyche reached the "universal" and "pan-human."[42] Thus the seeming artistic disorder of Dostoevsky's novels, which Robert Louis Jackson would explore much later as the novelist's "quest for form," actually conveyed a spiritual wholeness.[43] For Volynsky, Dostoevsky embodies a strain of antirationalism, disorder, and Nietzschean "supranormality" that directly contrasts with Tolstoy's "normality."[44]

It took Russians some time to realize the prophetic wisdom of this madness, however, which Volynsky relates by recounting his own experience hearing Dostoevsky speak as a student:

> A little bit hunched over, sickly, with a face displaying the features of a tortured satanism, with eyes that drilled into you—that was Dostoevsky. That was how I remember him in an early fleeting vision from my youth, among the student masses, which huddled around him at some public evening. He said something to this student crowd with his special language, and I recall that the young people absentmindedly laughed at his prophetic speeches, for which the time had not yet come. If he had appeared now, with the same speeches, even having not changed in them one word, a great mass of people would have surrounded him, listening to him without being bewildered at all.[45]

There is an ambivalence here about Dostoevsky's prophetic stature. While Volynsky allows that the time has come for Dostoevsky's "madness," he also notes its potentially "satanic" source, which lightly aligns with Rozanov's reading of "The Grand Inquisitor." Volynsky points out merely that there is now an audience for these ideas, but he does not incorporate them into a belief system of his own. Rozanov would later consider such hesitancy a major stumbling block for Volynsky as an interpreter of Dostoevsky. Reviewing a later collection of essays, *Dosto-evskii* (1909), Rozanov accused Volynsky's "Jewish-Hellenic-Roman face" of failing to understand what was actually Jewish about Dostoevsky:

> Despite his great love for Dostoevsky, for his "cult"—nevertheless, one must say that everything about this reasonable and abstemious Roman makes him a philistine next to the great drunkenness of Dostoevsky the aristocrat, Dostoevsky the Jew. Starting with Gogol and just entering Dostoevsky, a dirty and powerful "Yid-like" [*zhidovskaia*] wave—whether it was from the Dead Sea or from the waters of the Sea of Galilee, we don't know—crashed into the Russian element. But it is clear that it was *not* Aryan and *anti*-Aryan, but a kind of eastern, Asian wave with that pearly gleam that rests atop stinking puddles and the black richness of oil.[46]

We can already observe the antagonistic turn in Rozanov's writing about Jews and Jewish culture in this 1909 commentary. Drawing on the idea of contagion and a mix of both anti-Asian and antisemitic prejudices (which were occasionally conflated in that era), Rozanov claims that Volynsky's tendency to avoid the mystical extremes of Dostoevsky's religious ideas and failure to acknowledge his prophetic status had something to do with his Jewish background. Volynsky had once claimed that Dostoevsky's religious art was peculiarly Russian, as well as universal; however, Rozanov seemed to think its mysticism was due to the writer's authentic Jewishness—something especially assimilated Jewish critics, in his view, were unable to appreciate.

As he continued writing, Volynsky became more critical of the nationalism in Dostoevsky's novels. This topic would be the guiding thematic of *The Book of Great Wrath* (1903), which is devoted to an extended analysis of Dostoevsky's antirevolutionary novel *Devils*, while also offering additional thoughts on the nexus of the writer's religious and national ideas. In his preface, Volynsky pauses to explain why he chose the book's cover, a painting of the prophet Jonah by George Frederic Watts. For him, Jonah is the jealous prophet par excellence, too devoted to the idea of his own people as "god-bearing" to bring a divine warning to the pagan city of Nineveh, whose conversion is desired by God. Volynsky views Jonah as the selfish gatekeeper of the Jewish faith, which reminds him of Dostoevsky's national prejudices, which are often directly addressed to Jews. When Jonah returns from the whale's belly to fulfill his divine task, he "flares up with the same fiery rage at the wall of Nineveh," and when the inhabitants repent and receive his message with willingness, he "unleashes a reproach right up to the heavens."[47] "Until the last moment, [Jonah] does not see that his prophecy to the pagans not only does not diminish his people, but makes it a truly god-bearing people, widening its meaning for humanity, and by doing so strengthening its connection to heaven. Due to his great wrath and patriotic blindness, Jonah does not see that he is becoming the living link to a great evolution of a pan-human awareness of God [*bogoponimanie*]."[48] Glancing at Watts's painting, Volynsky writes, "You involuntarily recall the author of *Devils*, with his great wrath and great blindness for relating to Europe, to non-Orthodox peoples. He also threw burning pitch at everything that was beyond the boundary of his Byzantine purview; he also believed in the exceptional god-bearing quality of his people. . . . Like Jonah, he wanted to take away a prophetic blessing from other nations, and meanwhile with his powerful art served the human being in general, that is, all peoples regardless of their national divisions."[49]

The centering of Jonah's image in *The Book of Great Wrath* is possibly a direct challenge to Merezhkovsky's clamorous insistence on the transcendent universality of Dostoevsky's religion. Watts's painting (figure 2.1) is an especially dramatic depiction of Jonah's prophetic figure: it shows a man wasted away by nationalist zeal against a backdrop of chiseled depictions of divinely punishable sin. This depiction of Jonah contrasts sharply with a published image of Tintoretto's depiction of the muscular and commanding prophet emerging from the whale (figure 2.2, for comparison), published by Pertsov in an essay of the same year in the *New Path*.[50]

Even when national identity is the very object of his critique, Volynsky is reluctant to deny the potential for Dostoevsky's God to reach universal audiences. Like Rozanov and Merezhkovsky, Volynsky draws on ancient cultural mythology to craft a new portrait of Dostoevsky. Unlike his antisemitic colleagues, Volynsky draws on Jonah with a sincerity that is missing in Rozanov's ancient Egyptian fantasies of Dostoevsky's Jewishness and Merezhkovsky's prejudiced invocations of Old Testament themes and figures in his own book. Comparing Jonah with Dostoevsky, Volynsky suggests the tragedy of a writer whose moral-religious message was compromised by denying it to Jews and other peoples. While Dostoevsky and Jonah were of different faiths, they seem to have made the same mistakes as influential men of their times.

Figure 2.1. *Jonah* (1894) by George Frederic Watts

Figure 2.2. *Jonah Leaves the Whale's Belly* (1577–1578) by Tintoretto

Merezhkovsky's Antisemitic Criticism and Rozanov's Historical "Correctives"

Volynsky's appeal to the secularized framework of idealism and his nuanced critique of Dostoevsky's prophetic stature—along with the usual professional and intellectual sparring of peers—seem logical sources of Merezhkovsky's ire. But Merezhkovsky's baser prejudices superseded more intellectual disagreements and led him to attack Volynsky himself rather than the content of his criticism. Even when still on good terms with Volynsky, Merezhkovsky admitted that he was attracted to the "genuine purity, the naivete of philosophical ardor, the fiery and yet chaste passion of mind" of Semitic temperaments.[51] The fiery passion of Semites, argues Merezhkovsky, originates with their "thousand-year thirst for God," which has routinely served to nurture "peaceful Aryan cultures" that have succumbed to forms of materialism and positivism over the ages.[52]

Merezhkovsky's attacks were not limited to Volynsky but extended to his appraisal of Shestov's first book, *The Good in the Teaching of Tolstoy and Nietzsche* (Dobro v uchenii gr. Tolstogo i F. Nitsshe, 1900). In a letter to Pertsov, Merezhkovsky remarked, "His book is remarkable. Although it is undoubtedly 'Semitic,' written as if neither Christ nor Christianity ever existed. And indeed, as always with Yids (even in Spinoza), *it is that and yet not about that* or *it is about that and yet not that* [*to da ne o tom, ili o tom da ne to*]. But in any case, it would be curious to meet up with this Shvartsman [Shestov's given name]."[53] By the end of the 1890s, this condescending rejection of the "Semitic" critical work and temperaments of Volynsky and Shestov developed into much more forceful and negative attacks on Tolstoy's alleged Semitism in *L. Tolstoy and Dostoevsky*. Later, in the same issue of *World of Art* where Shestov's own essay on Dostoevsky and Nietzsche appeared, Merezhkovsky used phrasing identical to his letter to Pertsov to dispute the authenticity of Tolstoy's Christianity: "When he speaks about Christianity, one feels that he is not at all speaking 'about that'—it's all the same, true or untrue, but mainly— 'not about that.'"[54] In these responses to his Jewish peers, Merezhkovsky responded to two varieties of Semitism among critics who wrote extensively on Dostoevsky and Tolstoy. The first was the Jewish heritage and what he believed to be the Semitic minds of his Jewish rivals in literary-philosophical criticism (Volynsky and Shestov). The second polemic was leveled at Rozanov's anti-Christian promotion of Jewish culture and religion and his insistence on Dostoevsky's Semitism.

In the years Merezhkovsky was publishing *L. Tolstoy and Dostoevsky* in *World of Art* (1900–1901), Rozanov often publicly defended him against attacks from the press, which some interpreted as ideological solidarity. Indeed, Rozanov and Merezhkovsky were assumed to hold identical views by the clergy with whom they sparred at the Religious-Philosophical Meetings. The clear differences in their worldviews would emerge more clearly and more often beginning in 1903, when the recorded discussions of those meetings were printed in the *New Path*. According to Merezhkovsky, it was Nikolai Berdiaev who first succinctly and correctly characterized their views as oppositional. Berdiaev had seen what others did not, Merezhkovsky wrote, "No one suspected that this closeness of intersecting opposed extremes, is the closeness of opponents who are preparing for a fight to the death."[55]

Even as they projected an allied front, Merezhkovsky continued to express discomfort in his private correspondence about Rozanov's movement toward a Semitic outlook. In a letter to Pertsov in May 1900, Merezhkovsky wrote, "In Rozanov there really is an eternal Aryan; precisely even a passing into Semitism is beginning. Sometimes he is a pure Jew, not even an Egyptian. But in any case, we need him because he is an enormous talent."[56] Rozanov publicly demonstrated his alliance with Merezhkovsky when, a month later, with *L. Tolstoy and Dostoevsky* still far from its conclusion (it was only about a third completed), Rozanov published a glowing editorial note on the book's serialization in *World of Art*.[57] It appeared that Merezhkovsky needed the support. He was facing blowback for his attacks on Tolstoy's religious beliefs at a public lecture delivered to the St. Petersburg Philosophical Society on February 6, 1901, which was titled "On the Relationship of L. Tolstoy to Christianity."[58] The liberal press interpreted his critique of Tolstoy's Christianity as support for Lev Nikolaevich's recent excommunication. Rozanov came to his defense immediately, but, in typical fashion, he extended Merezhkovsky's critique of Tolstoy's Christianity to a general critique of Christianity itself.[59] No one seemed to notice a shift in Merezhkovsky's discourse amid his ongoing work on *L. Tolstoy and Dostoevsky*, which framed Tolstoy as an Old Testament, "Semitic" corruption of Christianity, who had rejected all positive, but dormant, pagan impulses that remained in his work. This criticism of Tolstoy was part of Merezhkovsky's broader attack on an imagined history of Semitic influence on Aryan culture, which he viewed as the true source of Christianity's life-affirming spirit. Following Nietzsche, he insisted on the joyful and youthful qualities of Aryanism; Semitism, on the other hand, he related to a denial of life, degeneration, and cold rationalism.

When Rozanov eventually reviewed Merezhkovsky's completed book in the summer of 1900, he continued to insist that Merezhkovsky had reason to label Tolstoy as a "pagan" (*iazychnik*), but for him the writer's unconvincing Christian belief reflected a deeper historical problem:

> In miniature, in the personal biography [of Tolstoy] we observe, if you will, an enormous collision of sorts between the Hellene and the Judean. But there in history, it was Hellenic soil that was decrepit, already plowed and re-plowed, and it had collapsed, passively accepting the Galilean seed. Tolstoy has the nature of Svyatogor,[60] the virgin soil of untold Rus'. It was this that was merely excited by the Galilean seed; but for all the "exhausted" powers of the giant, it just would not succumb to the seed.[61]

This passage is a good example of Rozanov's employment of sexual metaphor. Hellenic soil is cast as feminine and barely fertile, while the inseminating Judean element has animating power. As the Russian extension of the Hellenic virgin soil (one assumes that Rozanov is referring to Orthodox Christianity), Tolstoy has not permitted Judean influence and the soil remains exhausted and deprived of life. Though he may be a good pagan, there is nothing Jewish about Tolstoy.

Merezhkovsky seems to have immediately responded to this review, for in the next installment of *L. Tolstoy and Dostoevsky* he included a striking passage that returns to and rewrites Rozanov's account of Tolstoy's paganism and his uncultivated, anti-Judean Christianity.[62] That passage, which has received no critical attention, and Merezhkovsky's sustained attempt in his book to demonstrate Tolstoy's Semitism, appear directed against Rozanov: "Here for the first time the spirit of Semitism (*semitstvo*), the spirit of the desert and emptiness, breathed on the grandly, wildly grown, diverse, many-leaved, fabled forest of the Indo-European world. Although its venom poisoned only one already dried out branch of a still fresh, green Aryan tree, the poison was so strong that one drop was enough to infect the new Aryan races (*plemena*), having only just flooded in from Asia to Europe, which subsequently, due to their extreme youth, were defenseless before all of this cultural poison. The old man had infected the child."[63] Merezhkovsky's imaginary narrative of the fate of Indo-European culture reflects antisemitic stereotypes that were common at the time. Of a more sinister bent is the language of infection and invasion—as well as the explicit mention of race (*plemia*)—all of which introduce the possibility that biological specificity and cultural particularism have merged in this passage.[64]

No doubt alarmed that Semitism had begun to emerge in Merezhkovsky's book as a negative religious force, Rozanov responded to his colleague in the form of a short essay, "A Small Historical Correction" (1901). Here he disagreed with Merezhkovsky's characterization of Semitism as an ascetic religion, referring to his earlier essay, *The Place of Christianity in History*, to note that he too had once been similarly mistaken. Performing a final "Historical Correction" and concluding his essay, he appears to return to Merezhkovsky's image of the Aryan tree that has been poisoned by the "spirit of Semitism" and reverses the historical narrative: "The garden is Zion; Europe has stripped it, not having the strength to produce anything itself of the kind and now sells it in sardine tins."[65] Rozanov's Slavophilism continues to make itself known in his writings of this time; however, it appears as a philo-Semitic anti-Westernism to combat his colleague's rosy notion of an Aryan rebirth in the future of Christianity.

It seems that, at every stage of writing his book, Merezhkovsky had Rozanov, his defense of Semitism, and his penchant for aligning it with Dostoevsky's religion in mind. In such a way, the scapegoating of Tolstoy's Semitism in Merezhkovsky's book had the broader aim of reinforcing the essential Christianity of Dostoevsky and its still-vital potential. Both critics were struggling to align Dostoevsky with a cultural current that would place them in line to inherit his wisdom. Their writings on Dostoevsky were beginning to produce wild fictions about the author's core religious idea and the author himself, which was for Rozanov looking to the ancient past of Judaism, and for Merezhkovsky striving into a future Christianity that circumvented historical patterns of cultural development and that would culminate in apocalyptic revelation. While Rozanov relied on small samples of Dostoevsky's texts to support his Semitic interpretation of the author—and Merezhkovsky did the same toward opposite conclusions—their core dispute was over the proper interpretation of Dostoevsky's historical image and religious importance to their own projects. Their interpretations pointed to a new trend in writing about Dostoevsky: his religious ideas were now being viewed as inextricable from his art.

Merezhkovsky on Tolstoy's Semitism and Dostoevsky's Universal Christianity

In *L. Tolstoy and Dostoevsky* Merezhkovsky elevates Dostoevsky to the status of "new Christian" and presents Tolstoy as epitomizing Semitism.[66] Confusingly, at the same time he frames Tolstoy as a life-denying Semite, Merezhkovsky also returns to certain features of the novelist's worldview that he considers salvageable fragments of the Aryan cultural legacy. Where Tolstoy succeeded, he argues, is in the suppressed Aryan qualities of his vision of the world and human life. This seeming inconsistency in Merezhkovsky's book—how could Tolstoy be both Aryan and Semitic?—serves two purposes. First, the undeveloped promise of Tolstoy's latent "Aryan" nature provides a narrow path to synthesis with Dostoevsky's Christianity. Second, the complete racialization of Tolstoy permits a vision of Dostoevsky as transcending the earthbound typologies that so debilitate Tolstoy's spiritual promise.

Both the emergent role of race science and Merezhkovsky's use of metaphor and analogy should bear on a reading of *L. Tolstoy and Dostoevsky*. Merezhkovsky was above all else a poet, and his lifelong fascination with the history of religion put his metonymic talents as a versifier to new use. While his employment of Semitic and Aryan typologies in his book has eluded scholarly attention because such terms do not appear at a high frequency—"Aryan" appears nineteen times and "Semitic" appears sixteen times—their seeming inconsequentiality is overruled by their semantic valence. In an effort to counter Rozanov's "Semitic" Dostoevsky, Merezhkovsky mobilized similar cultural metaphors and stereotypes. It was not Dostoevsky, but Tolstoy, who turns out to be Semitic.

The most consistent argument that Merezhkovsky makes about Tolstoy's Semitic worldview is that his religion returns to an Old Testament morality. In 1899, Volynsky had also presented Tolstoy as "Old-Testament, almost Orthodox," but his comparison was not racialized and referenced the writer's similarity to the Greek titan Atlas, holding the ancient world on his shoulders.[67] But at various points in his book, Merezhkovsky employs Hebrew terms to mark Tolstoy's Semitic qualities with a negative connotation. Such references are to Israel, the fire of Sinai, the God "Adonai," and Lord "Tsebaoth" (of Hosts).[68] These terms indicate a common stereotype about the Jewish God's severity (the God of Judgment) in contrast to the New Testament God of love.[69] Frequent references in the book to Paul's Epistle to the Hebrews 12:29 ("For our God is a consuming fire") emphasize the threatening aspect of Tolstoy's morality, but Merezhkovsky reverses the original meaning of the biblical passage. Whereas in Hebrews, the Evangelist exhorts his Christian audience to resist the rising influence of Judaism, Merezhkovsky tells of how in a much earlier period, the Semites succeeded in subduing a diverse, life-affirming Aryan culture through the "all-consuming fire" of its cruel God.[70]

More generally, Semitic self-denial is associated with important metaphors of dryness, fire, and wind or breath, all of which combine in Merezhkovsky's favorite image of Semitism: the desert, a symbol of exclusion, punishment, and barrenness. The desert conveys the ascetic culture of the Semites as well as their isolation, resonating with a familiar trope of what is perceived as the Jews' self-willed exile, an extension of a self-hating and life-denying people, whose faith in God is rooted in fear rather than love.

This image of the God of Judgment is for Merezhkovsky nowhere more clearly illustrated than in the famous epigraph of *Anna Karenina*— "Vengeance is mine, I shall repay" (Deut. 32:35; Romans 12:19)—which he chooses to interpret in its Old Testament variation.[71] For him, the epigraph confirms the writer's affiliation with the Old Testament God and disavowal of Christ's mercy. Such a framing of the writer is sustained throughout the book. Tolstoy is later compared to the apostle Paul on the road to Damascus, whose famous conversion occurs after hearing Jesus cry out, "Saul, Saul, why do you persecute me?" (Acts 9:4). Merezhkovsky compares this experience to "L. Tolstoy, already 'breathing by the threats and murders' of Old-Testament, fleshless and bloodless *'circumcised'* Christianity."[72] The same circumcision trope appears again in the text with emphatic reference to Tolstoy's "Judaizing (*zhidovstvuiushchii*) Christianity."[73] Ironically, it was just such a Judaized Christianity that Rozanov had hoped for, but to Merezhkovsky it indicates Tolstoy's religious corruption.

In his response to Rozanov's Semitic Dostoevsky, it is possible that Merezhkovsky was also aware of and eager to dispute Tolstoy's view, attributed to Maxim Gorky, that "there was something Jewish in [Dostoevsky's] blood."[74] In his attack on the novel *Resurrection*, Merezhkovsky employs anti-Asian language in a critique of the character Simonson, who appears toward the end of Tolstoy's novel. Earlier in his writings, Merezhkovsky had linked qualities like mechanical regulation, abstract philosophy, homogeneity, and ascetic worldviews to both Semitic and Asian (to him, synonymous with Buddhism) typologies.[75] Simonson is a Jewish political prisoner and romantic partner of the novel's Russian peasant heroine, Katiusha Maslova. Simonson's devotion to natural science—particularly his interest in blood particles known as phagocytes—and his rather unpassionate but steady love for Maslova are for Merezhkovsky a sign of his intellectual and racial inferiority: "All these American Yankee Simonsons and Nabatovs, little Russian peasants, are reminiscent of yellow-faced positivists, little Chinese and Buddhist peasants. . . . [They] are correct, clear, smooth, naked and shamelessly healthy, like Edison's latest electromotors, phones, and phonographs; everything in them is made from aluminum or "made out of rubber." . . . They are terrifying already in and of themselves; but still more terrifying is the fact that Tolstoy looks on them like the flourishing of European and Russian culture, like the Christian salt of the earth."[76] Nineteenth-century Russians viewed the United States in terms of its highly developed culture of industry, which explains some of those comparisons, but the introduction of the epithet "yellow-faced positivist" marks Simonson, who the reader knows is Jewish, and underscores his racial difference. When Merezhkovsky holds Jews analogous to Asian types, he seeks to bring one race's perceived inferiority into the meaning system of the other.[77] Representatives of the purely rational, the purely mechanical, Simonson and his ilk are mere dehumanized metal and rubber. In the way that the Buddhist outlook often attributed to Asians signals for Merezhkovsky a sort of "spiritual" nihilism, his references to Jews' materialism follows what contemporary anti-Semites considered that group's presumed allegiance to socialism. John Klier has described how such "conservative Judeophobia" relies on the fallacy that the majority of nihilists were Jews.[78]

Alongside Merezhkovsky's case for Tolstoy's Semitism he maps out the writer's innate Aryan insight, with the result that Tolstoy's very person becomes symbolic of the destructive clash of Aryan and Semitic cultures. When he does praise Tolstoy as a "great Aryan" (*velikii ariets*), Merezhkovsky considers him a pre-Christian relic of a time when there were no hierarchical distinctions between living beings, when "God's creation" meant both "the man of God" and "God's beast."[79] Uncle Eroshka, a character from *The Cossacks* (1863), becomes for Merezhkovsky the primary symbol of Tolstoy's latent Aryanism and the figure who best characterizes his creator's healthy Epicureanism. While initially Eroshka stands as a positive figure for Tolstoy's insight into the flesh, as Merezhkovsky works to level Tolstoy's Christianity against Rozanov's Semitization of Dostoevsky, Eroshka becomes a signal of "Old Testament" values.[80] And so, at his very best, Tolstoy emerges as a latter-day figuration of the ancient Aryan struggle and ultimate failure to resist the poisonous influence of Judaism and Semitic culture. Following the path indicated by Dostoevsky becomes the only viable option.

Once his book was published as a separate volume, critics continued to note Merezhkovsky's concerted effort to tarnish Tolstoy's legacy, but the racial typologies employed in the process went unremarked upon.

The influential populist critic N. K. Mikhailovsky was one of the first to call out one especially "disgustingly frenzied takedown (*vykhodka*)," in which Merezhkovsky claimed Tolstoy's aristocratic lineage was defiled by its having been earned with his ancestor's work for the "Secret Chancellery," Peter I's governmental agency responsible for surveillance.[81] In a review of the book's second volume, where he frequently employs racial typologies, Mikhailovsky quotes the text in such a way that he can avoid engaging with antisemitic commentary about Spinoza, whom Merezhkovsky calls "a little Amsterdam *yid*."[82] Mikhailovsky likewise does not seem to attribute great significance to the place of Semitism in Merezhkovsky's historical consciousness: "All other kinds of paganism, as well as Judaism, Buddhism, and Islam, whose adherents as a whole currently comprise 70 percent of the world's population, remain outside the purview of Mr. Merezhkovsky; their role in the universal and otherworldly (*premirnyi*) struggle is unknown."[83] The widespread prejudice against Jews in these years provides a likely rationale for Mikhailovsky's silence about Merezhkovsky's consistent attacks on Judaism and Jewish culture.

Subsequent readers of the book would focus on the influential framework of "Dostoevsky's spirit vs. Tolstoy's flesh," but Merezhkovsky's polemic with Rozanov and his prejudiced views about Jewish critics provide a sense of the politics behind any reference to Dostoevsky's "spirit" and the stakes of his perceived spiritual superiority over a Semitic Tolstoy.

The polemic between Rozanov and Merezhkovsky indicates what we might describe as a new Slavophile-Westernizer debate, revamped in the era of race science and Silver Age literary criticism. The backward-looking glance of Rozanov's Semitic Dostoevsky suggests the lingering influence of his Slavophile roots. In the way earlier Slavophiles harked back to the traditional practices and religious culture of their (socially constructed) ethnos, Rozanov went even further into the past to find their mysterious, ancient sources. The result was a kind of "Semitic neo-Slavophilism," which he offered as a means of intervening in the role that Dostoevsky was playing in the flourishing of Russian religious thought. His Dostoevsky was meant to destroy, rather than restore, the church's role in private life. In one of his 1901 feuilletons, Rozanov wrote with subtle cynicism, "It seems we would not be mistaken if we were to say that in Russian society there is a current, a streamlet, a school of religious thought that begins and comes from Dostoevsky."[84]

Ever the provocateur, Rozanov claimed that Dostoevsky's discovery of God in the world (Ivan's "sticky leaves" or Zosima's channeling of St. Francis of Assisi) should pull Russian society *away* from Christianity and not toward it: "The 'materialist' movement of Christianity is its movement towards the resurrection within itself of the Hellene and the Jew."[85] Suggesting a return to Hellenism as a way of reforming modern Christianity was not new—Merezhkovsky of course held a version of this idea—but Rozanov foregrounded Jews and demonized Christianity in his vision and Merezhkovsky did the reverse.

By contrast, Merezhkovsky's concerted effort to associate Tolstoy's religious views with "Semitism" avoided any mention of Dostoevsky's ethnicity, apart from his European and Russian sensibilities. Dostoevsky's transcendence of the Aryan-Christian divide, indeed of racial categorization itself, reflects, in comparison with Rozanov's paradoxical neo-Slavophilism, Merezhkovsky's peculiar assimilation of Westernizer ideology. Rozanov often mocked his friend's "Westernizer" tendencies, noting in 1903 that "even though I knew nothing about his race [*rod-plemen'*], I didn't doubt the conclusion that somehow in his veins flowed impure Russian blood. There is an undoubted western mix in it."[86] Much later, after their definitive break and Rozanov's ostracism from literary circles, Rozanov agreed with a friend's thoughts sent to him in a letter: "I think Dostoevsky would have said to Merezhkovsky, had he known him, the same thing that Stavrogin told Shatov, *'I'm sorry, I cannot love you.'* Of course! Of course! Dostoevsky was all in it for Russia [*ves' bol' za Rossiiu*], to which Merezhkovsky was so interminably indifferent."[87]

If Rozanov had scoffed at Dostoevsky's emergence as a Christian prophet, Merezhkovsky privately lamented his growing eclipse. Writing to Pertsov in August 1899, he confessed his fear that "Tolstoy has overshadowed Dostoevsky. This is a conviction not at all held by all of our generation, but by our fathers, or even older brothers."[88] Of course, Merezhkovsky's polemic with Rozanov was just one reflection of a broader project to rewrite the history of Russian literature. As he worked on *L. Tolstoy and Dostoevsky*, he was also writing his novel about Peter I, and his increasingly critical orientation toward Tolstoy expressed itself in a sort of unlikely rapprochement between Peter and Dostoevsky (who was ambivalent about the legacy of Peter's reforms). In September 1899, Merezhkovsky admitted to Pertsov, "Only now I understand finally and unconditionally that the salvation of all Europe, of the whole world (that is, of the Earthly sphere) is in us, Russians, and *only* in us, and maybe precisely in *us* few (*terrifyingly few!*), the lawful inheritors of Russian Culture—of Peter, Pushkin and Dostoevsky, St. Sophia of Divine Wisdom, the Third Russian Rome—'and the fourth will never come.' "[89] The cultural imperialism exhibited in this confession illuminates the broader argument of Merezhkovsky's revisionist book: the reclaiming of Dostoevsky from the Slavophile critics (Strakhov et al.) and the transformation of him into a pan-European prophet, clearing the path for a new era in Western civilization through a flourishing Russian religious culture. Dostoevsky's well-known messianism is preserved in this new Westernized version; the geographical position of the "star that shines from the east" has not changed, but its cultural essence is a Western, ancient Hellenic one rather than one rooted in and emanating from Slavic lands and traditional Orthodoxy. Merezhkovsky's wresting of Dostoevsky from the descendants of the Slavophiles (emblematized in the figure of his friend and fellow critic Rozanov) is part of a larger cultural reckoning about the writer, his universal significance as a religious thinker, and the ethnic categories critics believed that he inhabited or transcended, as the case may be.

The critical debate between Merezhkovsky and Rozanov over Dostoevsky's cultural orientation created two futures for the writer's perceived religious idea. It either looked back to ancient notions of fleshy life after death (Rozanov's anti-Christian Semitic stance) or it faced forward, looking ahead to a transformed future of "consecrated flesh" (Merezhkovsky's future Christian synthesis). But whichever direction Dostoevsky's religious path led, the critical impulse demonstrated by Rozanov and Merezhkovsky to make Dostoevsky stand for a new page in the history of Christianity demonstrates the prominent role he was beginning to play in questions of national and religious identity. If the 1890s revealed a collective desire among critics to preserve the intimate links between Dostoevsky's texts and his biography, the close of that decade and the start of a new century ushered in a new critical approach that followed the religious projects of the critics themselves. Their interpretations are ordinarily viewed as "subjective criticism" and are considered less accurate than scientific approaches available in the imminently succeeding Formalist school. However, the portrait of Dostoevsky as a prophet of a new religious paradigm was arguably more lasting than the Formalists' program, whose changing political era helped them (initially) break free of nationalist ideology and idealist philosophy. In the interpretive work of Rozanov and Merezhkovsky, Dostoevsky's texts were mobilized as evidence of the two critics' reinvention of the author, who would become the figurehead of the future of Christianity in late imperial Russia. Their faithful critical reading engaged textual matter to craft an invented authorial spirit that could stand for their own cultural-religious stance. The ideology motivating their work was abhorrent, which scholars today must hold together with the fact of their lasting influence on subsequent critics' deep, cocreative interpretive work on the text of the novels. By reinventing the author via imaginative cultural-historical interpretation, textual mining, and a good deal of creative quotation, these critics only seemed to surmount the problem of "two Dostoevskys." They were able to do so by relying on the rhetoric of prophecy and nationalist ideology that the critics of the next era needed to confront and struggled to adapt to their comparatively progressive political agenda.

CHAPTER 3

Idealist Critics and the Reign of Character over Author, 1901–1905

Leading up to the revolution in 1905, Dostoevsky was already the subject of numerous new monographs, and his influence on the mood of Symbolist poetry and criticism was unmistakable. Dovetailing with a surge of interest in Nietzsche's Übermensch and moral philosophy, writers and thinkers were drawn to the figure of the rebellious hero in Dostoevsky's fiction, whose Underground Man and nonconformist young heroes like Rodion Raskolnikov and Ivan Karamazov posed burning questions to contemporaries about the almost divine power of individual action (self-deification) and whether morality could exist in a world without God. These audacious and violent fictional creations were also enormously compelling to Symbolists. For many, character types functioned as ancient pathways into a deeper understanding of human psychology: such modern Titans aestheticized the tragedy and ethics of transgressing divine command. Were such interpretations of Dostoevsky's heroes a sign of decadent apocalypticism, or was there something of more serious religious value about these "idea-characters," vestiges of nineteenth-century polemics about revolutionary socialism and its discontents?

Some Symbolists, like Konstantin Bal'mont, were still under the impression that the rebellious heroes of Dostoevsky's fiction were just facets of the author's own personal struggle. So Bal'mont wrote in his essay "On Russian Poets" (*O russkikh poetakh*), portions of which he delivered at the Taylor Institution at Oxford's Bodleian Library in 1897: "Incarnated by the Russian devil of nihilism, *podvizhnichestvo* [the saintly commitment to spiritual ends], and a tortured search for God that had been merged with Satanism, we might compare him with both Dickens—the creator of hero-criminals—and Edgar Allan Poe."[1] Rozanov had provocatively proposed that the Inquisitor was Dostoevsky himself, a sign that the writer had despaired of Christ's triumph over materialist philosophy and religious tyranny. But nearly twenty years after Rozanov's essay, the political economist and philosopher Sergei Bulgakov (1871–1944) would advance a new reading of Ivan's poem about the Grand Inquisitor that left Dostoevsky out of it. Although decades later, scholarly and critical evaluations of Dostoevsky were firmly under the influence of Nikolai Berdiaev, at the turn of the twentieth century, it was Bulgakov who had real credentials as a leading commentator on Dostoevsky's role in contemporary Russian society.[2] Distancing his analysis from the author, Bulgakov's lecture, "Ivan Karamazov as a Philosophical Type" (*Ivan Karamazov kak filosofskii tip*, 1901) would elevate character over author. Ivan, his tragic rebellion for an ideal that could never be, was the hero of Bulgakov's retelling. His faithful reading discarded Dostoevsky's authorship toward a view of character as a privileged source of truth in novelistic discourse. In this chapter, I will show how the idealist reading of Ivan elevated the hero over his author, a literary effect Mikhail Bakhtin would later proclaim was the distinguishing characteristic of Dostoevsky's novelistic art. While Vladimir Zakharov has criticized this tendency, naming it "Dostoevsky without Dostoevsky (the hero instead of the writer)," the idealists' privileging of Ivan over his author allowed them to transcend Dostoevsky—and his political views—in a way that would resonate with the more practical reformist politics of those affiliated with the idealist movement in philosophy.[3] What was this new idealism that so captivated Bulgakov's generation?

Bulgakov's lecture on Dostoevsky was not the chief aim of his philosophical activity, but it can be viewed as a response to Symbolist criticism of over a decade, part of a new turn in the worldview of some members of the intelligentsia: idealism. In the first years of the twentieth century, "idealism" was less a philosophical school and more a broad tendency in literature, philosophy, and criticism that positioned itself against nineteenth-century realist trends in art and the positivist critical modes of the previous century that accompanied them. Materialist critics had long promoted a view of reality upheld by sociological methods, which had been inherited by Marxist critics of the 1890s. Drawing on the work of Immanuel Kant, Volynsky had defined idealism simply as a privileging of subjective experience and metaphysical insight over sociological and materialist modes of representation in art or in critical analysis. In *The Struggle for Idealism* (1900), he devoted numerous essays to proving that trends in Symbolism were the best evidence of the rise of idealism and the need for criticism to adopt an idealist approach. In the foreword to the landmark volume *Problems of Idealism* (1903), to which Bulgakov contributed an important essay, Pavel Novgorodtsev offered a different definition of idealism than Volynsky, claiming that philosophical idealism is "first of all and primarily an expression of the progressive principles of moral consciousness."[4] By this he defines idealism as the rejection of positivist responses to moral questions, which can only be resolved by individuals who themselves seek to move toward ideals established by the "categorial imperative of morality."[5]

It can be challenging to define idealism based on who claimed it as a worldview, since others of this group, including Berdiaev (1874–1948), Semyon Frank (1877–1950), and A. S. Glinka (1878–1940, who wrote under the pseudonym Volzhskii), were different from most other critics affiliated with Symbolism or the new art movements.[6] Many of them were former Marxists and, even more remarkable, Bulgakov and some of his colleagues saw themselves in Dostoevsky's heroes.[7] Bulgakov would claim in his lecture on Ivan, "Of the entire gallery of types in this novel, this image [Ivan] is to us, the Russian intelligentsia, the closest, the most dear [*rodnoi*]; we ourselves are sick with his sufferings, we understand his grievances [*zaprosy*]."[8] It is through that lens that he and his colleagues would read Ivan as an archetype of their philosophical searching. This tendency among younger idealists to personally connect with Dostoevsky's heroes was a shift in previous strategies of critical affect.

The idealist context helps to explain Bulgakov's unusual intervention in Dostoevsky criticism of the time. While Vasily Rozanov and Dmitry Merezhkovsky focused on remaking the author to fit their own projects, Bulgakov and others reinterpreted the hero through the lens of their idealist worldview, which upheld the fundamental value of personhood as the arbiter of moral consciousness. The hero's voice began to surmount the presumed one of the author in the novels, and it permitted new, to some, radical interpretations of characters everyone had thought stood for one or another tendency. Ivan's moral failings are all the more compelling because of the acute moral conscience that seems to motivate his philosophical justifications for rejecting God. Of course, it is still possible to read Ivan as the architect of his father's murder, but Bulgakov helped make the religious significance of Ivan—and by extension, Dostoevsky—an independent phenomenon of philosophical interest that stemmed from the author's creation. Bulgakov and his colleagues in philosophical idealism would offer a practical interpretation of the ethical core of Dostoevsky's religious ideas that challenged the mystical, utopian, and nationalist lenses offered in the criticism of Merezhkovsky and Rozanov.

A New Century of Dostoevsky Criticism: Philosophical Idealism and Its Backgrounds

The epicenter of Russian philosophy and idealism in the last decade of the nineteenth century was the Moscow Philosophical Society, which began publishing its own journal, *Questions of Philosophy and Psychology*, in 1889 under the editorship of Nikolai Iakovlevich Grot (1852-99).[9] The idealists who gathered there reframed the philosophical and social problems of their time in terms of moral and metaphysical categories.[10] In the then rather small field of Russian philosophy, these critics of positivism saw Vladimir Soloviev as their predecessor—with good reason— as Soloviev's first major work, *The Crisis of Western Philosophy (Against the Positivists)* (1874), was a pioneering critique of positivism as the reigning doctrine of the age. The idealist critique of positivism in the early years of the twentieth century took on a more specific intellectual movement—Marxism—particularly the historical materialist theory of capitalist development (known as the *Zusammenbruchstheorie*). Idealists also took issue with Marxist dogmatism and its faith in the perfectibility of economic forms and social relations under socialism, which looked to them like a new religion. The idealists were some of the most vocal critics of ethical problems in Marxist theory about social and economic forms and, leading up to the 1905 revolution, many of them contributed directly to the political current in Russian life that sought democratic reform rather than revolutionary change.

There is also a good reason why younger idealists such as Bulgakov gravitated toward Ivan Karamazov, given the nature of the group's rejection of Marxism. They identified themselves with Ivan, making them part of an already established sociological phenomenon in Russian culture: the reenactment of literary types by the radical youth. As Nikolai Chernyshevsky's readers had been inspired to transform themselves into the revolutionary folk hero Rakhmetov in *What Is to Be Done?* (1863), so Bulgakov's generation identified with Ivan, who became the hero of their religious project and political ideals. In his lecture on the character, Bulgakov aimed to map Ivan's moral psychology and find an idealist philosophical and political path out of the dark place of atheist nihilism to which Ivan's protest leads. Having left Marxism for idealism, Bulgakov approached Ivan's trajectory in similar terms, insisting that Ivan "is a child of socialism, but one who is lukewarm, doubting. It's not necessary to consciously hold an idea of the age in order to be its son all the same; sometimes negation testifies to a far greater passionate relationship to a rejected doctrine, than its indifferent acceptance."[11] For Volzhskii, too, Dostoevsky's work became synonymous with the young man's own break from populism (*narodnichestvo*) and Marxism: "In Dostoevsky and in what he stood for—what was surrounding him—I suffered my own personal crisis of rationalism, both consciously and freely setting out towards authentic religion, not shying away from metaphysics, nor fearing mysticism."[12] According to Merezhkovsky, Berdiaev was a Dostoevsky character in the flesh: "Berdiaev has such tragedy about him that you're frightened for him—one wonders whether he will get out of it alive. This is the very same tragedy as all of the protagonists of Dostoevsky from Stavrogin to Ivan Karamazov: an unrelenting dividedness of mind and heart, of a will between higher and lower abysses, between 'the ideal of Madonna and the ideal of Sodom,' as Dmitry Karamazov phrased it."[13] Much later, in his autobiography, Berdiaev would claim Ivan as a spiritual mentor of sorts, noting, "Had I repudiated God, it would probably have been in the name of God."[14] Though these critics identified with Dostoevsky's characters, his political views—particularly his support of the autocracy, which this critical generation found abhorrent—were painfully at odds with the transcendent personhood reflected in so many of his characters.

The attraction toward Ivan among young idealist critics also marked an important shift away from the initial reception among student audiences of Dostoevsky's final novel and magnum opus, *The Brothers Karamazov*. Idealists were fond of quoting from one of the last entries of Dostoevsky's *Writer's Diary*, where he confessed, "Above all my hopes lie with the youth since they are the ones in our midst who are suffering 'with the search for truth' and longing for it."[15] It was to young people that Dostoevsky had addressed his final work. Indeed, Ivan relates a version of his creator's ideas when he remarks to Alyosha how "many, many of the most original Russian boys" end up discussing "universal questions" in stinking taverns.[16] But the novel's first young readers had initially responded not to Ivan but to his brother Alyosha, the novel's positive hero. That character's compassion and generosity resonated with the earnestness and "small-deeds" ethos of young populist readers, who were entering an era of political disillusionment. Rozanov had keenly observed in his 1891 essay on "The Grand Inquisitor" that "the image of Alyosha is everywhere in our literature, his name is already pronounced when encountering this or that rare and joyful appearance in life, and if we are fated to experience a rebirth at some point towards something new and better, it is very possible that he will be the guiding star of that rebirth."[17] Alyosha's idealism, however, was different than Ivan's *philosophical* idealism. Ivan turned out to be the idealists' guiding star, who offered a model of their idealist search beyond what they perceived as the utopianism of Marxist theory.

Even before younger critics like Bulgakov and Berdiaev began framing their views in Ivan's image, there were concerns among idealist thinkers about how to address Dostoevsky's repugnant politics. Soloviev's concern about properly aligning Dostoevsky with the idealist current shows up in the very founding of their movement's journal, *Questions of Philosophy and Psychology*. In a letter to its readership in 1891, Nikolai Grot expressed a commitment as editor to creating a space for philosophical debate about new currents and methodologies, which would help avoid the passive acceptance of outmoded ideas and provide fresh ground for new political agendas. Toward the conclusion of his letter, Grot invoked Dostoevsky to lend authority to his proclamation: "A truly Russian person, a Christian, by conviction of the best representatives of Russian self-awareness, is full of goodwill for all of humanity—for good, beauty and truth *in every mortal*." He goes on to write, "Dostoevsky is one of the most typical representatives of those principles, which to our profound conviction, should rest in the foundation of our unique national moral philosophy."[18]

Responding to Grot's letter, Soloviev did not dispute Dostoevsky's historic role in their movement, but he pointed to unresolved tensions in the writer's worldview that should provoke reservations about the too eager acceptance of the sweeping "formula of an all-encompassing, unifying, and all-conciliatory Russian and Christian ideal" proclaimed in his speech on Pushkin.[19] Soloviev continued, "If the memory of this brilliant visionary [*prozorlivets*] and sufferer is to be preserved unstained by the conscious rejection of his best ideals in service of the dark yoke of reality, then the contradictions between those ideals and the many unenlightened views in his works will also remain unresolved, and not one of us can wholly accept his spiritual inheritance."[20] It was Soloviev's wish that the movement look to Dostoevsky's "indubitable duality," while it built a worldview around "the Dostoevsky who defeated both the rabble and Slavophilism in his Pushkin speech."[21] Bulgakov followed this advice, but there is a tendency in his essays to frame Dostoevsky's heroes as evidence of the idealist faith in the primacy of personhood.

Dostoevsky's final novel was—and still is—perceived as the most affirmative testament of the writer's universally applicable religious ideas. As Bulgakov put it a decade later, "In that novel Dostoevsky appeared as that *universal person*."[22] The idealists held faith that the broad horizons of his religious vision in *The Brothers Karamazov* would help them overcome the lingering shadow of the novelist's nationalism and related xenophobia. Another way of softening Dostoevsky's political views was approached through nuanced intellectual-historical interpretations of the conservatism of the preceding decades. In an 1897 essay on Soloviev's contributions to Russian thought, Bulgakov distinguished between two camps of Slavophilism: a right one (Leontiev, Katkov, and Danilevsky) and a left one (Dostoevsky and Aksakov).[23] In his categorization Bulgakov was more tentative than his coeval Berdiaev, who portrayed Dostoevsky's "left" Slavophilism as though it were a strain of liberal Westernism.[24] This maneuver was easier to do with a writer who would conflate particular Russian traits with universal ones, which Dostoevsky does famously in his Pushkin speech: "To become a real Russian is to become entirely Russian, perhaps, and means only (in the end, you can underscore this) to become a brother to all people, to become a *universal person*, if you like."[25] Berdiaev quoted this passage in one of his essays, which attempted to sketch out Russian idealism as a national project, claiming Tolstoy and Dostoevsky as spiritual progenitors. Berdiaev added in a footnote, "[Dostoevsky] was a fiery patriot of the West, since for him the West was a dream of the universal person, and not gray reality, not dull prose, like that of the European person."[26] Relatedly, Bulgakov observed that Ivan demonstrated an undeniable reverence for the West in his conversation with Alyosha. Berdiaev's rhetoric reveals the defensiveness of the idealist critics, whose enemies dismissed them as reactionary. Indeed, Dmitry Filosofov's review of *Problems of Idealism* noticed this defensiveness.[27] The idealist insistence on liberatory elements in Dostoevsky's metaphysics—not just his personalism but even his version of Slavophilism—may be viewed as extensions of Soloviev's earlier efforts in his *Three Speeches* to incorporate Dostoevsky's religious ideas into nonreactionary, reformist currents.

Even without these efforts to establish the writer as a forerunner of philosophical idealism, Dostoevsky was already suited to the idealist critique of positivism. After all, Dostoevsky had been chief among critics of sociological theories borrowed from the natural sciences and had been consistently hostile to the nihilists' application of natural scientific discourse and theory to social and moral questions. In *The Annihilation of Inertia*, Liza Knapp has shown how Dostoevsky's novels took a consistent critical stance toward scientific theories since the Enlightenment. Knapp explains, "In his view, the laws of nature produced selfish and self-assertive behavior, the opposite of Christlike love; for this reason man must seek to be delivered from these laws."[28] It was these same natural laws that created Ivan's "Euclidean" worldview, which had led many critics to read him as a model nihilist. A brief summary of how Ivan was initially received will help establish how innovative (and strange) Bulgakov's idealist interpretation of Dostoevsky's hero truly was.

Ivan's Journey from Nihilism to Idealism: A Brief History of Ivan and the Critics

Even today, book 5 of *The Brothers Karamazov*, "Pro and Contra," is one of the most quoted portions of Dostoevsky's final novel. The author called it "the culminating point" in the story.[29] Two of its chapters, "Rebellion" and "The Grand Inquisitor," now account for many volumes of scholarship that have steered the international reception of Dostoevsky. Taciturn and morose in earlier scenes, in these chapters, Ivan Karamazov finally speaks uninterruptedly in monologues, giving an account of himself to his younger brother, Alyosha. Meeting at what Ivan calls a "stinking inn" (*voniuchii traktir*), Ivan and Alyosha sit in a room all to themselves while surrounding rooms clamor with the noise and activity of a typical tavern. And so, the physical out-of-placeness of the brothers foreshadows the equally awkward conversation they are about to have. Ivan, the most philosophical and cerebral of the brothers, will proclaim his anger that God allows the innocent to suffer in a world of his creation, while his pious younger brother, dressed in a monk's cassock, bears witness. The first reviews of book 5 showed either confusion or horror at Ivan's speech—particularly the dystopian "Legend of the Grand Inquisitor."[30]

It might have seemed improbable to Ivan's first readers that he would ever become a positive hero for idealist thinkers; Dmitry, who openly quotes German poetry and never loses faith in God, offers a more logical model. Whatever the rationale for the conflicting interpretations of Ivan over the years, the nature of his outrage is well known. Rejecting hundreds of years of Christian theodicy, Ivan claims that suffering could never be redeemed by a God who would allow it in the first place. For permitting especially the suffering of innocent children, God has betrayed his creation and made a joke of the promise of immortality, a paltry reward. The legitimacy of Ivan's anger and the soundness of his argument convinced readers for decades that Dostoevsky actually shared his character's anguish and denial of God.[31] In his letters, however, Dostoevsky was clear that Ivan was not a caricature of nihilism but was in fact supposed to represent its darkest ends. Writing to his editor at the *Russian Messenger*, where *The Brothers Karamazov* was published serially, Dostoevsky referred to Ivan as having crossed to the ideological point of no return, reaching what he called in one letter "the synthesis of contemporary Russian anarchism."[32] He wrote, "All of socialism has come out of and begun with the negation of the meaning of historical reality and reached a program of destruction and anarchism. . . . My hero takes up a theme that is, *for me*, irrefutable—the senselessness of the suffering of children—and deduces from it the absurdity of historical reality."[33] Unlike Raskolnikov, Ivan would have no "Epilogue"—the flash of redemption at the end of the story. Ivan's would be a grim tale of where socialism leads. The author promised his friend K. P. Pobedonostsev, a figure reviled in idealist and liberal circles, that Ivan's powerful argument would be soundly refuted in Zosima's teachings, which would be collected in book 6.[34] But twenty years after his assuring Pobedonostsev of that, the idealists did not turn to Zosima, or to Alyosha, to form their arguments against Marxian socialism, but to Ivan. It was Dostoevsky's nuanced portrayal of his hero's monstrous rejection of God that made Ivan's idealist makeover possible.

Although idealists had chosen an odd character on which to model the emotional and intellectual disintegration of their ties with Marxism, there was some historical justification for doing so. Nearly two decades earlier, *The Brothers Karamazov* enjoyed enormous popularity among the radical youth. In 1881, the eminent literary historian S. A. Vengerov (1855–1920) took up the subject of young people's recent attraction to Dostoevsky in the months before the writer's sudden death.[35] While he does not mention Ivan in his essay, Vengerov points out what young readers friendly to socialism already knew: though Dostoevsky wrote against their politics, they were his most ardent readers and the loudest participants at the literary evenings at which he read. It was not so much the conservative readers of the *Russian Messenger* that came to Dostoevsky's readings but predominantly "university students, men and women, students from the girls' schools and generally the 'stronghold of nihilism'—the youth who were in school—this is who raved, this is who raised the temperature of the room and drove out the chill of Petersburg stuffiness."[36] Initial reactions to Ivan in the critical press were mixed but confirm Vengerov's anecdotal observations. The first evaluations of book 5 in the spring of 1879 ranged from obvious incomprehension of Ivan to shockingly widespread acclaim, even among the most hostile "democratic" critics. One of the earliest reviews made no attempt to plunge into Ivan's moral crisis and the nightmare of his Grand Inquisitor, finding him only a stoic "without a soul" whose "mind is equally at peace when he is deciding that or another question for better or worse, pro or contra."[37] One wonders how carefully this reviewer read the book if he found Ivan's character so bland. On the whole, however, reviewers across the political spectrum found Ivan and the scenes in which he appeared compelling. According to the editors of the commentary to the thirty-volume edition of Dostoevsky's collected works, "In the criticism of 1879 and in the following years . . . there is not one disparaging evaluation of the chapters 'Rebellion' and 'The Grand Inquisitor.'"[38]

It was not until Vasily Rozanov that an era of more pessimistic readings of Ivan began. Among its most lasting contributions, Rozanov's 1891 essay identified Dostoevsky with the views of his despairing atheist character and concluded that the author had at the end of his life abandoned Orthodoxy: "The characters [*obrazy*] of the inquisitor, the student, the artist himself and of the tempting spirit, which stands behind all of them, flicker one after the other, lose the sharpness of their individual features, and merge into one entity, the voice of which we hear and understand, and whose very face and name we cannot distinguish from the others."[39] Rozanov's interpretation shows the influence of Konstantin Leontiev, who had been attacking what he perceived to be Dostoevsky's undogmatic Orthodoxy for some time. Leontiev would have liked Rozanov to adopt a more critical view, writing to him at one point, "I zealously pray to God that you quickly *outgrow Dostoevsky* with his 'harmonies,' which will never come to be and, besides, are not needed."[40] If later on the idealists worried about Dostoevsky's rightist tendencies, Leontiev had always believed the novelist was not conservative *enough*. In *Our New Christians* (Nashi novye khristiane, 1882), Leontiev held Dostoevsky's statements about "universal brotherhood" in his Pushkin speech and in his final novel as proof of the inauthenticity and corrupted Westernism of his Orthodox faith. He claimed, "In the speech at the Pushkin celebrations, his teaching was entirely clarified: it became clear that even Mr. Dostoevsky was like a great many *Europeans* and Russian *universal men*, believing in the peaceful and humble future of Europe, taking joy in the fact that us Russians, maybe even soon, would end up drowning and spreading out without a trace in the faceless ocean of cosmopolitanism."[41] Such a reading of Dostoevsky's religion contrasted sharply with Soloviev's (and the idealists') interpretation of the writer's universal Christianity.[42]

Bulgakov, who had been one of Rozanov's high school students in provincial Elets, would provide a counterpoint to both the Slavophiles and the radical demonization of Ivan in his 1901 lecture, seeking to reorient the character toward idealism and liberal currents. In his lecture, Bulgakov was drawn to the narrative arc of Ivan's religious crisis. He spoke of how Ivan's moral rejection of God's world (i.e., empirical reality, positivism) led him to noble but tragic ends. Ivan was neither a monster—the anarchist-nihilist that Dostoevsky intended earlier readers to identify with populist youth—nor a prideful and antidemocratic Übermensch cliché that emerged from the turn-of-the-century Nietzschean vogue: Ivan was a morally pure individual, an idealist.[43] Bulgakov also insinuated that this philosophical journey was linked to the tragic striving of the liberal subject and the polarized political scene of their time.

The idealist Ivan modeled a promising life path for critics who placed themselves ideologically and historically between autocracy and socialism. Ivan's tragic end in madness was perceived as a kind of warning, but his initial protest was presented as an alternative to blind faith in either God's mysterious ways or the panacea of scientific socialism. The idealists were not mystics; they also did not aim to engage with the more dogmatic features of Dostoevsky's religious ideas, such as the triumph of humility over egotism, the overriding message of *Crime and Punishment*. Ivan—not Zosima or Alyosha—became their hero because of his protest against God, which they chose to read as a protest against the other absolute of their time: Marxism. While they did not ever claim to be the originators of a new "secular" Dostoevsky, their reading of Ivan expanded the author's religious idea into a statement of moral protest that fit their times.

The New Ivan Karamazov: Bulgakov's Lecture and the Idealist Hero

Bulgakov's "Ivan Karamazov as a Philosophical Type" was delivered in 1901 as a public lecture when he was a professor at Kiev Polytechnical University teaching political economy.[44] His speech was met with great enthusiasm by the public, who, as Catherine Evtuhov has noted, were "accustomed to receiving lectures on grain prices."[45] University students tended to be on the political left, so we can read his lecture as an attempt to introduce idealism to a socialist audience. This intention seems clear in Bulgakov's admittance that his focus on Dostoevsky would be met with some hesitation or perhaps hostility. He acknowledged that to many people Dostoevsky was accorded the status of a "reptile of literature," whose "unique political convictions" were mistakenly identified with the "official representatives and keepers of those views."[46]

Bulgakov must have known that appealing to Dostoevsky's authority in any way to convince socialist audiences would be an uphill battle. Here—knowingly or not—he was contributing to a new direction in the liberal movement, which under the leadership of Pavel Miliukov (1859–1943) and Petr Struve (1870–1944) had by 1902 promoted a policy of "no enemies on the left"—a strategy aimed at attracting more socialists to their cause.[47] Anatoly Lunacharsky (1875–1933), who would later become a prominent Bolshevik but at the time was an unorthodox Marxist, ridiculed the pervasive presence of Dostoevsky, whom he called "Bulgakov's idol."[48] More broadly, reviewers of *Problems of Idealism*, in which collaborators attempted to convey the diversity of the philosophical idealist worldview, declared it a "new middle ages," prompting a sympathetic reviewer to ask, "Where does such hatred of idealism come from?"[49] One reviewer did not mention the influence of Dostoevsky in Bulgakov's contribution to the volume; however, he remarked that "the mystical tinge of his idealism . . . sounds so strange to us, people of the 20th century," recalling as it did unwanted memories of a "long-buried past."[50]

Among Marxists, Dostoevsky's name was synonymous with autocratic allegiance and obscurantism, to which a fascinating anecdote from Struve's tumultuous break with Lenin attests. Early in 1902, while they were residing in Munich, Lenin refused to receive Struve after many long disagreements over the latter's revisionism. Lenin's wife, Nadezhda Krupskaia, recalled reaching out to Struve afterward and recorded her impressions after the meeting. She wrote, "I went to see Struve at Vera

Ivanovna's [Zasulich] place. The meeting was very difficult. Struve was terribly offended. There was a heavy air of *Dostoevshchina*. He spoke about how others considered him a renegade and other things in that vein, that he felt bullied. Now I don't even remember what he said, I recall only the heavy feeling I had after leaving that meeting. It was obvious: this was an alien person from the enemy's party. Vladimir Ilych had been right. Later with someone who I already don't remember, Struve's wife Nina Aleksandrovna sent us greetings and a package of marmalade."[51] The mood Krupskaia describes in her reminiscence—even the marmalade, which echoes the namesake of the mystical drunk Marmeladov from *Crime and Punishment*—provides a colorful example of how repellent Dostoevsky's name was to stalwart Marxists.

If in his lecture, Bulgakov wished to provoke his audience by raising the specter of Dostoevsky, the antirevolutionary author of *Devils*, he did so with the motive of performing a parallel revisionism of the novelist himself: he would introduce the Dostoevsky that Soloviev had made possible to an audience of young, skeptical students. Seeking to establish common ground, Bulgakov argued in his lecture that "Dostoevsky looked upon the socialist worldview in just the same way he looked at Ivan's spiritual state—as something like a moral disease. But viewing it as a disease of growth, he saw it as a pivotal worldview that preceded a higher synthesis, which we might add, must consist in the merging of the economic demands of socialism with the principles of philosophical idealism and the justification of the first of these by the last."[52] This lecture would not rely on the clichéd antisocialist screed that many in Bulgakov's audience and readership may have expected of a recanting Marxist.

His lecture on Ivan was important for two reasons. First, it publicly marked his epistemological break with Marxism. Here Bulgakov "revealed himself as an idealist" after his colleagues Struve and Berdiaev had already begun adopting the ethical critique of certain principles of Marxist political economy.[53] This rapid pivot in Bulgakov's development as a thinker was tied to his idealist orientation; Evtuhov takes special note of his Marxist dogmatism just a few years earlier.[54] Second, his reading of Ivan would have an enduring impact on the international reception of Dostoevsky's religious idea in the coming decades. The idealists' success at aligning Dostoevsky's religious idea with liberal thought would culminate in Berdiaev's émigré, anti-Communist *Dostoevsky's Worldview* (1934).[55] Ivan also became the secular hero of existentialist philosophy in the same era. Albert Camus, whose character

Meursault in *The Stranger* is genealogically related to Ivan, even played the latter in a 1935 production of *The Brothers Karamazov* in Algiers.[56]

Bulgakov's analysis of Ivan is an ethical (rather than economic) critique of Marx's historical materialism, particularly the *Zusammenbruchstheorie*, which posited the inevitable collapse of capitalism. In his essay on the theory of progress, Bulgakov had argued that this view of history constitutes a theodicy: the inevitable victory of socialism over capitalism implies that sacrifices in the present would be justified by a future good. Bulgakov reads the progressivist justifications of Marxism as equivalent to the Christian promise of a future harmony that will deliver believers from suffering on earth. While the *Zusammenbruchstheorie* clearly posited an ideal, Bulgakov explained, Marxists never named it as such: "In the lexicon of strict Marxism, the word *ideal* is not even raised; here we hear the words: natural necessity, the law of development, the iron march of things, birth pangs, the wheel of history."[57] Improperly understanding the fundamentally "religious" problem of historical materialism was leading Marxists to mistakenly invest all of their hopes in future utopia, Bulgakov believed. As Berdiaev later wrote in the preface to *Sub specie aeternitatis*, "The sharp staging of the problem of socialism and anarchism exposes the religious meaning of universal history, helps us reject the temptation of the Grand Inquisitor—the violent construction of a kingdom of this earth, in which prosperity and peace would be sacrificed for freedom and eternity."[58] Both Berdiaev and Bulgakov concurred that idealism and Marxist historical materialism were in fact motivated by the same moral protest but that the latter led to a dead end and the former to more just, even if imperfect, ends.

Bulgakov claimed that Ivan rejected not only theodicy; he rejected all progressive theories of history, including the Marxist one. This interpretation was something new. Ruth Coates has claimed that Bulgakov was "either blind to, or deliberately overlooks, the obvious fact that Ivan is objecting not to the theory of progress and the socialist paradise, but to the Christian concept of heaven."[59] I propose that Bulgakov does not overlook the target of Ivan's protest; he equates the socialist desire to alleviate suffering on earth with God's promise of future harmony after death. Bulgakov believes that the socialist thirst for justice grasps for progressive narratives of history and rejects God; however, the moral basis of that search for future justice is still based on a belief in higher ideals bestowed by an Absolute (God). Marxism is just another religion, but it has removed God and thus commits moral blunders. This, Bulgakov argued, was the tragedy of Marxists, who like Ivan, were *actually* idealists, whose morality was undergirded by a metaphysics that their positivist worldview disallowed.

Ivan's lonely rebellion against God is, paradoxically, when his moral intelligence begins to acquire real value for Bulgakov.[60] Ivan is not simply an atheist who adopts Nietzschean amoralism, as some contemporary critics claimed; he is a formerly ardent socialist who has started to wonder if promises of a future just society are possible at all. As Bulgakov put it, "All of Ivan's doubts are directed against the reigning doctrine of progress, directed at the same time also against the theory of socialism, understood not only as an economic doctrine, but as a general worldview, I'll say even more broadly, as a religion."[61] This is the most important claim in Bulgakov's lecture because it is where he associates socialism with the promises of Christianity that Ivan so vehemently rejects. Ivan pits himself against the promises of both Christianity *and* socialism, neither of which guarantee outcomes compatible with his moral ideals.[62] This psychological state results in a painful state of being, one that the audience is encouraged to find admirable, even noble. Though Ivan now technically believes in nothing, a shred of moral feeling has survived. But how is it possible that Ivan's moral outrage—his guiding ideal—has survived what appears to be the triumph of atheism over faith, not just in God, but in socialism, too?

The transcendent "morality" of Ivan, so crucial to the idealist reading, was also its weakest, least convincing element for radical critics. Subsequent readers of the novel have scrutinized the strangely contradictory argument Ivan launches in his acceptance of God and his rejection of God's world. In fact, Ivan's exact utterance to Alyosha is phrased in a double negative, which enhances its cryptic and mysterious meaning: "It's not that I don't accept God, understand that, it is the world—the one created by Him—that I do not accept and cannot agree to accept."[63] In "The Ethical Problem in the Light of Philosophical Idealism" (1902), Berdiaev shares Bulgakov's portrait of Ivan as a moral individual whose ethical development was ongoing, arguing that true moral sensibility is possible only in the sort of liminal position between good and evil that Ivan occupies.[64] In this reading, Ivan is a free personality in becoming; he has not rejected God, but he is still perilously close to moral destruction if he succeeds in sustaining his rebellion against the divinely created world. In the first publication of this article in *Problems of Idealism* (1903), Berdiaev included an enormous footnote that speculated about whether Ivan's rejection of God's world could be understood as the hidden survival of his faith. The footnote was later removed when it appeared in *Sub specie aeternitatis* (1907). In *Problems of Idealism* it read, "It is not God that [Ivan] does not accept; it is God's world. But the world does not need to be morally accepted, for the world is *what is* (the kingdom of necessity); rather God needs to be accepted. God is *what ought to be* (the kingdom of freedom). Our task is to realize God in the world, since we conceive God not as the culprit of the world, but as its ideal."[65] Berdiaev's interpretation accords with the general idealist reading of Ivan, which sought to salvage the potential for his belief in God in his striving for freedom from necessity. It invites comparison to Ivan's namesake, the atheist Shatov in *Devils*, who exclaims passionately to his ideological tormentor, Stavrogin: "I will believe in God!"[66]

But not all critics friendly to idealism agreed with Bulgakov and Berdiaev that Ivan's faith in God had remained intact. Akim Volynsky held that for Ivan, as for the Grand Inquisitor, "there was no God, neither was there [His] world, but only the noble fiction of religion."[67] In "Dostoevsky's Religious-Moral Problem" (1905), Volzhskii still believed Ivan reflected the writer's own moral psychology. Dostoevsky, who was deeply invested in individual freedom and human welfare, could not bring himself to reject God and the suffering of Creation as Ivan had done, and his terrifying fear of religious doubt (which contemporaries linked to a kind of madness) led him to embrace religious dogmatism and Orthodox nationalism. Volzhskii continues, "The abysses of doubt and negation, the depth of penetrating into life, the unquenched thirst to decide the tortured questions of conscience, the torment for humanity, the holy pain of religious thirst—all of this led, with time, to moments of extreme attraction to the idea of soil and to the naïve cult of Russian reality, to a synthesis of the ideal and reality in the idea of necessity . . . as long as it was rooted in the soil."[68]

In their eagerness to prove Ivan's morality and acceptance of God, Berdiaev and Bulgakov were stumbling upon a deeper history. Debate over whether Ivan's potential atheism precluded moral feeling was already twenty years old. In 1881, the writer and radical critic Mariia Tsebrikova argued that "Dostoevsky shows illogically that negation leads to moral collapse."[69] She reasoned that Ivan's atheism does not stop him from helping a drunk peasant on his way back from a final meeting with Smerdiakov but does not mention that when he first passes, he withholds his help.[70] Much later, Aleksandr Dolinin would trace Ivan back to debates of the Petrashevsky circle, Dostoevsky's earlier period of socialist leanings, where once a paper was read about a variety of atheism that was "purely ethical."[71] In 1891, no less than Soloviev addressed the issue of whether belief is even a precondition for being a Christian. In "On the Reasons for the Decline of the Medieval Worldview," Soloviev challenged his audience to reexamine the assumption that doubt or difficulty believing was alien to Christian tradition and practice:

> When an unbelieving priest correctly performs mass, then Christ is present in the mystery for the sake of the people who need it, regardless of the unbelief and unworthiness of the performer of the rite. If the spirit of Christ can act through an unbelieving priest in a church mystery, then why can it not act in history through an unbelieving actor, especially when believers persecute him? The wind bloweth where it listeth [John 3:8]. Let even enemies serve it. Christ, commanding us to love our enemies, of course, not only can love them himself, but also knows how to use them for his deed. But to nominal Christians, proud of their demonic faith, it would follow to remember another person from the Gospels—the story of two apostles: Judas Iscariot and Thomas. Judas welcomed Christ with his word and embrace. Thomas revealed to him his unbelief to his face. But Judas betrayed Christ and "went to strike himself down," while Thomas became an apostle and died for Christ.[72]

Soloviev's understanding of true Christian belief, as well as the broader theme of Dostoevsky's faithful doubters, could have figured in the idealist tendency to overlook or soften Ivan's atheism.

One of Dostoevsky's letters to Pobedonostsev, which none of these critics would have known, serves to complicate the idealist vision of the morally intact Ivan, or at least its basis in *The Brothers Karamazov*. When planning the chapter "Rebellion," Dostoevsky suggested that the rejection of God's world was perhaps an *even more* radical stage of negating God's existence:

> I took up this stronger blasphemy, as I personally sensed and understood it; that is, precisely the blasphemy that is taking place now with us in our Russia *across all* (almost) the upper classes, but it is predominantly among the youth: that is, the scientific and philosophical refutation of the existence of God has already been abandoned. Today's *professional [delovye] socialists* are no longer preoccupied by it at all (as used to be the case in the entire past century and in the first half of the current one). On the other hand, the entire creation of God, God's world and *its meaning, is being negated* with all possible force.[73]

This passage indicates that Dostoevsky thought of Ivan's rejection of God's world as a rejection of the entire God-created universe and the morality associated with it. Hence Ivan's credo "all is permitted" because God and his world are an invention. While they did not know about this letter, the idealist defense of Ivan underscores how their reading clung close to the allowances of their own philosophical and religious convictions. Ivan was now *their* Ivan; it did not matter what the author intended to convey with his hero.

The portrait of Ivan that emerges in Bulgakov's lecture and that finds support in Berdiaev's writings became enmeshed in a more general project of modeling the "idealist persona," along with his or her subjectivity and philosophical journey. In his essay "On the Realistic Worldview," Bulgakov reiterated that the wellspring of Ivan's sickness—his inability to continue his rebellion against God—is philosophical idealism itself, which functions like the trailhead to a path: "Philosophical idealism is a necessary path toward religion, presenting a station which the modern person cannot bypass in his striving towards a religious worldview. The right to unbelief, just like the right to believe, must be acquired through thought."[74] This point threatens to undermine their propagandizing of idealism itself. "To become an 'idealist,'" Bulgakov wrote, "one needs to pass through a long trial and undergo more or less continual independent work."[75] In "The Spiritual Drama of Herzen" (1902), Bulgakov noted that both figures were tormented by moral philosophical questions, but while Ivan is still looking for answers—still seeking moral gratification—Herzen, who ultimately adopts Slavophilism, "has entirely prepared answers."[76] Herzen's path was leading to "religious 'contact with the other world' (as Dostoevsky loved to phrase it)," but his desire to resolve all doubts by an all-embracing dogma brought him to the historical salve of Slavophilism.[77] This portrait of the idealist persona, its affirmation of sustained intellectual crisis over the desperate adoption of ready-made dogma, would seem to be a difficult program to offer satisfied Marxists—or anyone for that matter. On the one hand, Ivan resonated with Bulgakov's colleagues in idealism as the hero that their movement and lived experience demanded; on the other, the idealist, antiutopian persona to which Ivan had given form and story was vulnerable to critical attacks and was less attractive than the solid promises of Marxism.

The rise of liberal politics in Russia between 1903 and 1905 and Bulgakov's effort to distinguish between the liberal "idealist" and the Marxist "utopian" worldviews amplified the critical investigations into the "striving" or "searching" (*iskanie*) literary type, whom Ivan came to exemplify. The language of "striving" or "searching" in the journals of this period is ubiquitous. Indeed, the theme of "searching" was central to the idealists' self-definition, which conveyed an accurate description of a shared starting point that allowed for the diversity of their views. As Berdiaev explained, "Idealists are united not so much by a defined and homogenous positive worldview and belief system . . . as [by] their *searching* and negative relationship to the limitations of positivism, the dissatisfaction of the knowing spirit."[78] Despite these more positive connotations of the "searcher" type, critics were quick to note the futility and impotence of the practical potential of their opponents' idealism. The "successful" idealist, for them, was a person who was by necessity destined to fail, for the reason that an ideal functions only as a horizon. Adding to this pessimistic vision of the idealist was the question of whether religious belief in Russian society had survived positivism at all. The debate surrounding the idealist persona was just beginning, and Dostoevsky remained one of its touchstones.

Critiques of the idealist persona returned to the problem of character function and type from debates over "positive heroes" in the 1860s and 1870s. In a protracted response to Bulgakov's lecture on Ivan, Lunacharsky brushed against this history when he asked, "What's all this about theodicy and all this Russian Faustianism?"[79] The Faustian hero was certainly a prototype for Ivan.[80] But what Bulgakov staged as an ethical problem epitomized in Ivan's suffering Lunacharsky understood as an ontological one, which he suggested raised such alternative questions: "It is worth living at all? And if it is, then how? For oneself or for others? This is the healthy kernel of the Karamazov question, which has nothing in common with the problem of theodicy."[81] For Lunacharsky, Ivan's character function more closely mirrors Hamlet's "to be or not to be," not Faust's epistemological (*gnoseologicheskii*) crisis, depicted in lines from Goethe's work quoted by Bulgakov in his lecture on Ivan: "And see there is nothing we can know! / It fair sears my heart to find it so."[82] Lunacharsky's concluding analysis of Ivan shows the influence of Darwin and is staunchly positivist: "A human being is not satiated, they guard and create ideals, they go forward and, dying, pass on their testaments to children and grandchildren, not for the sake of justifying the world and not under the duress of a tortured conscience, but because in the difficult struggle for existence, a human being has been made a creator and a fighter."[83] For Lunacharsky, Bulgakov had mixed up his characters by mistakenly presenting Ivan as an idealist seeker of faith.

V. V. Vodovozov, who served as a commentator to a lecture on Soloviev that Bulgakov delivered in 1903, voiced a similar critique of the idealist persona. Following the lecture, the *New Path* published a transcript of the discussion. Vodovozov was not a Marxist, and thus not as antagonistic to Bulgakov's ideas as Lunacharsky was, but he still took issue with the attributes of heroism in essays that Bulgakov had published up to that point. While he does not mention Ivan, Vodovozov makes extensive references to Bulgakov's 1902 Herzen essay, in which the author claimed that Ivan and Herzen share similar character functions. For Vodovozov, idealism suggested a kind of passivity toward metaphysical and social problems, a dedication to an endless, possibly fruitless, struggle. As a corrective to this pessimism, Vodovozov suggests that the Greek hero Hector is a more accurate model for the struggle of the contemporary individual: "Although in front of him he glimpses not only his own death, but also the destruction of that goal for which he has been fighting."[84] Echoing the spirit of Lunacharsky's critique, Vodovozov insists, "The thirst for struggle and activity is lodged in human nature, and it is not metaphysical or scientific convictions, but temperament, that urges it on to struggle."[85] Bulgakov's response to Vodovozov rejected especially the claim that his own and Soloviev's philosophies amounted to a pessimistic worldview. For him, the idealist position embodied precisely Ivan's healthy skepticism—the "questing, striving skeptic" as opposed to the "cynical skeptics" represented by Socrates.[86] It was Vodovozov's accusation of pessimism that upset the idealists and presaged their retooling of the idealist persona in 1904.

Though Bulgakov had insisted on the positive quality of Ivan's skepticism, a gradual shift in philosophical idealism—and the liberal political scene with which it found accord—was underway. More and more, idealists sought to frame accusations of pessimism as a positive, "realistic" alternative to Marxist utopia.[87] In his essay "Chekhov as a Thinker" (1904), attributes Bulgakov had earlier identified with Ivan were revised with more contemporary material. The "world-weariness" (*Weltschmerz*, or *mirovaia skorb'*) exhibited in Chekhov's work, Bulgakov wrote, reflects a philosophical position he terms "optimopessimism."[88] "True, this was not a victorious faith, which sees in barely born growths a flourishing future and solemnly greets it; this is a melancholy faith, longing and restless, but according to its way, strong and unwavering."[89] But as he had earlier noted about Ivan, it remained "impossible to live in rebellion, and this mood or this worldview must be somehow overcome or survived, otherwise there is no exit."[90] The Chekhovian hero is part of the "realistic" turn in idealism, an even more positive formulation of what began as Ivan's new idealist identity. Idealist critics had attached to Ivan, their philosophical mentor and prototype, a way to strive toward a fallen world without losing sight of constructive ideals, without despairing. Their own emotional relationship to that character, it might be suggested, helped them articulate their moody and imperfect idealist response to Marxism.

What did this new reading of Ivan reveal about the state of criticism in the years leading up to the 1905 revolution? It shows not just the broad shift from the authority of the author to hero but also reflects a new stage in the divide among the intelligentsia between socialism and reformist, liberal political projects. Beginning as an underground political organization that some of the idealists joined, the Union of Liberation (*Soiuz Osvobozhdeniia*, 1904–1905) sought to bring together a coalition of political actors opposed to the autocracy, including more conservative *zemstvo* liberals, social democrats, and socialist revolutionaries, with the broader goals of realizing equal rights and creating a constitutional democracy. The statutes of the Union of Liberation stressed its fundamentally "democratic character," as well as the need to address not only political problems but also "a whole range of economic and cultural problems."[91] After the events of the 1905 revolution, which led to the establishment of the First Duma, the first (legal) liberal political party, the Kadets (Constitutional Democrats), won a majority of seats in the 1906 election.

It should be stressed that the liberation movement as a whole was a motley crew—its members abandoned Marxism for a range of reasons that did not necessarily align with the goals of the more metaphysical idealists. The liberal reformists' prominent voices, Miliukov and Struve, did not look to Dostoevsky the same way the idealist inheritors of Soloviev did. Unlike their friend Struve, Bulgakov and Berdiaev tended to approach political-economic problems through religious-philosophical ones.[92] The seeds of their differences with Struve's reticence about religious topics were present almost at the outset of their friendship. In a letter to Struve from 1899, the first year of their acquaintance, Berdiaev wrote, somewhat repentantly, about the metaphysics haunting his Marxism: "I'm afraid that you, too, will find in me an already too risky metaphysical tendency. On the whole I must confess that I am an innate metaphysician and that Marxism hasn't healed me of it. My most passionate desire is this: to raise Marxism to transcendental [*zaoblachnye*] heights, to impart it an idealist character when all is said and done."[93] Given this backdrop, and amid their efforts to bring people over from Marxism to the liberation movement with which they were affiliated, the fact that Bulgakov and Berdiaev took up a new sympathetic interpretation of Dostoevsky's flawed hero could be seen as a rather confusing contradiction of their political movement's reformist agenda.

Despite Miliukov and Struve's disinterest in metaphysical problems, Randall Poole, the foremost scholar of Russian philosophical idealism, has shown how idealism was an important element in the development of liberalism in late imperial Russia. Poole has argued that the Moscow Philosophical Society's study of Kantian metaphysics established the philosophical foundations for Russian liberal thought "by grounding the value of the human person in transcendent being (personalism)."[94] "The idea that human beings bear an absolute value and dignity because they are persons or, in Kant's terminology, ends-in-themselves," while not explicitly raised in Bulgakov's analysis of Ivan Karamazov, is nonetheless a core idea in his investigation into Ivan's protest against God and in Berdiaev's earliest theories of the individual personality.[95] In their reception of Dostoevsky, idealists managed to merge a notion of personhood drawn from Kant with Dostoevsky's consistent privileging of the individual's free will in God's world. While Dostoevsky's political views are now received as discontinuous with liberalism, the idealist reading of his work deepened Soloviev's argument in *Three Speeches in Memory of Dostoevsky* by considering the liberationist potential of the writer's sweeping religious ideas, decoupled, of course, from their nationalist leanings.[96] After Soloviev's death, the idealists attempted to reconcile liberal theories of individual value and Dostoevsky's fictional articulations of the religious ideal of Godmanhood.[97] The idealist reading helped reshape the positive value of Dostoevsky's fiction and made it possible for a lesser-known critic to claim in 1905 that "Dostoevsky's significance is not in his sermons, but in the 'questions of the personality'" posed in his work.[98]

As the reform movement gained momentum and acquired further legitimacy in 1905, its members' perception of Ivan as an idealist archetype was under constant attack from radical critics, who actively rejected the metaphysical approach of Bulgakov's reading. In response, idealists opted to frame Ivan's struggle more and more in terms of the language of "optimism" and "realism," perhaps having realized that framing one of Dostoevsky's most tragic characters as an idealist hero sounded paradoxical at best and at worst incomprehensible. Their reading of Ivan also reveals the limits of the idealists' metaphysical preoccupation in spheres where more practical political issues were constantly debated. What Rowan Williams has noted about Bulgakov could be said of his idealist colleagues: "[He] was apolitical in the sense that he had little sense of political strategy and little taste, energy or gift for the bread-and-butter business of planning and negotiating."[99] The story of Ivan's transformation—from nihilist to idealist and, finally, to budding liberationist—is a snapshot of how Dostoevsky's faithful readers creatively reimagined the political tendency of his work, realigning his religious ideas with their liberatory struggle to end the autocracy that the writer had openly supported.[100]

The idealist reading of Ivan's protest against God's "narrative" of the world, which permits the suffering of innocents, can be read as a kind of subversion of the author by the character, which Bakhtin once argued defined the aesthetic effect of Dostoevsky's work. Bakhtin's theory of Dostoevsky's "dialogic" narrator in *Problems of Dostoevsky's Poetics* accords with the idealist rejection of the limits of historical materialism to the free development of the human personality (which can be likened to how the monologic narrator intervenes in the formation of characters' autonomy in the novel). Dostoevsky's heroes are, on the contrary, "not only objects of authorial discourse but also subjects of their own directly signifying discourse."[101] Elsewhere, in his essay "Author and Hero in Aesthetic Activity," Bakhtin examined the mode of "confessional self-accounting" as an instance where the roles of hero and author cease to exist: "Author and hero are fused into one: it is the spirit prevailing over the soul in process of its own becoming, and finding itself unable to achieve its own completion or consummation, except for a certain degree of consolidation that it gains, through anticipation, in God."[102] But Bakhtin carefully noted some exceptions and alternative developments of self-accounting, which provide insight into how idealists read Ivan. While usually self-accounting involves neither author nor hero—and thus finds itself alien to any aesthetic organization, "when my act is a specifically ethical act, then my reflection upon it and my account of it start determining me as well and involve my own determinateness."[103] Bakhtin goes on to note that when "tones of faith and hope" begin to predominate, then self-accounting becomes endowed with "aesthetic moments."[104] Ivan can be said to represent an example of the hero's self-accounting in which negative images of "tones of faith and hope" begin to take over. The aestheticization of his self-accounting unfolds almost exactly the way Bakhtin describes it. Ivan gives an account of himself to Alyosha, which then takes shape as an *aesthetic* "moment": the "narrative poem" (*poema*) "The Grand Inquisitor." In this way, Ivan's self-accounting realizes itself in a rebellious ethical act—his protest against God—which not only begins to determine his development as a person but also leads to his authoritative position in the text as an author. Of course, Bulgakov and the idealists did not view Ivan's development in these terms, but Bakhtin's detailed investigation into the aestheticization of self-accounting sheds light on the idealist interpretation of Ivan as an authoritative personality in the world of the novel.

Pursuing this view of Ivan as an author himself—one who could voice an ethical act that they could believe in and connect with their liberal views—helped them challenge Dostoevsky's own authority. In short, the idealists were refuting the view, launched first in Rozanov's seminal essay, that Ivan was simply the direct voice of Dostoevsky himself. In the idealist reading, Ivan is accorded his own status as a separate entity with his own authority, ethical calculation, and pain. Desiring as they did the liberation of Dostoevsky's core moral message from the illiberal political affiliations he once held, the idealist interpretation of Ivan led by Bulgakov offered a real opportunity for reparative readings of Dostoevsky. The search to find the author through his hero was one route to salvaging what they perceived to be the redemptive idea of his life's work.

But it was not only those in their political milieu who might have found their mobilization of Dostoevsky misguided, for Bulgakov and Berdiaev faced criticism from their colleagues in literary spheres as well. In the fall of 1904, Bulgakov and Berdiaev took on the editorial responsibility of the *New Path* as it transitioned to its third and final year under the name *Vital Questions* (Voprosy zhizni, 1905).[105] If Bulgakov had begun to invoke Dostoevsky in his search "from Marxism to idealism," the God-seekers (Merezhkovsky et al.) who had formerly steered the agenda at the *New Path* drew on the authority of the same novelist to propose a more ambitious goal: "from idealism to mysticism."[106] "On this path," wrote Dmitry Filosofov, "both the decadents, who have gained knowledge of the inner recesses of the human being, and the shamelessly love-stricken realists [Gorky, Andreev et al.], who have come to love, in Dostoevsky's words, life before the very meaning of it, must inevitably set out."[107] While most everyone affiliated with the Russian religious renewal agreed that Dostoevsky had articulated best the spiritual search for the ideal that they placed at the center of their worldview, their views about the spiritual practices necessary to pursue this ideal showed a difference of opinion.

As they assumed editorship of the *New Path*, Bulgakov and Berdiaev continued to explicitly frame idealism as the philosophical basis of the liberation movement, more and more underscoring the "realism" of idealism. Berdiaev rejected the accusation that the metaphysical freedom posed in philosophical idealism "turned its back to liberationist social progress."[108] The two men would assert that their movement had little to do with the "decadents" over at Valery Briusov's journal, *Libra* (Vesy); theirs was a synthesis, a hybrid: "ideal-realism."[109] Earlier in 1904, Bulgakov concluded an essay on the realist outlook by quoting Dostoevsky's famous definition of himself as a "realist in a higher sense," suggesting the term "Gospel realism" for the work of both Tolstoy and Dostoevsky.[110] Dostoevsky was still an authority, but the status of his work as "realism" (and what that actually meant) was growing more unstable among Silver Age critics and thinkers.

Although initially Bulgakov and Berdiaev were eager to present themselves as true "realists" and not at all part of the religious mysticism of the Merezhkovskys and the "Dionysianism" of the increasingly influential Viacheslav Ivanov, the impotence of liberal politics after the First and Second Duma pushed both of them into exclusively religious-philosophical terrain. By the time Ivanov and his colleague Georgii Chulkov collaborated on their volume *On Mystical Anarchism* (1906), which unapologetically based its worldview on Ivan's nihilist "nonacceptance of the world," Ivan's moral stance had been allowed to collapse into its inherit tragic conditions, which cleared a mystical path. Mystical anarchism, the subject of chapter 4, would turn Ivan's metaphysical anguish and moral tragedy into an unlikely utopian politics, something Bulgakov had never attempted, and that was by far the most radical reimagining of Dostoevsky's religion up to that point—and possibly in the history of criticism on him. This shift from philosophical idealism to mysticism spelled out what Filosofov had wanted to see from the idealists all along, and it initiated more critical negotiations of the limitations—even the dark corners—of Dostoevsky's religious idea.

CHAPTER 4

Symbolist Critics and the Death of the Author, 1905–1910

At the beginning of 1905, Russia was at a crossroads. Both Marxists and those in the religious renaissance greeted the 1905 revolution as a way out of centuries of autocratic rule and what seemed to some as the birth of a new society. However, for those such as Dmitry Merezhkovsky and Sergei Bulgakov, who had by then recovered and adapted Dostoevsky's religion and art to their times, the revolutionary years brought on a need to reevaluate what the writer, who had been so famously antisocialist and openly supportive of the autocracy and the Orthodox Church, meant in such a new world. To any reader familiar with the past ten years of criticism on Dostoevsky, Merezhkovsky's new position on the writer must have been striking.[1] Recalling the tragic events of Bloody Sunday, Merezhkovsky wrote, "It would seem that one need only answer faith with faith and a miracle of love, a miracle of the tsar's union with the people would be accomplished. It would seem so, according to Dostoevsky. But alas, we know what happened and how the regime [*vlast'*] responded to the people."[2] Dostoevsky's work was no longer speaking to the present in the same way.

This period was the most divisive era of Russian criticism on Dostoevsky up to that point. The literary scene was as tumultuous as the political one. A few years after a wave of new art movements had sprung up in the aftermath of the *World of Art* journal, by 1906, there were separate camps of poets and critics, all staunchly opposed to one another's aesthetics and politics. Beginning in 1904, Valery Briusov's "Decadents" were putting out innovative poetry and criticism at *Libra*. Religious-philosophical poetry and criticism dominated the pages of the *New Path*, which had been renamed *Vital Questions* in 1905 when it transitioned to Bulgakov's editorship. Zinaida Gippius, Dmitry Filosofov, and Merezhkovsky (henceforth, "the Merezhkovskys") would soon leave for Paris, while in 1906 a new journal called *Zolotoe runo* (the Golden Fleece), featuring groundbreaking cultural criticism from the Symbolist theoretician and poet Viacheslav Ivanov, would attempt to resurrect the dream of *World of Art*, which had once facilitated cooperation among the creative intelligentsia, despite differences in taste and politics.

This new literary climate, the 1905 revolution, and the twenty-fifth anniversary of Dostoevsky's death collided and forged a new era of critical work on the writer. It is incorrect to claim, as some have, that Dostoevsky's stature in relation to Russian art and culture declined during this period; rather, the mode of critical evaluation of him was being adapted to respond to a revolutionary political landscape.[3] Of course, some critics were not at all compelled to enlist him or any other writer in the revolutionary times or to question their talent in light of current events. Briusov, editor of *Libra*, often preferred to keep politics out of criticism. He responded to a newspaper survey organized by the critic Kornei Chukovsky toward the end of 1906: "F. Tiutchev was a 'rightist,' N. Ogarev was a 'leftist,' F. Dostoevsky was a 'rightist,' N. Nekrasov was a 'leftist.' What is the relationship between the revolution and literature? The revolution can furnish a few themes for the writer, who treats them either with or without talent. That's about it."[4] Meanwhile, the second-wave Symbolists Andrei Belyi and Aleksandr Blok wrote about Dostoevsky as a failed prophet, whose forecasts led only to a false sense of liberation. These younger Symbolists did not see themselves as the blessed disciples of a prophet; they were the abused progeny of a mad visionary.

Bulgakov's Christian socialist party, the Union of Christian Politics, continued to adapt Dostoevsky to idealist philosophy, which earned steady criticism from the Merezhkovskys. They had been devoting their literary activity to founding a new church, while the Symbolists who gathered at Ivanov's "Tower" salon articulated a rather nondenominational philosophical worldview—mystical anarchism—among other things, a reconciliation of the art of their day with ancient mystical rites. For their part, Ivanov and his close colleague Georgii Chulkov—the founder of mystical anarchism and, later, a pioneering Dostoevsky scholar—followed a path cleared by Vasily Rozanov.[5] While they could never surpass Rozanov's flair for provocation, they saw in Dostoevsky's sketches of the human personality a path to mythic and liberationist social structures: from anarchism to mystical eroticism.[6] For these critics, the way to maintain faithful readership was for the critic to finally overcome the author and to assume his mantle: reparative readings of Dostoevsky, aimed at recovering certain ideological dimensions of this work, became possible only through this empowerment of critic over author. While their motivations and styles may have differed, what is common to the critical work of Bulgakov, Merezhkovsky, and Ivanov—as well as Rozanov—in the revolutionary years is their reparative intent and the critic's primacy.

As always, we can look to Rozanov for the most provocative example of this critical trend. In the final issue of the *Golden Fleece* of 1906, Rozanov republished the second (1901–1906) and third (1906) prefaces as an "afterword" to his 1891 commentary on the "Legend of the Grand Inquisitor," a text that "turns against its creator," which he wrote in the second preface.[7] "The ideological content of Dostoevsky is enormous, although twenty years after his death, if you take a pencil you can always point to where he did not reach what was necessary, where he overstepped what is needed. . . . We must go further than Dostoevsky."[8] Having confused "metaphysical" questions with "historical" ones, Dostoevsky's "aberration of the mind" was, Rozanov believed, better left to the present moment: "God has brought us to a talented *moment*. Will *we ourselves* manage to be as talented?"[9] To Rozanov, critics should take over the resolution of problems posed but incorrectly addressed by the writer, and in this suggestion, he comes remarkably close to Michel Foucault's reassignment of the author's role as a function of discourse in "What Is an Author?": "The author is an ideological project, since we represent him as the opposite of his historically real function."[10] What faithful readers perceived as redeeming aspects of Dostoevsky's work could only be restored to contemporaneity through the critic's own artistic—and spiritual—insights. Whether they renounced him or clung tighter to his image, Bulgakov, Merezhkovsky, and Ivanov attempted to take Dostoevsky into an uncertain future at a time when his ideas were breaking apart and participating in the discursive rearrangement that is the critic's privilege.

This chapter provides an account of the reckoning over Dostoevsky that took place surrounding the 1906 jubilee. It is significant that new and radical discussions of Dostoevsky's work occurred in a year that commemorated his death; critics were beginning to look for new entry points into his work in order to fill in his disappearance. Foucault wrote about the space opened by the author's disappearance, presenting this new presence as discourse: "The author's name manifests the appearance of a certain discursive set and indicates that status of this discourse within a society and a culture. It has no legal status, nor is it located in the fiction of the work; rather, it is located in the break that founds a certain discursive construct."[11] It was no longer Dostoevsky's work that needed interpreting in this era of criticism, but criticism itself that was generating a new "discursive set," whose intent was to faithfully render the author's ideas through their own experience of history as it played out around them.

The Twenty-Fifth Jubilee: Commemorating the Author in a Revolutionary Year

Anna Dostoevskaia had big plans for the twenty-fifth anniversary of her husband's death.[12] As the stenographer of his novels, she perhaps knew the author and his texts better than anyone else did. A jubilee edition of Dostoevsky's complete works was in the midst of publication (it came out between 1904 and 1906 in fourteen volumes), and a small section of the Russian State History Museum dedicated to the writer's life and work had opened in Moscow in 1906. Both projects were accompanied by a detailed guide to texts written by or about the writer, intermingled with catalogues of objects owned and used by him, compiled personally by Dostoevskaia. Though the prominent critic A. G. Gornfel'd called Dostoevskaia's guide a "lifeless book"—lamenting that there remained serious biographical and textological research to be done on the writer—it is now recognized as a watershed in Dostoevsky studies.[13] Some of the objects cataloged by her—the desk on which he wrote *The Brothers Karamazov*, his cigarette case, and the last newspaper issues he read just before the pulmonary hemorrhage that killed him— point to the physical and very real life of the author.[14]

The sequence in which the volumes were published seems to have been coordinated with current events. The first volume to come out was the fourteenth, containing the popular *Brothers Karamazov*. The eighth volume, which contained Dostoevsky's controversial novel *Devils*, came out in the revolutionary year of 1905. In its own time, it had been considered only a tendentious lampoon of revolutionary socialism; however, Symbolist and religious-philosophical readings of the novel focused on its Christological symbolism and its postulation of Russia as a "god-bearing" nation. The eighth volume also included materials relevant to the composition of *Devils* but ended just before the famously excised portion, "Stavrogin's confession," in which the protagonist confesses to a monk his gravest sin: the violation of a child who subsequently died by suicide. The complete text of the confession was published by Leonid Grossman only in 1929. These notes on *Devils* showed a clearer glimpse into Dostoevsky's crafting of the novel's religious symbolism. A note accompanying the publication of these items explained that the notebooks to *Devils* had been prepared by Strakhov for the 1883 edition of Dostoevsky's complete works but that they had been set aside for one of the future editions "due to certain circumstances."[15] By ensuring that the volume containing *Devils* and its author's notebooks came out in 1905, Dostoevskaia sought to frame her late husband as not only a religious writer but an antirevolutionary writer as well.

When it came to looking for a suitable critic to write an introduction for the edition, Dostoevskaia encountered some problems. Virtually all critics writing about Dostoevsky, under the influence of profound collective outrage against the autocracy, had grown more critical, more suspicious, of the writer's politics. Dostoevskaia approached Merezhkovsky first, since no critic had attached himself as closely to Dostoevsky's legacy, but 1905 was a transitional time for the Merezhkovskys. Personal conflicts had prompted them to leave Russia for an extended stay in Paris in February 1906, but they continued to contribute to Russian journals from abroad.[16] While away, the Merezhkovskys connected with prominent socialist revolutionaries in Paris, an association that no doubt influenced Merezhkovsky's shifting views on Dostoevsky.[17] However, their Paris years were hardly radical in a conventional sense of the word; their goal in joint efforts such as *Le tsar et la révolution* (1907) was to frame the 1905 revolution for European audiences as a religious crisis that only socialism (of a more populist flavor than the Marxist variety) could rectify.[18]

Since publishing his popular book *L. Tolstoy and Dostoevsky* (1902; see chapter 2), Merezhkovsky had already been revising his thinking about the writer. The essay he offered to Dostoevskaia, "Prophet of the Russian Revolution" (*Prorok russkoi revoliutsii*), documented Dostoevsky's support for the autocracy and the Orthodox Church, nevertheless (and confusingly) arguing for the hidden, revolutionary religious agenda emerging from the novels.[19] The old Merezhkovsky was muted in this new essay, which sketched a portrait of a writer with undoubted revolutionary spirit but who was ultimately incapable of rejecting the institutions of church and state, the reactionary chimera tormenting liberation movements and frustrating religious renewal.[20] E. A. Andrushchenko has completed a study of Merezhkovsky's various versions of this essay at his archive at the Institute of Russian Literature in St. Petersburg, proving that he had been writing two versions at the same time: a gentler, shorter version for Dostoevskaia and a longer, strident one.[21] Even after having seen the softened version, Dostoevskaia was still forced to reject it, but as if in deference to Merezhkovsky's past commitment to her husband's legacy, she decided to publish a letter by Merezhkovsky with an explanation. In his message, which appeared just after the title page of the first volume of the collected works, he offered an explanation to Dostoevskaia and any readers who had anticipated finding an introduction written by him: "The views expressed in my essay on a few of the most cherished beliefs of F. M. Dostoevsky—autocracy, Orthodoxy, and nationality—are so out of alignment with the established opinions about the works of this writer in Russian society, that I then agreed with you that maybe an article such as mine has no place in a classical Jubilee edition."[22]

With no evidence of Akim Volynsky or Lev Shestov ever having been considered for the honor of writing the introduction, Dostoevskaia wrote to her husband's friend S. I. Smirnova to ask if she might consider the honor. Considering Smirnova a reliable potential contributor, Dostoevskaia wrote, "How many times has it occurred to me that in our time of trouble [*smutnoe vremia*], only you alone, perhaps, could clarify for our reading public the essence and true meaning of Fedor Mikhailovich's works, which have foretold so much in contemporary reality."[23] Were there really no critics left who were sympathetic to her husband's work and legacy?

Dostoevskaia eventually secured Bulgakov to write the introduction, and Merezhkovsky's rejected contribution was published in *Libra* in two parts. Originally it was pitched to and rejected by Petr Struve's journal *Polar Star* (Poliarnaia zvezda), an editorial decision that did not surprise Merezhkovsky. Writing to Briusov about that rejection, Merezhkovsky claimed that Struve had found it "religious, *to a fanatic degree*," but Merezhkovsky conceded that his recent thinking naturally didn't fit with the "measured K. D. [Constitutional Democrat]-greyness and warmth of *Polar Star*."[24] He wrote to Briusov again several days later, noting how Struve had been "afraid of my mysticism," and had demanded certain changes to the piece that he had refused.[25] Merezhkovsky's letters to Briusov indicate that he personally considered his recent thoughts on

Dostoevsky to be radical, unpalatable to liberals like Struve and the "established opinions" of Dostoevskaia alike.

The contrast between Bulgakov's portrait of Dostoevsky, which aimed to disassociate the writer from both autocratic and church power, and Merezhkovsky's rejected "Prophet of the Russian Revolution" will be addressed in the following section. Both critics remained dedicated to Dostoevsky as a figurehead of their own religious worldviews, and their essays represent attempts to assume the author's authority by adopting a reparative approach in their critical discourse.

Commemorating Dostoevsky: Religious Revolutionary or Christian Socialist?

Merezhkovsky's lengthy essay "Prophet of the Russian Revolution" accuses Dostoevsky of unwittingly serving the forces of the autocracy, while also predicting the cultural and social upheaval of the 1905 revolution. The writer had insisted on the national superiority of Russian Orthodoxy as a gateway to universal Christianity and famously claimed that the Russian people were as invested in the Tsar as they were in their faith. Merezhkovsky takes issue with these positions in this essay, assembling an archive of passages from Dostoevsky's journalism and private writings that are often edited to avoid his conversational style and notoriously complex sentences. With such stylistic revisions, Merezhkovsky establishes his intellectual and cocreative authority in the essay. Of special relevance is a famous passage in *A Writer's Diary*, which Merezhkovsky quotes three separate times as a kind of refrain. The passage is from Dostoevsky's last notebook entries from 1881: "The Russian people are wholly in the Tsar and in the idea of him. Nothing else is in them and they have nothing else—and they don't need anything else because Orthodoxy is everything. Orthodoxy is the Church, and the Church is the crowning edifice now and forever. . . . The person who does not understand Orthodoxy will never understand anything about the people. Not only that, such a person also cannot love the Russian people."[26]

Merezhkovsky calls this notebook fragment "Dostoevsky's basic idea and basic mistake": by conflating the people and the Tsar, Dostoevsky conflates Orthodoxy and the state.[27] Despite their differences, the Western and Eastern churches perpetrated the same corruption of the institution's spiritual mission on earth: the Roman Catholic Church turned into the state, while the Russian Empire reorganized itself under Peter I and subsumed the Orthodox Church.[28] Merezhkovsky's strategy is to reveal the reactionary core of the writer's journalism in the first part of the essay before turning to his fiction in the second part. If the *Diary* condemns Dostoevsky, the fiction absolves him—a familiar strategy among readers, even today.

In the second part of the essay, Merezhkovsky indirectly returns to the polemic with Rozanov a few years earlier. Shatov's exchange with Stavrogin in *Devils* about Russia as a god-bearing nation is considered evidence of Dostoevsky's prophecy that a "Russian Christ" will come to defeat social disintegration and atheism. Merezhkovsky assumes that Shatov voices Dostoevsky's views and he arrives at the conclusion that the writer's national chauvinism overwhelmed and possibly eradicated his belief in God. But as Shatov is one of Dostoevsky's most enigmatic positive characters, some background about his "god-bearer" theory would help to contextualize Merezhkovsky's outlandish interpretation of it in his essay.

"Unsteadiness" (his name comes from *shatkii* or "unsteady") captures well Shatov's emotional hot-headedness and verbal incoherence in *Devils*, but the scene in which he speaks the "god-bearer theory" back to Stavrogin, who initiated Shatov into the idea but who now cynically denies it, is one of the most powerful religious moments in the novel and in Dostoevsky's entire body of work.[29] In the tense scene between them we learn of the theory's key features. Nations (*narody*) are not naturally conditioned to build their worldviews on science and reason, Shatov explains; they seek moral guidance—distinctions between good and evil—in religious belief systems led by a god unique to their culture and experience. In this way, each nation generates its own god, the survival of which reflects the strength or unity of the nation, as well as its moral health.

Dostoevsky based Shatov's explication of the theory on what he perceived as the false role of Orthodoxy in Nikolai Danilevsky's pan-Slavic nationalism, famously elaborated in his work *Russia and Europe* (1869).[30] For Dostoevsky, any unified national response to the atheist West depended on the special role of Russian Orthodoxy: it was not the nation, but the religion of that nation, that mattered. In an 1869 letter to his editor Nikolai Strakhov, who supported Danilevsky's work, Dostoevsky expressed his belief in "our native Orthodoxy . . . [as] the essence of our future civilizing role, and the resurrection, perhaps of all of Europe, and the whole essence of our mighty future."[31] But by lending his views to what one critic has called the "rabid Slavophile" Shatov, Dostoevsky distances himself from his character.[32] Joseph Frank held that Shatov, unlike Kirillov, was "along the path that Dostoevsky certainly considered that of salvation, but the symbolic pattern of the book requires that his path also be blocked by the fatality of Stavrogin's doom," not to mention Shatov's own tragic demise.[33] One can read the annihilation of the Shatov family—his wife and child die in childbirth and he is murdered—as his punishment for a faith based not in God but in nationalist kinship.[34] Shatov's spiritual trajectory is interrupted, yet crucially, unlike Stavrogin, he voices the hope that the god-bearing nation will fulfill its national destiny and bear not only the decadent West, but also him, to God. And so, though it would seem that killing off Shatov signals the resounding defeat of the god-bearer thesis, critics have suggested that Dostoevsky hinted only at its present impossibility or sought to warn readers of the cost of abandoning it.

It is striking that Merezhkovsky overlooks Dostoevsky's disagreement with Shatov's position. Mobilizing the antisemitic frameworks he had once used to dispute Tolstoy's religious beliefs, he employs similar rhetoric to Dostoevsky: "From faith in the national Messiah, which was incarnated in an entire nation-godbearer, to faith in Christ, which was incarnated in a single human-godbearer, in the tsar—that is, from Yid-ism [*zhidovstvo*] to the Flagellants [*klystovstvo*]—such is the path of Dostoevsky from Orthodoxy to autocracy."[35] Merezhkovsky claimed that "true 'Yids' are not Jews, but those Christians who turn from the New Testament to the Old, from the universal Christ to the people's Messiah."[36] These antisemitic asides permit Merezhkovsky to challenge Dostoevsky's religious commitments, making him as barren of faith as Shatov, and enhance his own critical authority.

The sharp rhetoric, contradictory messages, and offensiveness of Merezhkovsky's essay explain why Dostoevskaia could not publish it in the jubilee edition. But, ever the faithful reader—and despite his rejection of Dostoevsky's reactionary views—Merezhkovsky does not read suspiciously between the lines but subjects his analysis of Dostoevsky to the test of faith itself. While he does not explicitly articulate it, Merezhkovsky argues that Dostoevsky's reactionary positions were so blatantly opposed to his sincere love for the Russian people and the strength of his faith in Christ that the critic must speculate about a radical pivot in his reactionary development. He asked, "How could Dostoevsky not pronounce this word, how could he obscure his greatest truth with the greatest lie—his religious revolution with political reaction, the face of the holy rebel Father Zosima with the face of the cursed torturer, the Grand Inquisitor. How could he accept the kingdom of the devil for the kingdom of God!"[37] According to this reading, Dostoevsky did not manage to transcend his trust in the autocracy, choosing to hide behind the mask of autocracy and the Grand Inquisitor, but his real religion was articulated in the conversation between Ivan Karamazov, Father Paisy, and Father Zosima in book 2 of *The Brothers Karamazov*. The tragedy of Dostoevsky's life, Merezhkovsky concludes, is that he opted for political reaction instead of the truly radical promise of Father Zosima's free theocracy.[38] Merezhkovsky thus reinterprets Zosima as a dissenter against the state in an effort to show how Dostoevsky's inner radical tendency developed in parallel with his external public support of the autocracy. In this way, Merezhkovsky implies that, having reached the ultimate extreme of one view, the writer would have found himself fully aware of its failure and would begin approaching the opposite extreme: true theocracy triumphing over the state and the liberation of the people in a new church.[39]

It is impossible to ignore the conflicting emotions directed at the critical object in Merezhkovsky's essay, where the critic's affect merges scathing critique with painful devotion. In order to salvage Dostoevsky for the revolutionary years of 1905–1907, Merezhkovsky implies that doing so rests in a creative merging of the work, author, and critic, writing "only Dostoevsky can unmask Dostoevsky, only Dostoevsky can justify Dostoevsky. With him I am against him and with him I am for him. What I do, he would have done himself."[40] "We are not the denouncers, nor are we really the followers of Dostoevsky," Merezhkovsky wrote. "We are his accomplices."[41] This is how, despite its tone of outrage, Merezhkovsky's jubilee essay is still a far cry from what Paul Ricoeur would later call "suspicious"—the dominant affect of criticism. His critical stance sounds rather like a statement merging unrequited love and fealty: "When we raise that sword, which has not been sharpened by us, for a struggle that we did not initiate, when we pronounce the severing word, "the autocracy is the Antichrist"—we speak, I repeat, as if we are against Dostoevsky, but in reality we are for him; we act the way he would have himself if he had brought his religious consciousness to its conclusion."[42] This rhetoric draws on the style used by the Grand Inquisitor in *The Brothers Karamazov*, when he tells Christ, "We are not with you, but with *him*—there's our secret!"[43] It is as if Merezhkovsky demands, "Don't think that we are against Dostoevsky, we are with him," but by echoing the Grand Inquisitor, he hints at the notion that remaining with Dostoevsky in a revolutionary time will be construed as siding with the forces of evil instead of with Christ. For Merezhkovsky, it is a question not of proving Dostoevsky's unsuitability for the times but of having faith in his future suitability.

Roland Barthes once observed that "the reign of the Author has also been that of the Critic."[44] In Merezhkovsky's rejected jubilee essay the affective landscape is more complex. He performs an act of devotional submission in order to gain a dominant foothold on what the author ought to have done or could have done. Much in the way that Merezhkovsky attempts to show Dostoevsky's revolutionary spirit emerging at the extremes of his reactionary devotion to the state, the critic himself finds authority wearing a mask of submission. The message of the text is purified by the critic who submits it, indeed *performs it*, as the author would: "We are not adding anything of our own to this prophecy, we are only completing it, leading it to the stage of our religious consciousness and repeating together with Dostoevsky, the first prophet of the Holy Spirit, Holy Flesh: 'So be it, so be it.' "[45] Dostoevsky is the prophet of a new religion, but only the critic can interpret its missteps, revise it, and carry it to its conclusion.

No such anguish appears in Bulgakov's essay; however, his treatment of Dostoevsky's work shows a similar impulse to radically reorient the author in contemporary discussions of socialism, particularly its diverse forms. In a programmatic statement from his Union of Christian Politics (*Soiuz khristianskoi politiki*) published in *Vital Questions*, Bulgakov had noted that "Christianity" and "socialism" were erroneously placed in opposition to one another, even in the case of thinkers such as Dostoevsky and Soloviev, "who may themselves even, to a well-known degree, be numbered among Christian socialists, if not in their programs, then at least in their general tendency."[46] In *The Brothers Karamazov*, the connection between Christianity and socialism is handled with irony. In book 2, the liberal landowner Miusov, who participates in the debate about church and state, conveys a view allegedly told to him by a secret police agent of the French state, detailed with surveilling socialist revolutionaries: "A Christian socialist is more terrifying than a socialist atheist."[47] The devout Father Paisy immediately objects to this comparison—and is abruptly cut off by the next plot event—but the notion of a future synthesis of the two ideologies is hinted at.

Though Bulgakov did not name Dostoevsky as the direct forerunner to his Union, his words recalled one of the final entries of *A Writer's Diary* from January 1881 that provocatively addressed socialism in Russia. The entry in question originally functioned to refute the claim of many socialists that atheism ran deep in the Russian people, although it can be easily read out of context as the writer's conditional assent to a form of socialism. Writing about his atheist opponents, Dostoevsky clarified, "I am talking about our Russian 'socialism' (and I am adopting a word that is inversely opposed to the church precisely to clarify my idea, however strange it may seem), the goal and outcome of which is the national and universal church, which exists on earth insofar as the earth can contain it. . . . Not in communism, not in mechanistic forms is contained the socialism of the Russian people: the people believe that salvation is possible only in the last and final *global unification in the name of Christ*. That is our Russian socialism!"[48] While Bulgakov only mentions Dostoevsky once in his first major statement on the Union of Christian Politics from 1905, the very name of the organization returns the reader to the above quotation: twenty-five years earlier Dostoevsky had called for a "union in the name of Christ." Bulgakov reconciled Dostoevsky's polemical Russian socialism with his new political movement, an idea that migrated to his jubilee essay. He sought to prove the socialist basis of Dostoevsky's religion, which therefore renders unconvincing the *"purely political* blunder" of his support of the autocracy and his supposedly strong adherence to the official church.[49] This point is in direct disagreement with Merezhkovsky, for whom Dostoevsky's faith in the autocracy was not a mere "political" mistake but a flaw in his religious idea.

Bulgakov sets out to prove Dostoevsky's religious compatibility with socialism by relating it to the writer's well-known abhorrence of Catholicism. In this line of reasoning, which relies on a fallacy of relative privation, Dostoevsky is seen to have "related . . . more mildly to socialism than Catholicism," which for him indicates his receptivity to or potential inclination toward socialism.[50] This kind of argumentation goes further than apologia; Bulgakov's essay mobilizes textual evidence to support his claims of a more left-leaning Dostoevsky, reflecting a collective desire among many Symbolist and religious-philosophical critics to find in the work what the author's political stance contradicted.

As part of his project to associate Dostoevsky with socialism, Bulgakov also wished to separate Dostoevsky (as well as himself) from ties to the official church. This last goal was perhaps a response to his critics, among them the Merezhkovskys, who were skeptical of Bulgakov's political ambitions with his Union. Gippius later noted about Bulgakov and the other contributors to *Problems of Idealism* (see chapter 3), "For them, 'idealism' was just a stage, a transitional step towards religion (which was also a transitional step to the church)."[51] To her, only the bleak emptiness of the church could provide a refuge for the range of views held by Bulgakov and others in his Union. Even one of her opponents, Georgii Chulkov, agreed with Gippius's assessment.[52]

But Bulgakov was not only defending his own political work; he sought to claim that Dostoevsky in fact never proposed the "existing Orthodox Church" as a model for the future transformation of society through Orthodox faith.[53] He never conflated Orthodoxy with "the church administration, whose members are insincerely selected from government adherents, by a significant degree according to political motives, and he acknowledged that the 'church is paralyzed.'"[54] About the question of Dostoevsky's support of the autocracy, Bulgakov understood it as an entirely separate phenomenon, not connected to his Orthodox faith at all. Dostoevsky's "idiosyncratic adherence to the autocracy" was simply a feature of his "democratism [and] faith in the creative powers of tsarist power and the autonomous political development of the people" and also of his "lack of faith in the possibility of parliamentarianism in Russia."[55] Elsewhere, in a lecture he delivered in Kiev several months earlier—"A Crown of Thorns"—whose title likens Dostoevsky to the crucified Christ, Bulgakov employed hypothetical fallacies to soften the writer's support of the autocracy. In that essay, Bulgakov explained that Dostoevsky's "idealization of the autocracy" made more sense in 1860s than it did to an audience in 1906. He further reasoned, "Of course, if Dostoevsky and I. S. Aksakov and other honest Slavophiles had lived to our time of internal and external Tsushima they would have attached themselves—in this I am totally convinced—to the liberation movement, although, of course, retaining their particular voice, they would not have lost themselves in the many-voiced chorus."[56] This argument's form parallels Merezhkovsky's: Dostoevsky would have been with us, despite what evidence from his work demonstrates. Bulgakov finds democratic motivations even when Dostoevsky was at his most Orthodox and imperialist, such as his now infamous proclamation in *A Writer's Diary*: "Constantinople sooner or later must be ours."[57]

Negative appraisals of Bulgakov's essay and doubts about the contributions of Dostoevskaia's bibliographical guide confirmed that new approaches to Dostoevsky were badly needed. Reviewing the jubilee edition, Volzhskii preferred the "lifeless" bibliographies to the leading critics' tendentious rewriting of Dostoevsky's political and religious commitments. He remarked, "However interesting the articles by Bulgakov and Merezhkovsky are in and of themselves, after 25 years

Dostoevsky does not require any further recommendations. A strictly scholarly introduction, even if drier in character, would be more desirable and appropriate now."[58] The philosopher Lev Shestov, who had already devoted a serious book-length study to Dostoevsky, joined the chorus, reflecting in 1907, "Berdiaev . . . just like Merezhkovsky and Bulgakov only due to a misunderstanding consider themselves the continuation of Dostoevsky's cause [*delo*]. When Dostoevsky hung on the cross, he doubted himself in everything and doubted himself until the end. . . . It seems that because, under torture, Dostoevsky wrenched himself from sweetness, it does not at all follow that Berdiaev, Merezhkovsky, or Bulgakov suggest drinking vinegar mixed with bile."[59] More and more, critics and leading voices in the journalistic discourse were settling on the author's work, which looked like a refuge of possibility compared to the conflict and dissent surrounding the author himself.

Konstantin Bal'mont, the most popular Symbolist poet of his time, concurred in remarks from a 1907 survey of literature, which advocated for the complexity of Dostoevsky's word over previous critical attempts to force the synthesis of author and text: "Whatever Dostoevsky conjured [*zagovoril*], his word was exact, his achievement was like the sharp aim of an Indian's lasso. His positions were unexpected; each one of his ideas was piercing. And he was equally good at describing a room, a speech to God, a political essay, or reflecting on poems."[60] Bal'mont's evaluation, though it joins calls to leave the author behind, is a dispassionate outlier during this period. In two other camps—one occupied by Andrei Belyi and the other by the mystical anarchists to whom Belyi was passionately opposed—there were tensions within Symbolist criticism about the positive or "revolutionary" potential of Dostoevsky's religion.

Belyi pointed to the false prophesies underlying the author's religious thought, while the mystical anarchists attempted to create a new movement that revolved around the rebellious mysticism of Ivan Karamazov. Belyi demanded an "overcoming" of the author, apparently unconvinced that he could be separated from his historically contingent false prophesies, while the latter looked to texts *within* Dostoevsky's texts—the protagonists' own spoken discourse and writings by fictional characters—toward recovering the author's religious insights into new critical formations. The Symbolist fascination with fictional characters as character-symbols, whose words resonated beyond their author, is one point of origin for Bakhtin's theory of polyphony in Dostoevsky's novels.

Andrei Belyi's 1906 Anti-Jubilee

As Merezhkovsky and Bulgakov refashioned Dostoevsky—one offering a religious revolutionary and the other a Christian socialist—Belyi rejected the idea of inheriting the novelist's project altogether.[61] In a review of Volynsky's 1906 collected essays on Dostoevsky, Belyi confessed that despite all that Volynsky's generation of critics had contributed to understanding the writer, they seemed unconcerned that Dostoevsky's promises about religious liberation were not coming true. Belyi wrote, "Only later we began to understand more definitely that plunging one-self into Dostoevsky did not lend itself to creating new values, but that whatever had plunged into Dostoevsky was the dawn of an untold religious renaissance."[62] Dostoevsky's inheritance was merely a reminder to keep searching for spiritual insight, a journey that must continue without the author. As for their time: "We are once again in the mountains. On the rift towards a better future the fog comes to meet us. We are alone once again."[63] The sons were seeing their brilliance reflected in the murky pools of their literary father, Dostoevsky, not the other way around. In his review of Volynsky, he concluded plainly, "It's necessary to overcome Dostoevsky."[64]

In another essay from this period, "Ibsen and Dostoevsky," Belyi even more stridently attacked Dostoevsky, identifying him as Rozanov once did with the Grand Inquisitor. He offered two ways of "overcoming Dostoevsky's tastelessness": either forward to Nietzsche or back to Pushkin and Gogol. "To Gogol and Pushkin—those initiators of Russian literature—is to whom we must return in order to save literature from the seeds of decay and death that have been lodged into it by the inquisitor's hand of Dostoevsky."[65] Belyi thus urges his contemporaries to look to Ivan's "poem" about the inquisitor, not the author himself, as the true source of Dostoevsky's legacy. But even more serious was Belyi's assault on the religious core of Dostoevsky's art. He held that "Dostoevsky is religious, but the fire of his religion does not go beyond the literary description of real experience. These descriptions are awkwardly shrouded by the vestments of Christianity."[66] In his review of Volynsky's criticism, he accused Dostoevsky of encouraging his descendants to expect an apocalyptic resolution that would never come: "We understood that we had come out of the suffocating underground, and there, while we were tearing ourselves out of it, was Dostoevsky's work illuminating our paths. But one more step and the apocalyptic delirium of his heroes turned out to be hysterical, unnecessary, an inheritance before the eternal sun of the Apocalypse. We wanted an ending, but the spasms, screams, and demonic possession were not for us."[67] In the essay on Henrik Ibsen, Belyi even repurposed motifs from *Crime and Punishment* to attack Dostoevsky's barren religious vision: "We've heard a lot of promises in little taverns, where mystics befriend police officers, where the police station is more than once passed off as eternity even though it is in the image of 'a banya with spiderwebs.' "[68] Dostoevsky had brought only darkness and cold, a critique that Belyi's peers were accustomed to hearing from Gorky and the realists at *Znanie*—not from one of the leading Symbolist poets. After all, as a young poet, Belyi had been nurtured by none other than Merezhkovsky, the critic who was fighting the hardest to bring Dostoevsky into the revolutionary reality of their times.

Among the younger Symbolists, Aleksandr Blok echoed Belyi's concerns when he implicated Dostoevsky in the stagnation that had paralyzed Russian life: "A fat spider kept warm the sensuous icon lamp at the peaceful hearth of simple and good people."[69] Despite having dreamed of "God, Russia, and the establishment of universal justice," Dostoevsky could manage only "a moment of blinding happiness" and managed to deliver characters like the *Idiot*'s gothic villain Parfen Rogozhin, "the incarnation of chaos and non-existence."[70] These were examples of what Belyi had identified as Dostoevsky's farsightedness—his focus on prophesying the future but his failure to create a clear view of the life unfolding around him. This sentiment directly contradicts what Soloviev had written and what Ivanov would claim about Dostoevsky. For these young poets, the promise that Rozanov and Merezhkovsky had seen in Dostoevsky's dialectics and predominantly darkly sketched religious dreams had become, with the revolution, simply a gaping void.

Horrified at the turn in his friend's recent articles, Merezhkovsky wrote to Belyi right after the two essays appeared in the January and February 1906 issues of *Libra*, sharing an idea that he had expanded in his jubilee essay: "If Dostoevsky had not existed, we would not have existed. Destroying him, you destroy us."[71] Belyi's support of Ibsen over Dostoevsky read to Merezhkovsky like a Karamazovian rebellion against God: "Asserting that Dostoevsky did not know the path, but Ibsen did, you are doing the same thing as asserting that Christ is not the way and that the way is an uprising against Christ—'*an ascent to the heavens*'—titanism!"[72]

The rebellion of Belyi and Blok attacked the once-living writer, calling for the removal of the prophet's mantle of authority while mobilizing images from the text that had now entered the cultural discourse as shorthand symbols of spiritual despair—the spider motif, the murderer Rogozhin. These crystallized fragments of the work are the meaningless leftovers of a destroyed faith and an art deprived of joy. While Belyi had not abandoned God in these years, he was moving away from the critical practice of turning the author into a devotional object, a tradition that the earlier generation of Symbolist critics sustained. The mystical anarchists were advancing this trend, working toward a more sophisticated reconfiguration of the religious feeling at the heart of Dostoevsky's worldview, seeking meaning in critical reflection on the work and leaving the author behind.

Mystical Anarchism and the Author's Annihilation

Mystical anarchism (1905–1907) was perhaps the most radical reconfiguration of Dostoevsky's religious ideas to arise out of the revolutionary years, but the ridicule it earned in literary journals has tarnished its critical legacy.[73] Among the group's fiercest critics were the Merezhkovskys and Belyi, who published frequent attacks in *Libra*.[74] Despite the fact that its founder, Georgii Chulkov, had the support of the widely respected Ivanov, mystical anarchism is still viewed as lacking philosophical rigor and contributing little to contemporary debates about religion and society.

The only artistic project proposed by mystical anarchism, the theater project "Torches" (*Fakely*), was never realized, but it assembled some of the best talent in the dramatic arts.[75] "Torches" was intended to reconcile Symbolists with the realist writers at Gorky's collective *Znanie*, which included the popular dramatist and author of short fiction Leonid Andreev. While it came to naught, the project was more than theater and demonstrated the impressive reach of the mystical anarchist coalition. In a letter to Briusov in early January 1906, the eminent theater director Vsevolod Meyerhold shared a proclamation uttered by Gorky, demonstrating the hope that the theater collective could help transform the broken state: "In wretched Russia only art exists, we here are its 'government.' We underestimate its meaning too much; we must *powerfully* rule and our theater should be realized on an enormous scale. This must be a theater-club that could unify all literary factions."[76]

The mystical anarchists promoted a nondogmatic mystical worldview (it was not a religion), which, its theoreticians believed, was capable of generating a revolutionary energy that could overcome contemporary factionalism and the lonely individualism brought by modernity.[77] The movement rejected both the Merezhkovskys' determination to found a new church as the way out of the political and spiritual crisis facing their generation and Briusov's apolitical, aestheticized worldview at *Libra*. The iconoclasm of mystical anarchism makes sense considering Chulkov's background. Before becoming the literary editor of *Vital Questions* and contributing theater reviews to literary journals, he had been sentenced and exiled to today's Amma in the Sakha Republic (then Amga, Yakutia) for political activity deemed dangerous to the state. In Nizhny Novgorod, where after his imprisonment he was living under police surveillance, he was apparently working with the local branch of the Social Democrats. He wrote later in his memoirs that this activity "combin[ed] a devotion to Dostoevsky with revolutionary practice in the spirit of Bolshevism."[78] Filosofov once referred to Chulkov as an "involuntary 'Social Democrat,'" which he meant as an insult.[79]

In *On Mystical Anarchism* (O misticheskom anarkhizme, 1906) Chulkov led the group's first effort to formally outline its worldview. Despite its explicit references to Dostoevsky, Chulkov's volume has not received attention as a direct response to ongoing contemporary debates on Dostoevsky in the jubilee year. The volume opened with an introductory essay by Ivanov, "The Idea of Nonacceptance of the World and Mystical Anarchism." The title directly references Ivan's speech to Alyosha in *The Brothers Karamazov* in which he "returns his ticket" to God. Ivanov thus links Ivan to the mystical anarchist project, articulating the movement's core idea of nonacceptance. It is not exactly rejection, for the term's phrasing seems to encourage the liminality between acceptance and rejection. Ivan's ability to model the experience of being suspended between an old ideal and a future one is what makes him such an appealing poster child for mystical anarchism.

Ivanov's pioneering interpretation of the mythological dynamics of Dostoevsky's fiction, "Dostoevsky and the Novel-Tragedy" (*Dostoevskii i roman-tragediia*, 1911), is palpable in his essay on mystical anarchism.[80] In his later, more influential essay, the notion of nonacceptance reappears in relation to the three "mystical roots of guilt," a central concept to the Christian worldview. Ivanov writes of "an individual's preference for one deity over another, their inability or disinclination to piously combine in their soul *acceptance* [my emphasis] and respect of all gods, of all divine wills and energies of the world."[81] Such is the tragic guilt that Ivan faces when he refuses to accept God's world in favor of some unknown truth. One of the fundamental differences between Bulgakov and Ivanov's attraction to Ivan Karamazov is that for the latter, Ivan is a clearly drawn tragic figure, whose nonacceptance leads to mystical transformation at the cost of rebelling against all that is human and all that is sacred.

Just as Rozanov and Merezhkovsky had rooted Dostoevsky in the ancient past—the former situating Dostoevsky among the ancient Jews, the latter framing Dostoevsky as a prophet of a transcendent Aryanism that could heal Christianity in his day—Ivanov applied his knowledge of the cultural history of ancient Greek religion to place the novelist into an older mythological tradition, this time in the origins of the mystical cult of Dionysius.[82] Ivanov's reading of Dostoevsky's novels as more recent manifestations of ancient myth and religious energies helped render the writer's corpus into a discourse about spirituality and the nature of artistic creativity—all central values of the Symbolist worldview. The novels had long been received as an archive of human psychological experience, but Ivanov would also extend some of Rozanov's readings to account for the texts' mystical insights. This communal agreement about what the object of study signified can be compared to the gathering of believers to hear the liturgy.[83] This ritual gathering, of which reading and critique is a part, is enabled by elites—priests in a religious context or critics in a literary one—who read and interpret the corpus toward the creation of a new discourse. As we will see, Ivanov's interpretation of Ivan demonstrates a new mode of faithful reading that seeks to replace the author with theory and the critic's vantage point.

Author versus Author: Ivanov's Mystical-Anarchist Reading of Ivan

Before turning to Ivanov's essay, a brief discussion of his theory of artistic creation is necessary. In his early statement on Symbolist art and artistic creation, "The Symbolics of Aesthetic Principles" (1905), Ivanov had turned to *The Brothers Karamazov* to liken artistic creation to resurrection. In that essay, he paraphrased the novel's famous epigraph (John 12:24) as an echo of Ivan's nonacceptance of the world—an unusual reading being that the verse is normally associated with Alyosha and Zosima. Ivanov's version is "Whoever separates himself from the world for the sake of the world, dies for the world; he must exhaust himself and die; just as a seed will not grow if it does not die."[84] For Ivanov, who outlines the meaning of the creative act in this essay, the two parts of creation involve the artist's ascent (roughly equivalent to inspiration) and their descent (the creation of the work). He explains, "Ascent is rupture and separation; descent is the return and good tidings of victory. . . . Ascent is a 'No' to the Earth; descent is the meek ray of a mysterious 'Yes.' "[85] This notion of creative "ascent" as a tragic affirmation of the personality resulting from a self-sacrificial separation from the collective appears later in the essay on "nonacceptance of the world." The act of separation is theomachy (a war with god or the gods), an exercise of the individual's free will that is necessary to the overcoming of the individual's isolation and eventual mystical communion with others.[86] One of the clearest articulations of this state of rebellion against God appears in Ivanov's "Crisis of Individualism" (1905), where theomachy is defined as "a change in the structure of the religious and universal self-determination of the personality, from relationships of accord and dependence to relationships of antagonism."[87] For Ivanov, there is paradoxically no route to mystical communion with God without theomachy, making it possible for him to read Ivan's rebellion as a spiritual synthesis of freedom and necessity.

Merezhkovsky had looked to the novels for evidence of revolutionary religious ideas that could overcome Dostoevsky's reactionary journalism, ultimately deciding that it was the critic who needed to realize the unfulfilled religious project of the redeeming fiction. In his critical work on Dostoevsky, Ivanov is less concerned about the relationship of author to text, looking to the novels as echoes of mythic wisdom that the critic need only bring to the surface and pose as a general principle. In other words, Ivanov's reading attempts to redeem the religious message of the novelist with literary theory. Ivan's rebellion is not Dostoevsky's but an example of the dynamics of artistic creation itself and even of certain character functions of the tragic hero. Ivanov's reading is faithful, however, for it assumes and grasps at an inherent value in the religious idea in Dostoevsky's works, at which he arrives not by forging patterns in the corpus of the novels or resorting to Dostoevsky's biography. Ivanov's reading brings Dostoevsky into the historical vastness of artistic creation and religious experience, lifting Dostoevsky out of the contingencies of his work in which other critics become ensnared in contradictions.

In "The Idea of Nonacceptance" Ivanov defines mystical experience as tragically dependent on a falling away from God, which he believes Ivan's rebellion exemplifies. Chulkov, too, had once noted how the state of rebellion was a crucial preliminary stage of mystical insight. Writing about a performance of Sophocles's *Antigone* (in fact, translated by

Merezhkovsky), he touched on the heroine's theomachy as its central meaning: "Antigone's rebellion is not limited by the bounds of the empirical world: she consistently enters into other circles—ones that reflect the experience of the god-warrior [*bogoborets*]."[88] Antigone is at odds with the gods' laws, just as Ivan indicts God for a suffering world.

If Bulgakov had looked on Ivan's nonacceptance of the world as a moral protest leading first away and then toward God, Ivanov made the more complex theoretical argument that Ivan's creative work, his poem "The Legend of the Grand Inquisitor," contained the core ethics of his religious-philosophical rebellion. Referring to it significantly by the genre Ivan himself gives it (*poema*; in the Russian tradition, a long narrative poem), Ivanov argued that "The Grand Inquisitor" represents two ways of rebelling against God. Christ represents a rejection of the world and the Inquisitor rejects God.[89] Ivan holds both potentials within him, a tension possible if we read him as an archetypal artist. Ivanov explained, "In [Ivan's] creative ecstasy, he joins with Christ, he already sees the Father; but since he merges with the mask [*lichina*] of the Grand Inquisitor, he does not believe in God."[90] Notably, it does not matter to Ivanov who wrote *The Brothers Karamazov* and it is irrelevant that Ivan failed to choose the path of Christ that he immortalized in his own poetic creation. What matters is that the *poema*, the created work, affirms Christ even if its *author* (Ivan) did not and at the moment *cannot*. Ivanov seems to ask: If Ivan's own speech and his authorship of the *poema* do not contradict the ultimate truth of the *poema*, which is the rebellious and life-affirming image of Christ, then why do Dostoevsky's views have any bearing on how his texts are read and what values they signify?

In a different essay from the same time period, Ivanov provided general reflections on the poet's relationship to the created text that further illuminate his reading that Ivan's *poema* is the true expression of his acceptance of God, a process that results from going to war with God on the everyday plane: "*Poetry's* knowledge is fated to spring from the depths of the subconscious through the layers of contemporary knowledge. Its religious soul is to shoot up from the valleys of the contemporary ignorance of God [*bogonevedenie*] through the storm clouds of theomachy to the white peaks of a face-to-face vision of the divine. When it overcomes abstract individualism and 'the Euclidean mind,' when it attains a vision of divine countenances in the world, it shall write on its tripod the words: Chorus, Myth, and Rite."[91] Ivan's poem is the "overcoming of . . . individualism" and rationalism that condemns him in the novelistic reality; however, his artistic creation puts him into contact with God. Put differently, in "The Grand Inquisitor," Ivan reveals Christ's correct path as though it were "supraconsciously and prophetically" determined, while the Inquisitor's false path reflects the negative, "intellectual featurelessness" of Ivan's rational mind. After all, just like the Inquisitor, Ivan is ruled by his atheism in ordinary life; he is not capable of affirming his inner, divine nature, as Ivanov understands it to be revealed in his *poema*. While Ivan fails to achieve the exercise of "suprapersonal will" that his own artistic image of Christ achieves, the *poema*—the creative act itself—is proof that "in the soul and on the lips of Ivan Karamazov," he has adopted a "nonaccepting" stance and has had a mystical experience. In Ivanov's reading, Ivan's own text is evidence of a religious rite, which becomes inscribed on the sacrificial tripod of the people's religion (which mystical anarchism is thought to articulate in an initial way).

It should be clear by now that, like Merezhkovsky, Ivanov assumes a significant degree of critical authority. In "The Idea of Nonacceptance" Ivanov turns to a first-person mode of philosophical discourse, experimenting with the boundary between critic and autonomous hero: "We remain, in this sense, religious and outside the bounds of positive doctrine if we dare to resist the obvious and necessary reality of our inner voice. In us the seed of mystical action is alive and we, whether we are aware of it or not, are the organs of religious creation."[92] Employing an idealist critique of the positivist privileging of empirical reality, Ivanov goes further than Bulgakov by intimating that Ivan has an intuitive sense for mystical experience, but incapacitated by the compulsion to understand the incomprehensible (i.e., as a member of the intelligentsia), he cannot actively respond to it. Ivan's tragedy is the rift between will and reason, as Ivanov's own sonnet in alexandrines, "Nonacceptance of the World," helps illuminate: " 'I'—mutters the Will—'do not accept the world.' / Wisdom reproaches the Will: 'The world is your own appearance after all.' "[93] By reminding the reader that Ivan is a poet, whose creative product holds the actual truth of his divine insight, Ivanov accords authority to the author's creation—and to the poet-critic—rather than to the author himself. A bit later in the essay, Ivanov more explicitly elevates hero over author, this time addressing inevitable criticism that mystical anarchism was a philosophy of negation and its positive interpretation of "nonacceptance" was merely a preliminary step toward the self-willed obliteration of the personality, or nihilistic atheism.

Like his idealist colleagues, Ivanov was fond of the path as a metaphor for the radical spiritual potential of even the most committed

FIGURE 4.1.   Theotokos of Smolensk (c. 1500) by Dionisius

atheist. It is therefore meaningful that he compares mystical anarchism with a scholarly methodology known as "Hodegetics" (from the Greek ὁδός, or "path").[94] Ivanov likely encountered this word while studying in Germany, where he completed his dissertation, but his employment of it in his essay on Ivan resonates beyond the now defunct methodologies of nineteenth-century academia. According to Ivanov, mystical anarchism is like Hodegetics, in that it is the "philosophizing about the *paths* (not the goals) of freedom."[95] It should also be noted that the term "Hodegetics" describes a genre of Eastern Orthodox iconography called the Hodegetria (Russian, *Odigitriia*), which shows Mary pointing to the infant Jesus, indicating that he is the path. For an example of this icon genre, see figure 4.1.[96]

Throughout the essay, Ivanov makes several connections between Christ as the pathway to inner freedom, not just in reference to Ivan's Christ in "The Grand Inquisitor" but also in a seemingly extraneous survey of Renaissance masters' portrayals of Christ. Finding ideological insufficiencies in Michelangelo's *Last Judgment* and Raphael's *Transfiguration*, Ivanov wrote of Leonardo's Christ in *The Last Supper*, who "*accepts* the world of betrayal and sacrifice that did not accept Him, accepts with the sad acquiescence of a humbly divine and beautifully spiritual visage and with a sunny-meek gesture of pale hands extended at the table—one turned with its palm downward, the other sacrificially open."[97] These impressions resonate with the earlier description of Ivan's Christ, who "does not accept silence, does not accept humility; with a kiss He struggles for His world and realizes it with His very own existence."[98] Ivanov places Ivan in the context of an extensive visual landscape of painting and iconography, at the center of which is Christ. Ivan Karamazov now joins the ranks of da Vinci as a poet of Christ, a mystical anarchist, and "The Grand Inquisitor" becomes incorporated into the canon of Western artistic visualizations of Christ as "the way."

Ivanov's reading of Ivan achieves theoretical rigor and introduces the troubled rebel into the pantheon of religious artists, an interpretation that is at odds with the predominant understanding of Dostoevsky (and Ivan) as conflicted believers. Leaving the author out of the equation, Ivanov's portrait of Ivan as a prototypical rebel, as "a god-warrior, loved by God more than all others," likewise attracted Chulkov to Dostoevsky's texts as much as it earned the mystical anarchists harsh criticism from the Merezhkovskys and Belyi.[99] To their opponents, the mystical anarchists were identifying a rebellious quality in Christ, an idea that can be glimpsed also in smaller contributions from their colleague Konstantin Siunnenberg (Erberg).[100] While mystical anarchists rejected the view of Christ as humbly accepting God's demand for sacrifice, they also seemed to accuse Dostoevsky of spiritual cowardice. If Ivanov had held up Ivan as a model for their movement and distanced himself from the author, Chulkov did the same when he challenged the revolutionary potential of Dostoevsky. In one essay, Chulkov suggested that Dostoevsky and Soloviev were, unlike Ibsen and Nietzsche, unable to overcome the limitations of "Historical Christianity," which, in "prophesying submission to God, has hid from us the rebellious face of Him, who from the heights of Golgotha appealed to a Higher Power: 'Eli Eli Lama Sabachthani?' [My God, my God, why hast thou forsaken me?]"[101] The insinuation here is that Dostoevsky's revolutionary potential was compromised by a debilitating impulse toward humility as a supreme ideal. The mystical anarchist perception of Ivan's rebellion against God as holy, not demonic blasphemy, brought on a flood of criticism from the Merezhkovskys and others.

Mystical anarchism's fiercest critics were aware of its close spiritual affiliation with the novels of Dostoevsky. In a lampoon of its leaders, Belyi referenced key iconography from Dostoevsky's fiction to joke about how mystical anarchists were due to set up a school for new adherents, where "on Saturdays, pupils will be led to 'a bathhouse with spiderwebs' or to 'nasty little taverns,'" to "visually study the apocalyptic morbidity of life."[102] Belyi mostly preferred to mock mystical anarchism, but the Merezhkovskys and, early on, Bulgakov considered its political connotations a heretical break from the religious programs both offered as responses to the political upheaval of the revolution.

While there is no documented response from Bulgakov about the role of Dostoevsky in mystical anarchism's program, it is clear that he did not wish to tolerate such heresy at his journal. In the final months of the *New Path*, Chulkov's editorial decisions and the trust that Bulgakov and Berdiaev had placed in him made him an instant enemy of the Merezhkovskys, especially Gippius.[103] Later on, it seems Bulgakov came to regret pushing out the Merezhkovskys, and his relationship with Chulkov came under strain. It was when Bulgakov was away at his dacha in Crimea that Chulkov took the liberty of printing a brief note "On Mystical Anarchism" in the July 1905 issue of *Vital Questions*, which Bulgakov called "a tasteless little article."[104] Considering the article in part an attack on his views, Bulgakov wrote soon after its appearance, "Something broke for me in relation to him after that little article."[105] The Merezhkovskys' response to Chulkov and mystical anarchism was far stronger.

In the scandalous essay "The Coming Boor" ("Griadushchii kham"), Merezhkovsky took aim at two groups: the realists at *Znanie*, whom the Merezhkovskys often referred to as *bosiaki*, after the itinerant workers of Gorky's fiction, and those he called "decadent-orgiasts," a clear jab at the mystical anarchists.[106] The last of these, he argued, were guilty of inciting a war against God as dangerous as the realists' ideological atheism (many of them were socialists). Merezhkovsky labeled Ivanov dismissively as the newest offshoot of "Nietzscheism" (by which he meant godlessness) in contemporary literature: "The *bosiaki* took one half of Nietzsche and the other went to our decadent-orgiasts. Jig-Leg didn't have time to hide before the devotees of the new Dionysus broke out in song: 'raise your dithyrambic legs higher!'"[107] In this baroque and, to anyone unaware of the debates of 1905, totally obscure literary insult, Merezhkovsky imagines that Jig-Leg ("Pliashi-noga"), a character from Gorky's short story "Chums" (*Druzhki*, 1898), has been caught in one of Ivanov's Dionysian orgies, whose call to dance is a parody of Briusov's decadent, mildly obscene one-line verse poem, "O Close Your Pale Legs" (1894).[108] This characterization of his lectures on Dionysus pained Ivanov, who wrote a letter to Merezhkovsky saying as much.[109]

Merezhkovsky understood the mystical anarchist slogan "nonacceptance of the world" not as the first stage of the personality's reconciliation with God through the collective but as a reactionary stance aimed at destroying the revolutionary potential of religion.[110] "If retribution in the afterlife, by the way, consists of the departed seeing the fruits of their own deeds, then Ivan Karamazov and Nietzsche, beholding the incalculable swarms of Übermensch of their own creation, must experience truly hellish torment—as though they were sinking into a stinking swamp."[111] But Merezhkovsky's grandiose evocation of eternal hellfire is ultimately not his worst denunciation of the mystical anarchist personality who rejects God's world. "It is difficult for a person to fight with God, but it is even more difficult to reconcile with God. In any case, for Russian revolutionary society this is the most difficult thing: more difficult than uprooting the autocracy and establishing a social-democratic republic," he writes after quoting Dostoevsky's call to "love life before the meaning of it."[112] Both this citation—which appears also in Berdiaev's essay "The Grand Inquisitor"—and the sentiment that the time for fighting God was over united Merezhkovsky and Berdiaev against Ivanov and the mystical anarchists. This review of the polemics over mystical anarchism is intended to illustrate how Dostoevsky's work was employed as discursive material in new debates about religion and society. Often just his mere name and the dark images (spiders, bathhouses) and religious themes associated with his work were employed as shorthand accusations of decadence and atheism.

Lurking in this polemic is an anxiety about how the appropriation of Ivan as a prototypical mystical anarchist seemed to suggest that Dostoevsky the author would have been behind the vague leftist orientation of the mystical anarchists. As I have tried to show, in reality, mystical anarchists did not claim Dostoevsky in this way—they were moving beyond the identification of author with hero—but the critical establishment was unused to such approaches to Dostoevsky's work, driven more by theory than biography. Whatever their approach to criticism, the separate camps mobilized Dostoevsky in ways that suited their religious projects or their preferred interpretation of art's relationship to society. Since most of these disagreements played out in the jubilee year and drew on Dostoevsky's work in various ways, it is odd that opponents of mystical anarchists did not remark on the incongruousness of their Dostoevskaian slogan and Chulkov's obvious sympathies for the Social Democrats. Neither the more decadent critics at *Libra* nor the Merezhkovskys could abide the mystical anarchist association with socialists, not least because it showed an unwanted rapprochement between one wing of the Symbolists and Gorky's realist faction, many of whom rejected Dostoevsky for ideological reasons. To the extent that Symbolists and idealists alike considered the Social Democrats positivists, Briusov and the Merezhkovskys were contributing to an accusation initiated by Belyi in 1905, which framed Ivanov's Dionysian worldview as another form of positive knowledge, despite its being understood by many as exhibiting a contrary, mystical gnoseology.[113] Belyi's counterintuitive insistence on the positivist inclination of the Dionysian was refurbished by Briusov and the Merezhkovskys during the controversy over mystical anarchism in 1907. Although the mystical anarchist reading of Dostoevsky was dismissed, I have tried to show that it fostered one of the first instances of faithful reading that overcame the author by offering a unified theory of the work's artistic dynamics, helping to center the critic and making possible alternative political futures for the novels. Ivanov proposed reading the novels in the tragic mode, which made it possible to understand how the novelist's work could transmit a harmonious message despite the dark corners of the author's life and the themes of the novels themselves. As Ivanov wrote in a 1909 essay, "True artistry is always theodicy; it was for good reason that Dostoevsky himself said that beauty would save the world."[114]

The debates aroused by the heresy of mystical anarchism presaged the crisis in Symbolism that lessened the movement's influence on Russian culture. Still, long after the peak of the attacks on mystical anarchism, Ivanov's protégé Sergei Gorodetsky still pointed to Dostoevsky as the initiator of the Symbolist search for a "balance between analysis and synthesis": "We remember who stands at the head of the new Russian prose, whose first son was Dostoevsky. It was he who, separating all experiences into separate elements, knew at the same time how to synthesize what was most important, creating images of colossal stability and capaciousness; he, whose ghost (*ten'*) will soon hover above us mournfully and majestically, reviewing the century. He in large part created our singular, undiminished national pride—our language. He preserved it and created it in us. His name unites us in the coming days."[115] Referring to Dostoevsky as the undisputed initiator of new creative potentials of the Russian language, Gorodetsky relies on the image of the author as haunting and surveilling the ongoing development of his influence. Ivanov's interpretation of Dostoevsky as a tragedian and a theoretician of the individual's war with God and its ensuing mystical experience had also acknowledged the centrality of Dostoevsky's talent without necessarily demanding that his biography or politics find reconciliation with the image of his creative work and religious vision. After all, Ivanov's reading of Ivan made the point that Ivan was an atheist but that his mystical experience of God had been crystallized in the artistic product of "The Grand Inquisitor." Ivanov gave future critics a useful formula: take the artwork, apply a theory, and you will be liberated from the author.

When comparing the strategies of Ivanov and Merezhkovsky, it is clear once again that faithful reading yields different results; however, both critics seek to elevate the critic over the author. Interpretation of the aesthetic object becomes more important than the fact and conditions of its creation. Ivanov had liberated the critic from reconciling author and text, but Merezhkovsky insisted that the critic share the author's fate when he wrote in his jubilee essay, "We are not the denouncers, nor are we really the followers of Dostoevsky; we are his accomplices."[116] Merezhkovsky refused total rejection of the author whom he had once visited as a teenage poet and whose art he hoped could be restored in a new religious movement. Faithful to the writer's body more than the body of work, Merezhkovsky the critic joined his fate with Dostoevsky. Ivanov, on the other hand, whose politics and religious worldview differed in scale and substance, based his faith in the artwork, but his reading of Ivan Karamazov still balanced on the edge of apologia. The atheist creature of *The Brothers Karamazov* is suddenly the archetypal artist guiding readers to rebellion, mystical contemplation, and liberation, rather than a philosophical argument against totalitarian socialism. In the years leading up to the First World War, the worsening political climate continued to shape how critics wrote about Dostoevsky. The intelligentsia was about to grapple with the writer's most profound statement against the left, as the Moscow Art Theater prepared to stage the antirevolutionary novel *Devils*. That production and the critical discourse surrounding it is the subject of chapter 5.

The Moscow Art Theater's Rewriting of *Devils*, 1910–1914

Theater adaptations of Dostoevsky's novels continued to play a role in the intelligentsia's shaping of his moral-religious ideas at a time of political and social crises. One of the most important of these in the years leading up to 1917 was *Nikolai Stavrogin*, which was staged by the Moscow Art Theater and premiered on October 23, 1913. This scenic adaptation by the leading playwright and director Vladimir Nemirovich-Danchenko (1858–1943, hereafter Nemirovich) of Dostoevsky's *Devils* has been viewed as a pale sequel to the Art Theater's revelatory performances in *The Brothers Karamazov* (1910), which theater historian Inna Solov'eva has called the "highest . . . affirmation of 'Stanislavsky's system' on the material of tragedy."[1] But by contrast, after *Stavrogin*'s final run of fourteen performances in St. Petersburg at the Mikhailovsky Theater during the 1914 spring season, one reviewer announced, "These are the stages of decline."[2] *Stavrogin*'s biggest claim to fame, however, has little to do with its theatrical value (or demerits, as the case may be) and speaks directly to the view among progressive critics that Dostoevsky the reactionary could not be separated from his work.

Maxim Gorky's "On Karamazovism" has been the focus of most scholarship on *Stavrogin* to this day.[3] Indeed, it remains the reason why many have heard of it at all. Writing from exile in Capri, Gorky decried the antirevolutionary politics of the novel and (he assumed) Nemirovich's production, stirring debate on censorship and the social value of Dostoevsky. Most liberal critics of the day defended the Art Theater's right to stage *Devils*, agreeing with the theater that Dostoevsky's surreptitious but affirming spiritual message would unite, not incite, audiences. Responding to Gorky's public opposition, the theater collective called attention to *Stavrogin*'s (and Dostoevsky's) artistic and spiritual value in equal measure: "For you [Gorky], *Devils* is nothing other than a pasquil of a temporary political nature; you blame Dostoevsky, the great god-seeker and profoundest artist, for the decomposition of society."[4] But for Gorky and radical critics the Art Theater's choice to stage Dostoevsky was effectively an endorsement of the autocratic regime and an attack on socialist activism.

For his scenario, Nemirovich initiated a break with the earlier adaptations of Dostoevsky's novels examined in chapter 1. His production of *Stavrogin* was a faithful rendering of much of the direct speech of the characters in *Devils*. He continued the Symbolist and religious-philosophical critics' orientation toward textually based, reparative reading rather than a focus on the author's biography. But his play attempted a difficult synthesis between character dialogue and the liberty of the adapter to rearrange and reinterpret the atmosphere and plot structure of *Devils*. Rearranging scenes, removing certain characters from the action, and privileging certain events in the plot over others, Nemirovich preserved the dialogue of the main characters but dared his audience to dismiss the novel as merely an antirevolutionary *roman à thèse*. The biggest revision of the novel's plot was his decision to remove the radical atheist Kirillov and the group of conspiratorial revolutionaries—the result was a play rich in religious symbolism and cleansed of its political critique of the radicals. Nemirovich's faithful reading of the words of the characters over the authority and political views of their creator produced a version of *Devils* that highlighted the religious-philosophical idea of the novel, which idealists and Symbolist critics, and even Anna Dostoevskaia, had been attempting in their own separate ways.

Nemirovich's decision to dampen the antisocialist politics of *Devils* is a somewhat surprising turn for a director whose author-focused methodology is somewhat of a scholarly cliché. Though scholarly interest in Nemirovich as a playwright and director compared to his more famous collaborator Konstantin Stanislavsky has lagged, the two have traditionally played diametrically opposed roles in histories of the Art Theater. If Stanislavsky was the true artistic genius, Nemirovich was a skilled business manager; if Stanislavsky was the true innovator of the actor's method and training, Nemirovich was faithful to the author's original plan. After all, it was his dislike of the "System" and its shift of focus toward the actor and away from the playwright that had created tension between them.[5] As Rebecca Gauss has noted, "Nemirovich, the playwright, saw theatre as a servant of literature, meant to provide a living illustration of the text."[6] Nemirovich's devotion to the text was even considered an existential threat to set designers: "The poor artistry of the designer! They have banished you from life, driven you from the square and streets, driven you from rooms and here now, finally, they have banished you from the theater, where you had hoped to find your final refuge!"[7] Fidelity to the author's word, at least to those advocates of set designers, was still the measure of a play for Nemirovich. The balance of textual fidelity and emotional intensity that he brought to his *Stavrogin* scenario may even owe something to Osip Dymov's early essay on adapting Dostoevsky with greater fidelity to the originals. Dymov recalls meeting Nemirovich for the first time while he was working with Alexander Kugel' at the review *Teatr i iskusstvo*. Nemirovich said to him, "I have read your series of articles on Dostoyevsky, published in your magazine. They are very interesting and original. I wanted to meet their author personally."[8]

There is some indication that Nemirovich studied the text of *Devils* extremely carefully. He engaged with the supplementary materials related to *Devils* in volume 8 of the jubilee edition of Dostoevsky's collected works, which offered clues as to the author's guiding plan for the characters Stavrogin and the younger Verkhovensky. One such revelation was the character Golubov (evoking the word *golub'*, or dove), who was discarded from the final version of the novel after having appeared in conjunction with Shatov. This detail allows for the possibility that Nemirovich's playscript for *Devils* at the Art Theater was perhaps inspired by the notebooks published in the jubilee edition and new evidence of the alternative paths the story may have taken. These new materials had prompted Volzhskii to remark on their power and even their perfection compared with the final manuscript version of *Devils*: "The most remarkable in these fragments is the conversation between Stavrogin and Shatov. Here there are places, in power and significance surpassing what went into the novel."[9] Nemirovich's creative work adapting the novel parallels increasingly rigorous scholarly study of Dostoevsky enabled by materials published in the jubilee edition. There was a desire to see the novelist's texts as experiments rather than finished works—they could be seen now as entirely malleable things, open rather than closed to the future.

This chapter is devoted to excavating the *Stavrogin* production to discover what Nemirovich's faithful reading made from *Devils*. Archival versions of the script and Nemirovich's correspondence reveal a centering of the novel's core religious ideas, revealed in the tense exchange between Shatov and Stavrogin about Russia's status as a "god-bearing people" (*narod-bogonosets*).[10] This conversation about faith and national identity emerges as the "main idea of the novel."[11] Given Nemirovich's fascination with Shatov, it is not surprising that this scene would be given select treatment and his editing of it has clear narrative-dramatic and ideological implications. Nemirovich's particular framing of the relationship between Shatov and Stavrogin had political consequences that were part of the intellectual fabric of those times, echoing the already substantial body of criticism on Dostoevsky by Symbolist and religious-philosophical critics. Many of those critics were members of the Religious-Philosophical Society (RFO), which had long been claiming Dostoevsky as the forerunner of their religious and aesthetic views. *Stavrogin* was an adaptation rendered from faithful reading, placing it in line with the critical project that had been progressing for almost two decades—led by the poet-critics Dmitry Merezhkovsky and Viacheslav Ivanov—of reinterpreting and themselves "adapting" Dostoevsky's ideas into new usable frameworks.

A new look at *Stavrogin* moves away from summaries of the play's act and scene divisions, working toward a veritable "adaptology" of it.[12] If a significant element of adaptation is intertextuality, a central claim in Linda Hutcheon's *Theory of Adaptation*, then a comparison of the original with the scripts and its various drafts reveals *Stavrogin*, to use Hutcheon's language, as "its own palimpsestic thing."[13] Close analysis of Nemirovich's published correspondence reveals some clues as to what kind of adaptation he was preparing, but it remains unclear how or whether he chose to alter, revise, or edit dialogue within the scenes he included in the script. On this point, scholars have assumed that the playscript did not diverge significantly from the original plot of the novel to warrant comparison with the original text. Elsewhere, descriptive overviews of the play's structure have substituted for a close analysis of the scripts, which would account in part for Nemirovich's editing choices.[14] But since it has long been considered an unsuccessful transposition of Dostoevsky to the stage, the playscript has not been explored in detail. Before turning to that script, however, broader context about adapting and interpreting *Devils* is warranted.

Why *Devils* in 1913?

Why did Nemirovich choose to adapt this novel at this precise moment? His work on the very antisocialist *Devils* raises questions about the nature of his social and political views. While artistic conservatism does not guarantee a politics to the right of center, Nemirovich's original dramas reflect the light social commentary of the 1880s bourgeois stage and demonstrate the worldview of a typical liberal of his time.[15] As an example, *The Price of Life* (1896), considered his best play, dealt with the theme of suicide and contemporary social fracture. Regardless of how his dramaturgy has stood the test of time, his contemporaries bestowed serious honors on it. The selection committee for the Griboyedov Prize awarded *The Price of Life* its top honor over Anton Chekhov's *The Seagull*, a striking decision in retrospect and at the time one that caused Nemirovich himself to admit his play's inferiority to Chekhov's.[16] Despite his key role in the history of Russian theater, as this book went to press, no scholars since the Soviet period have dedicated monographs to Nemirovich's dramaturgy, further study of which could provide insight into his philosophy of dramatic adaptation and the impact of his political views on such work more broadly.[17]

Whatever Nemirovich's political views may have been, radical (and later, Soviet) commentators considered any staging of Dostoevsky to be reactionary.[18] Scholars seeking to move past the production's political controversy looked at *Stavrogin*'s seemingly apolitical "atmospheric" and psychological drama, noting Nemirovich's glaring omission of the revolutionary drama. This descriptive-historical approach in particularly Western scholarship on the play has resulted in two assumptions. First, many critics have argued that *Stavrogin* adopted a kind of apolitical track, a theory that for many is confirmed by Nemirovich's ostensible focus on the romance plot and discarding of the revolutionary plot. At the same time, a related assumption has persisted that if the Art Theater's production did in fact stay out of politics, surely this came at the artistic expense of the play.

Although Solov'eva claims that Nemirovich was under pressure to suppress not only the radical but also any potentially conservative elements of Dostoevsky's novel, in his correspondence one observes a sustained interest in the novel's religious ideologue: Ivan Shatov, theoretician of the god-bearing nation.[19] Nemirovich's interest in Shatov demonstrates that he was in fact profoundly attracted by the nationalist-religious arguments of *Devils*, which, like Sergei Bulgakov, he seems to have read separately from Dostoevsky's critique of radical socialism. No evidence in Nemirovich's letters or in the production's archival material indicates that his removal of Kirillov and the revolutionary cell was politically motivated. Looking at Nemirovich's letters, it appears that he was simply not as interested in the intrigues of the revolutionary cell as he was in the story's religious problems, centering on Shatov and the tragedy of Kirillov. In fact, Nemirovich had planned a second play, to be called "Shatov and Kirillov," but I will discuss that further later on in the chapter. Collectively, his approach resulted in a version of *Devils* that ignored Dostoevsky's criticism of revolutionary competence and organization. He instead showed his audiences a constructive version of the novel and a national idea that its characters gesture toward but fail to realize. Whereas Dostoevsky had originally presented Shatov's nationalism as toothless due to its disassociation from Russian Orthodoxy, Nemirovich adopted a sympathetic portrait of Shatov and by extension advanced a salvageable national idea. Merezhkovsky had of course rejected Shatov's "god-bearing nation," framing it antisemitically as the drifting of Orthodoxy toward Judaism. Nemirovich's reframing of Shatov gave the story something close to a patriotic hero, as a consequence of which the revised plot directed its audience to have a conversation about faith and country, rather than the revolutionary critique that radicals had been so vigorously protesting since first hearing of the Art Theater's plans to stage the play. Ascertaining the political orientation of *Stavrogin* holds considerable value for charting the cultural reception of Dostoevsky's nationalist views in the period just before the First World War and revolution.

Devils was not the usual choice for any of the playwrights who tried their hand at adapting the major novels in previous decades. In addition, its controversial and divisive politics made it unattractive for private and imperial theaters alike. One glaring exception to this lack of interest in *Devils* is a tendentious production of the novel in 1907 at publishing mogul A. S. Suvorin's Petersburg Theater of the Literary-Artistic Society.[20] In the year before its premiere, Dymov wrote of Suvorin's theater as heralding the end of theater itself: "Theater as a force of old and profoundly just psychological causes is inevitably collapsing, incessantly collapsing."[21]

Nemirovich may have read the script when it was published in 1908. Coauthored by writer, literary critic, and vicious parodist V. P. Burenin and his young colleague M. A. Suvorin (A. S. Suvorin's son), the play was a far more conservative treatment of the novel than Nemirovich's

Stavrogin would turn out to be. Burenin and Suvorin's *Devils* treated the revolutionary theme openly (and satirically) while avoiding the novel's religious idea. With the more repressive political atmosphere ramping up after the tsar's dissolving of the Second Duma in June 1907, it was still a sensitive time to adapt such a novel. The theater review *Obozrenie teatrov* noted that the censors had banned it as late as August 18, 1907 (it premiered in late September 1907); however, according to the same journal it passed a month later.[22] An unabashedly partisan review in the *New Times*, the newspaper owned by the elder Suvorin, commented that Dostoevsky's lampoon of the socialist-revolutionary struggle paled in comparison with the more violent socialist movements of 1907, in which "today's organizers not only know how to raise their hands for a vote, not confusing their right with their left, but they even shout to the others 'hands up!' "[23] The respected theater critic Alexander Kugel' made a similar point, but it was toward a critique of Dostoevsky's satire in light of the seriousness and importance of the recent 1905 revolution: "Whatever view one holds about the revolutionary move-ment in Russia, already *a posteriori*—on the basis of lived experience—we can say that this event by its magnitude is not at all of a high-school (*gimnazicheskoe*) quality."[24] It was high time to take the revolutionaries seriously, but Burenin and Suvorin's conservative *Devils* doubled down on Dostoevsky's original caricature of their ideas and social behavior. Burenin's parodic and exaggerated treatment of the revolutionaries can be glimpsed in an illustration included with the published play in figure 5.1.

By adapting *Devils*, Burenin moved from the role of literary critic to rewriter. This creative act perhaps exemplifies the remarkable longevity of his literary career and personal spite. In his 1871 review of Dostoevsky's original, he had reserved special criticism for Shatov and Kirillov, whose "mystical" personalities among the contemporary younger generation had little basis in social reality: "To foist on the contemporary youth an inclination to theories that are founded on generalizations with a mystical veneer is to not understand the times."[25] He sympathized with Dostoevsky's critique of socialism, but he rejected the "philosophical" (by which he meant "religious") ideas of the novel's heroes. For him, their rejection of socialism and collapse into atheism was mere mono-mania (Kirillov) or philosophical dilettantism (Shatov), rather than the tragedy of a generation caught between socialism and loss of faith. And so having virtually begun in Burenin's journalistic activity in the 1870s, Burenin and Suvorin's adaptation of *Devils* was a throwback, indulging in outmoded satire in the shifting political climate of 1907.

FIGURE 5.1.   Illustrated title page of V. P. Burenin and M. A. Suvorin's adaptation of *Devils*

Guided by their antimystical approach to the novel, they removed Kirillov's speech about the Mangod and, crucially, Shatov's explanation of the god-bearing nation.[26] Adding to this political line, the role of Mar'ia Lebiadkina, whom Viacheslav Ivanov named the novel's symbolic representative of an ailing and spiritually thirsting Russia, was largely insignificant; her one-on-one exchanges with Stavrogin (included by Nemirovich) and with Shatov (which he left out) are gone. Records indicate that in 1907 the censors would have allowed the conversation about the god-bearer but that Burenin and Suvorin had intentionally chosen to remove it.

Georgii Chulkov, the only Symbolist to write a review of the production, was offended by its artistic failures and cynical political motives: "We don't want to make conjectures about the source of Karmazinov in Turgenev, nor about other figures of that time in other personae of the novel. What matters to us are these *eternal* masks, behind which are hidden a kind of unified, terrifying and meaningful face."[27] For Chulkov, Burenin's abandonment of the "mysticism" (religion) of the novel, what in Dostoevsky's entire work Symbolist critics had long hailed as his highest achievement and the living link to their own programs, missed the point of the novel entirely. Taking aim at the hyperrealist staging, Chulkov also noted the oddity of such a reworking of Dostoevsky during the heyday of experimental drama that had been moving away from naturalist settings and melodramatic performances: "The director stood on that superficial point of view that in *Devils* illuminates only 'realistic' satire. As usual, the sets were stupid [*glupy*] and crude; as usual the actors were tormented in the cage of directorial cliché, a suitable fate for the usual repertoire of this theater, but completely inappropriate for Dostoevsky, that great ancestor of symbolist art."[28] Nemirovich's *Stavrogin* shows how responsive the Art Theater was to symbolist leanings of the kind expressed in Chulkov's review of the production. The disappointed and angry debates about the value of Dostoevsky's work had cooled since the 1906 jubilee, when *Devils* was received especially badly by critics of all political leanings. To Nemirovich, it was time to begin his own faithful reading, taking the spiritual core of *Devils* seriously and re-creating the novel as a national epic of the Russian faith.

The Art Theater's reputation was founded on its naturalist renditions of Gorky's well-received plays, *The Lower Depths* (1902) and *The Merchant Class* (1902), and of course Chekhov. These productions earned it a radical reputation in its first years.[29] This groundbreaking work prepared them for staging Dostoevsky in the 1910s, which began with the celebrated production of *The Brothers Karamazov* in 1910.[30] *Stavrogin* and *The Village of Stepanchikovo* (1916) followed, and they would feature works by contemporary playwrights who wrote in the novelist's shadow. Merezhkovsky's Dostoevsky-inspired *There Will Be Happiness*, about revolutionary failure and spiritual illness, was produced by the Art Theater in 1916. Soon after, Leonid Andreev's *Dear Specters* (1917) was staged, a play that dramatized Nekrasov's elated first reading of the manuscript of Dostoevsky's debut, *Poor Folk*. These works, which will receive attention in the epilogue, demonstrate how Dostoevsky's novels offered not only promising dialogue for the stage but also living material with which Silver Age dramatists could develop their own ideological platforms and artistic credos.

While stage adaptations of Dostoevsky prior to 1913 (mostly of *The Idiot* and *Crime and Punishment*) concentrated on the novels' modern psychologies and melodrama, their religious and political themes had not been directly and fully explored on the stage. The continued influence of the Russian Orthodox Church on the new comparatively liberal censorship regime following the 1905 revolution explains why especially religious treatments of Dostoevsky's work on the stage were not as frequent prior to *Stavrogin*—the Art Theater's *Brothers Karamazov* in 1910 had faced difficulties with the Zosima character, for instance.[31] But the Art Theater was different from other private and imperial theaters that had staged Dostoevsky. It had already been experimenting with Symbolist and pseudoreligious drama (Maurice Maeterlinck's plays, for instance) and had in Nemirovich a playwright whose reading of Dostoevsky shared key features of leading religious-philosophical thinkers.

Shatov's God-Bearing Nation and Its Religious-Philosophical Commentary

Of special importance in Nemirovich's scenario was the role of Ivan Shatov and his proselytizing of the "god-bearing nation," a concept introduced in chapter 4. New conversations about the god-bearing nation and *Devils* itself were at the heart of broader conversations that took place at the RFO shortly after the Art Theater's St. Petersburg premiere of *Stavrogin* in February 1914. Those speeches were thereafter published in the leading journal *Russian Thought*: Sergei Bulgakov's "Russian Tragedy," Viacheslav Ivanov's "The Foundational Myth in the Novel *Devils*," which appeared in the same issue as Bulgakov's essay, and Nikolai Berdiaev's "Stavrogin."[32] It is possible that Nemirovich had even read Ivanov's earlier and more famous essay on the "novel-tragedy," which concludes with a sophiological reading of *Devils*.[33] Thus, in an unusual and, it seems, uncoordinated rapprochement of the theater elite and the cultural intelligentsia, RFO members argued for the central importance of the novel's religious idea, attempting, like Nemirovich, to transcend its divisive antisocialist critique. Not only that, *Stavrogin* staged a new interpretation of the novel in its foregrounding of what RFO critics had considered its key religious-symbolic triangle: Mar'ia Lebiadkina, Nikolai Stavrogin, and Ivan Shatov.

Bulgakov and Ivanov engaged in a separate recorded debate at the RFO, which went unpublished until 1999. They were the first critics to take Lebiadkina seriously as the essential religious force in the novel. As Stavrogin's secret wife, she possesses an uncanny ability to see the truth in others, even as her deteriorating grasp of reality causes the reader to doubt her cryptic utterances. While those in the revolutionary cell might still see the charismatic and princely Stavrogin as the secret weapon that will help them incite the common people to armed rebellion, Lebiadkina sees what Shatov is only starting to see, which is that their leader is a pretender. In the novel, Lebiadkina and Shatov both become deeply disillusioned with Stavrogin because he cannot live up to the lofty religious idea that he knows he represents to them: he should be the Russian Christ—his name derives from "stavros," Greek for "crucifix"—but he can neither save nor nurture the world. Ivanov and Bulgakov identified Lebiadkina with the sophiological concepts of the "world soul" and "mother-earth" and they interpreted Stavrogin as the self-affirming masculine principle who fails to merge with the feminine principle, a union that would restore harmony to the world. Ivanov's response to Bulgakov's paper at the RFO made clear the high regard this group accorded *Devils* in Dostoevsky's body of work. For Ivanov, "*Devils* is at its foundation a religious work . . . precisely *Devils* more than any other of his works."[34] And for the same reason, Ivanov would also be the first to call it a novel-tragedy. Victor Terras would later write, in full acknowledgment of Ivanov's critical insight on the novel, "Dostoevsky's tragic impulse prevailed over a desire to assert a belief in the existence of divine justice and order on this earth. Once again, Christ is not of this world."[35] Stavrogin, the failed Christ, and Shatov, his failed prophet, were to them a hopeful admonishment—not a condemnation—of Russia's spiritual potential.

In the recorded discussion between Ivanov and Bulgakov, one observes the high stakes of reconciling these characters' failures with the positive religious idea that they represent. Bulgakov took a hard line, naming Shatov a nationalist heretic and Stavrogin a faceless entity, a provocateur. Indeed, much earlier, Bulgakov had ended his introduction to the 1906 jubilee edition with the image of the god-bearer.[36] Ivanov argued heatedly against both claims, reasoning that "in Shatov there is no trace of nationalism [*net nikakogo natsionalizma*] and he is distinguished by what he says not about nationalism, but about the people [*narod*]."[37] Stavrogin earns Ivanov's compassion, as well, a sentiment that resonates with Nemirovich's playscript and diverges from other commentators, such as Volynsky, who named the protagonist an archdecadent.[38] For Ivanov, Stavrogin is "revealed to be . . . both god-bearer-apostate and god-bearer-traitor." Ivanov continues, "It is characteristic that in these new works about the god-bearer, about what the god-bearer is, works about Christ, all of this Stavrogin has discovered and found." According to this reasoning, Stavrogin cannot be a simple provocateur but rather "simply Judas, about whom it is said that Satan went into the heart of Judas [Luke 22:3]. And this person, the cursed Judas, is Nikolai Stavrogin." This reading of the protagonist accords with Leonid Grossman's research on the excised chapter "At Tikhon's" (*U Tikhona*), whose purpose is central to the moral-religious fabric of the novel. That chapter, published posthumously and which Dostoevsky's editor Mikhail Katkov refused to print, was supposed to counteract the image of the hero "torn from the native soil" with Tikhon's example of "national [*narodnaia*] morality."[39] Ivanov's idealized defense of Stavrogin extends to his pupil, Shatov, both of whom receive his sympathy as tragically flawed propagators of the god-bearer thesis. We have already seen how, in the case of Ivan Karamazov, Ivanov's critical tendency is to view the fallen characters, rebels, and atheists as the paradoxically affirming agents of the works' guiding tragic religious vision.

Seeking to justify Dostoevsky's novel as a religious work and the moral-aesthetic beauty of the god-bearer thesis itself, Ivanov does not contextualize it in contingencies of Russian religious culture, literary history, or nationalist politics. Given the close correspondence between the god-bearer thesis and Dostoevsky's own views about Russian faith and culture, Ivanov insists on Stavrogin's ultimate religious signification even though he betrays Christ and his bride, the symbolic representation of Russia. Finally, Ivanov's archetypal comparison of Stavrogin to Judas partakes in universalist narratives of Christian mythology, a clear attempt to ennoble the suffering of the disgraced protagonist. In Nemirovich's playscript, Stavrogin's hanging body is the blunt conclusion to his spiritual tragedy: his inability to assume the role of god-bearer, a task he leaves to his eager pupil. In his play, Nemirovich would develop Ivanov's optimistic and highly symbolic interpretation of *Devils* by offering a vision of Shatov—and of Dostoevsky's Russian idea—that feels like an ongoing project, rather than a doomed theory.

Nemirovich's *Stavrogin*

Alexander Burry, with reference to James Agee, argues in his book on adaptations of Dostoevsky that an effective transposition fulfills "a need for *both* some sort of connectivity *and* a 'transfiguration' that turns it into an entirely new work," pointing to Linda Hutcheon's insight that "repetition with variation" provides "the comfort of ritual combined with the piquancy of surprise."[40] In this way, adapting and transposing one work to another medium is itself a kind of ritualistic return to an original. Signaling the spiritual connotations of transposition evoked by Burry and Hutcheon toward his own work, Nemirovich begins his play with a reference to Orthodox ritual, *"na paperti,"* on a parvis, the church entrance where Stavrogin's elegantly dressed mother, Varvara Petrovna, first encounters the disabled and bedraggled Lebiadkina. I view such a reworking as a "transpositional opening," a term Burry uses "to describe material that gets reactivated in order to mine a text for potentials."[41] By beginning with Lebiadkina's public audience with Varvara Petrovna at the church, Nemirovich strategically "reactivates" the novel's plot toward the overarching question of religious faith and its tragic absence and away from the novel's antirevolutionary argument.

Rearranging the *fabula* in such a way, Nemirovich highlights the spiritual role of the lame woman and prepares the audience for the following scandalous scene in which Stavrogin's secret marriage to her is announced. Nemirovich's choice to begin at the church also serves to decentralize the narrator, Anton Lavrent'evich, who is made a character in the scenario. The removal of the narrator was an innovation in Nemirovich's adaptations of Dostoevsky; the script for *The Brothers Karamazov* included a narrator to structure the scenes.[42] The second scene is the only instance in which Nemirovich reorganized the plot events, placing Stepan Trofimovich's conversation with the narrator directly after Varvara Petrovna's visit to the church.[43] After the first scene shows the encounter between Varvara Petrovna and, unbeknownst to her, her daughter-in-law (Lebiadkina), the second scene finds Stepan Trofimovich complaining to his confidant about his own "secret" and hasty engagement to Dasha. In this way Nemirovich brings the love plot (Stavrogin and Liza) and the marriage scandals of the first part of the novel into a condensed first act. However, by beginning with Lebiadkina at the church, he emphasizes Stavrogin's legitimate union and its religious significance. Underscoring her symbolic import, Lebiadkina appears in more scenes in Nemirovich's script than Stavrogin's actual romantic interests, Dasha and Liza.

Mstislav Dobuzhinskii's set designs helped concentrate the religious mood of *Stavrogin*.[44] Their minimalist execution and symbolist inspiration was a palpable shift in the usual palette and style of Art Theater productions up to that point, consciously departing from the production of Ivan Turgenev's *Month in the Country*, which directly preceded *Stavrogin*: "In contrast to the symmetry, the calm colors and lines—those suggested in the good-humored Turgenev plays—the dynamic of Nikolai Stavrogin and the entire teeming atmosphere of *Devils* required something absolutely different."[45] Worrall contends that the designs were "hampered by Dobuzhinskiy's 'atmospheric' settings which, with the exception of one or two scenes, appeared out of keeping, both tonally and spatially, with the novel's predominant moods."[46] Rzhevsky disagrees, noting that "the result was a well designed production, thanks to . . . Dobuzhinskii's sense of harmony and proportion, but without Dostoevsky's ideological intensity."[47] An awareness of the deliberate religious motivations of Nemirovich's script allows us to appreciate Dobuzhinskii's pared-down "atmospheric" approach to the various mise-en-scènes. Reproduced images of the sparse and gloomy sets of the Skvorechniki interiors viscerally convey the novel's dreadful mood, which intensified with each successive scene. In Dobuzhinskii's sketches for the final two scenes, the crimson glow of the fires begun by arsonists alights the room where Liza and Stavrogin meet for the last time; the orangey red of that scene returns in the discovery of Stavrogin's hanging body, which concludes the play.[48]

I return to archival scripts and production materials to argue that Nemirovich deemphasized the revolutionary plot not only to appease Gorky but also as part of a conscious reparative critical strategy to rearticulate the stakes of how religion is represented in the novel. In doing so, Nemirovich presents Shatov as a positive symbol of a viable theory of the god-bearing nation. As part of this reframing of Shatov as heroic, we can better assess the artistic and political intentions behind Nemirovich's omission of Kirillov, which had the effect of elevating Stavrogin and Shatov to nobler roles.

On July 6, 1913, Nemirovich wrote to Alexander Benois, who that spring had joined the Art Theater as head of stage design. In the letter, he hinted at personal motivations for wanting to stage *Devils* that justified the closer study of his adaptation offered in this chapter:

> I am still afraid to confirm it, but more recently I suddenly felt, to express it with elevated style, a kind of clarity on account of precisely the revolutionary portion of the novel. I felt that within me some curtain has been torn and has freed me from different considerations, the consequences of which what is tragic in that part of the novel has acquired that spiritual breadth and depth at which point there is no place for specific tendentious considerations of a social character. . . . There appeared an unconquerable

temptation to illuminate from the highest points of view precisely what still seem like fresh wounds. In this I am also fortunate that I possess an historical perspective for events not irrelevant to the interest of a volatile contemporaneity.[49]

Nemirovich's sympathy with the religious-philosophical reading of the novel could not be more clearly stated in this passage.

In the same letter, Nemirovich indicates that the spotlight is shifting from Trofimovich to Shatov, who will become the moral center of the story: "In Shatov, his faith in the people-god-bearer, his story with his wife and death, in Kirillov—there, in them, around them, is the source for that charm which so gripped in *Karamazov*. . . . There you have it around Shatov (Moskvin!)."[50] Shatov of course was supposed to appear again in the play's second part, a future production titled "Shatov and Kirillov." The archive at the Art Theater has no materials on this second adaptation, suggesting that Nemirovich never wrote the script. The play was likely abandoned because it would have taken too much time for the censors to pass its themes of religion and suicide; in retrospect, it would have been fitting to stage this second play at such a time, with Russia's government in continual disorder. The country was only a year away from war with Germany and the beginning of the end of the empire itself.[51] Even if the second play was never written, a letter to Stanislavsky from July 25, 1913 (O.S.), provides some clues as to its focus: "'Shatov and Kirillov' . . . is more profound, but less scenic. And *very* dark. Here of the female roles there is only Shatov's wife (also Mar'ia Petrovna) [Lilina].[52] The last scene—the murder of Shatov and the suicide of Kirillov."[53] In this second production, Nemirovich anticipated that "the highest point of the drama's denouement will be the scene of Shatov's murder," yet another indication that Shatov's character was being built up in the first play for a tragic fall in the second.[54]

But with his plans to stage the second part of the play unrealized, in *Stavrogin* Nemirovich removed all scenes with the conspiratorial terrorist cell (excepting Petr Stepanovich)—including, to many reviewers' dismay, Kirillov. Bulgakov explained Kirillov's absence by claiming that his figure was simply unrepresentable: "In the scenario of *Devils* on the stage of the Art Theater this character [*obraz*; i.e. Kirillov] is still completely absent: the stage could not bring across this captivating drama."[55] In yet another letter to Benois, Nemirovich wrote about his desire to concentrate on Shatov, considering his scene with Stavrogin "not entirely necessary for the development of the plot" but for its "being one of the most amazing scenes of the novel in terms of its power in the idea that it conveys (the people as 'god-bearer').""[56] Let us turn now to that scene that so gripped this generation of critics.

Scene IV: Shatov and Stavrogin

Nemirovich's scenario divided the action into four sections with a total of fourteen scenes. He begins at the church with Mar'ia Timofeevna and Varvara Petrovna and ends with an epilogue, with Dasha's reading of Stavrogin's suicide letter. The final stage direction reads only *"slyshen krik"* (a scream is heard), as Varvara Petrovna glimpses her son's hanging body.[57] As in the Art Theater's earlier production of *The Brothers Karamazov*, Nemirovich used carefully selected dialogue from the novel. For *Stavrogin*, he reorganized the text of many dialogue exchanges—especially with the most gregarious characters, Stepan Trofimovich and Petr Stepanovich—but very little if any text was added that did not appear in the original text of the novel. The structure of his scenario maintains the novel's *fabula*, with the already mentioned omissions, except for scenes I and II in the first act of the play.

Consulting Nemirovich's letters and the script, one can see that Kirillov's removal was not just a loss or a sacrifice of the novel's integrity but a way of reworking the play's dramatic economy and tempering the Orthodox nationalism of the novel. By removing Kirillov, the ideological and dramatic tension becomes focused on Shatov and therefore also on Stavrogin's role in promoting a *single* idea to his pupil. This concentration of the novel's philosophical debates takes full advantage of Kirillov's absence and avoids the tendentious critique of his Mangod theory and his alienating nihilistic extremism. The focus on Shatov's god-bearer testimony also had the advantage of concentrating the spectator's attention on Stavrogin's lapsed religion and tragic rebellion. Nemirovich economizes the suicides of the plot as well; with Kirillov gone, the pathos of his suicide is arguably absorbed into Stavrogin's, which concludes the play. If realized, "Shatov and Kirillov" would have drawn even tighter links between the suicides, for Nemirovich had intended the celebrated tragic actor Vasily Kachalov to play Stavrogin in one and Kirillov in the other.

Kugel', long hostile toward the Art Theater, was profoundly uninspired by the production but praised the fourth scene between Stavrogin and Shatov. He wrote, "The scene between Shatov and Stavrogin in the sublime, talented performance of [Nikolai] Massalitinov and with the noble and precise representation by Kachalov is . . . of undoubted theatrical value."[58] Bulgakov viewed the scene as the production's attempt to bridge the theater with religion: "After the elevated artistic [*vysokokhudozhestvennogo*] incarnation of this character [Shatov] on the stage of the Art Theater, it is not necessary to recall the spiritual drama of Shatov: as if from the ambo, from the stage is heard cherished, eternally moving words about the people [*narod*] as the body of God, about the god-bearing people."[59] Of special note is Bulgakov's mention of the "ambo," from which the priest delivers the liturgy before the background of the iconostasis. In this sense, Bulgakov suggests that it is the content of Shatov's *message* that conveys the scene's pathos, not primarily, as Kugel′ suggests, the performance of Massalitinov. I now turn to this scene in Nemirovich's scenario.

Throughout the play, there were seven rounds of edits once the actors began rehearsing the playscript. In the case of scene IV ("U Shatova" [At Shatov's]), most additional cuts to the playscript version once rehearsals were underway were made in the second and third versions and then appeared finalized in the final version of the script. For the most accurate sense of the performed version of the script, I used the prompter's copy as a guide in an effort to keep track of any last-minute omissions made as the first performance approached. The rehearsal diary indicates that rehearsals of this scene and the following one, which featured the conversation between Stavrogin and Mar′ia Lebiadkina, were consistently led by Leopold Sulerzhitsky (known as "Suler"), a Tolstoyan and close artistic collaborator of Stanislavsky and his famous First Studio.[60]

When considering how to stage this conversation, Nemirovich envisioned a simple mise-en-scène that would focus audience attention on the characters' dialogue, writing in his memoirs, "To powerfully impress the public, it is necessary to present scenes about the people [*narodnye*] in the full glare of the footlights. But there Ivan Karamazov and Smerdiakov or Shatov and Stavrogin would hold their conversations in the light of a single little lamp for a full forty minutes and the public would be absorbed in the scene every instant."[61] The simple setting invites greater concentration on the words of both characters, but it also shows his faithfulness to the physical setting of their conversation in the novel (for instance, close to the beginning of their conversation, one of Nemirovich's stage directions preserves the novel's detail of Shatov moving as if to open the *fortochka* [a window for ventilation]).[62] By rooting the enacted scene in its original language and environment, Nemirovich achieved a convincing veneer of fidelity to the text, even if the ensuing conversation between Shatov and Stavrogin displayed meaningful alterations to yield a more hopeful presentation of the god-bearer thesis.

As a consequence of Nemirovich's edits and continual cutting of dialogue in the chapter entitled "Night," Stavrogin is both humanized and legitimized as the founder of the god-bearer thesis; his cynical betrayal of his pupil's ideological dependence on him is far less damning. For example, in the novel, Shatov's mention of a long letter to Stavrogin while in residence in America spurs a brief digression about the impoverished conditions of that trip ("lying for three months on hay"), when he spent the entire time with "that unfortunate, that maniac," Kirillov, who had been fed an idea by Stavrogin diametrically opposed to the one Shatov treasured about "God and homeland [*rodina*]."[63] After this utterance in the novel, it is revealed that Stavrogin merely glanced at the letter in which Shatov tried to express in his own words the meaning of the god-bearing nation.

Nemirovich's omission of large portions of Shatov's references to his trip to America softens Stavrogin's callous neglect of his pupil. In the play scenario, the audience does not hear Shatov's bitter recollection of the traumatic American journey, Kirillov's divergent theory, or Stavrogin's careless reading of his sincere letter. The scenario thus removes the interpersonal betrayal of the American adventure and centers the entirety of the dramatic focus on the god-bearer thesis. Excising mention of the letter, the dialogue moves to Shatov's pleading question: "If you go back on those words about the people now, then how could you say them then? . . . That is what weighs on me now." The scene then turns to Shatov's remembrance of his conversation with Stavrogin about the theory with certain glaring omissions. Those are reproduced below:

SHATOV: Do you remember your expression: "An atheist cannot
  be Russian; an atheist would instantly cease to be Russian."
NIKOLAI VSEVOLODOVICH: Yes?
SHATOV: You're asking me? You've forgotten? [*Text omitted*:
  Meanwhile that was one of the most exact explanations of one
  of the most important features of the Russian spirit that you've
  determined.] Could you have forgotten that? [*Text omitted*: And
  I will remind you that you also said then: "A non-Orthodox
  person cannot be Russian."][64]
NIKOLAI VSEVOLODOVICH: If I had faith, then without a
  doubt I would have repeated what I said again now. [*Text deleted*

and relocated: But I assure you that this repetition of my past thoughts is having a very unpleasant effect on me. Could you please stop?]

SHATOV: If you had faith . . . [*Text omitted*: But wasn't it you who told me that if it could be mathematically proven to you that the truth was outside of Christ, that you would agree that it is better to remain with Christ than with the truth? Didn't you say that? Didn't you?][65] [*Text omitted; deleted and relocated*: Stavrogin: Permit me to ask you finally . . . where is this hasty and . . . spiteful exam leading? Shatov: This exam will end for all time and you will never again be reminded of it. Stavrogin: You're still insisting that we are outside space and time . . . Shatov: Shut up! I am stupid and awkward, but let my name die in mockery. Please let me repeat to you the main idea you had then. . . . Oh, only ten lines—the conclusion alone. Stavrogin: Repeat it if it's only the conclusion . . .]

NIKOLAI VSEVOLODOVICH: But I assure you that this repetition of my past thoughts is having a very unpleasant effect on me. Could you please stop?

SHATOV: If you had faith?

NIKOLAI VSEVOLODOVICH: Permit me to ask you finally. . . . Where is this hasty and . . . spiteful exam leading?[66]

The removal of the lines referencing fidelity to Christ over rationality and the symbiosis between Orthodoxy and Russianness—which censors would have flagged—reduces the religious stakes of this tense confrontation between close associates. In the novel, Shatov's outrage at Stavrogin's cool disavowal of his previously held beliefs returns us to Dostoevsky's critique of Nikolai Danilevsky, who neglected the role of Orthodoxy in Russian and pan-Slav identity. The novel's version indicates how Dostoevsky imbedded his disagreement with Danilevsky into Stavrogin's ideological betrayal of Shatov. Giving credence to Shatov, it appears that Stavrogin's former religio-nationalist beliefs are obviously a counterpoint to Danilevsky's rather populist neo-Slavophilism, which advanced a secular iteration of Slavophile ideology. The removal of these lines thus reorients the ideological polemic of the novel's exchange. Shatov appears faithful to the author's insistence on religious identity in national destiny contra Danilevsky; however, the absence of specific details from the novel, particularly the role of Christ and Orthodoxy, takes the conservative edge off Dostoevsky's chief attack on

Russia and Europe. The politics of this scene are softened; Shatov appears patriotic without performing as the religious zealot by which many of Dostoevsky's critics may have identified him. The novel's pathetic Shatov, Stavrogin's misled student, emerges in Nemirovich's scenario as a noble disciple of the god-bearing thesis, an idea whose promise Stavrogin has tragically abandoned.

After the previous exchange, Stavrogin affirms that he recognizes in Shatov's résumé precisely what he told him two years ago, but he notices a troublesome change in Shatov's "reduction of God to a simple attribute of nationality." In the novel, Shatov angrily contests this critique, but in the playscript, it is crossed out in the second and third versions and finally disappears in the final version. The novel's text appears below with omitted portions in the playscript parenthetically indicated:

> NIKOLAI VSEVOLODOVICH: I don't think that you've violated them. You have accepted them ardently and ardently regenerated them without noticing it. [*Text omitted*: The very idea that you reduce God to a simple attribute of nationality . . .]
>
> SHATOV: [*Text omitted*: I reduce God to a simple attribute of nationality? On the contrary, I am elevating the nation to God. And when has it happened differently? The people are the body of God. (*Shatov moves to explain the contributions of Jews, Greeks, and French socialism.*)] If a great people do not believe that in them alone is the truth (precisely in them alone and exclusively), if they do not believe that they alone are able and called to resurrect and be the salvation of all through their truth, then they will instantly cease to be a great people and will instantly turn into ethnographic material. [*Text omitted*: rather than into a great people.] A truly great people could never reconcile themselves to a secondary role in relation to humanity, or even to a primary role—but would only accept with certainty and exclusively the first role.[67]

In the novel, Shatov is outraged by Stavrogin's quibbling, resulting in the pupil's prolonged discussion of the "religious" contributions of various civilizations, altogether a longer, more didactic response. In the playscript, Nemirovich seems to have never considered including Shatov's historical summary of past great nations and, having discarded Stavrogin's rebuttal in the final version, resolved on a much less antagonistic commentary from Stavrogin, which is met not with Shatov's outrage but with his development of the idea on the way to suggesting that the Russians are the only god-bearing nation. Nemirovich not only condenses and makes more accessible Shatov's summary of the god-bearer thesis, but he also avoids the antagonistic turn in their conversation. Stavrogin's comment "I don't think that you've violated them. You have accepted them ardently and ardently regenerated them without noticing it" takes on a new meaning in Nemirovich's script. It does not come across as a provocative, condescending correction to Shatov's understanding of the idea as it does in the novel. Rather, Stavrogin now affirms and endorses Shatov's passion for an idea that he himself can tragically no longer believe in. He passes the torch, as it were. Shatov, who continues to struggle with faith, emerges a hero in Nemirovich's script for his commitment to the god-bearer thesis. As Shatov passionately insists, "I will believe in God." At play's end, we do not even hear of Shatov's death—nor those of his wife and son—but only of the murders of the Lebiadkins committed by Fedka the convict. It seems Shatov and his idea survive in Nemirovich's scenario while they are extinguished in Dostoevsky's original.

Nikolai Stavrogin reveals tensions in reading Dostoevsky that build on the examples of reading, interpreting, and adapting discussed in previous chapters and that continue into the present day. The religious-philosophical reception of Dostoevsky, the first to envision him as a Christian thinker, had worked to disentangle his conservative politics from the universal potentials of his religious thought. The initiator of this trend, Vladimir Soloviev, had earlier worked toward such an "all-inclusive," universalist Dostoevsky.[68] This reframing of Dostoevsky was possible in large part because its proponents had a noninstitutional view of religion, believing, as Ivanov clearly did, that Dostoevsky's universality, despite its nationalist Slavophile overtones, overcame his loyalty to the autocracy. In seeking to move *Devils* away from its conservative politics, Nemirovich forged links between its author's capacious Orthodox message and the potential patriotic value of a god-bearer thesis for the twentieth century. The historical timing of such an interpretation was impeccable.

In August 1914, several months after the St. Petersburg premiere of *Stavrogin*, Russia entered the First World War, which provided an ideal patriotic atmosphere for this line of Dostoevsky reception. What Dostoevsky meant in this cultural climate is clear in an anecdote recorded by a contributor to the popular theater weekly *The Footlights and Life* (Rampa i zhizn'*) about a recent literary evening. Amid a host of luminaries, which included Konstantin Bal'mont, Fedor Sologub, Ivanov, and Teffi (Nadezhda Lokhvitskaia), the visiting Polish poet Tadeusz Miciński rose to speak on Polish and Russian friendship, featuring Dostoevsky in his remarks. When he had finished a great silence fell over the listeners. Ivanov stood to acknowledge his words and said "Happily taking advantage of what the Polish poet had considerably and enthusiastically [*s vostorgom*] mentioned: 'I will quote for you just one word of the very same Dostoevsky: 'So be it! So be it!' [*Budi! Budi!*]."[69] Though he attributes this quotation to the author, Ivanov is quoting Father Paisy's ecstatic response to Father Zosima's prophecy in part 2, chapter 5, of *The Brothers Karamazov* that Orthodoxy will establish a theocracy for all people. Merezhkovsky had quoted the same passage in 1906 in his jubilee essay as proof that the wisdom of the author's creations could redeem his political blunders.

In the context of Dostoevsky's notorious and unwavering anti-Polish views, Ivanov and Miciński submit an expansive interpretation of the writer's legacy that accords with Nemirovich's adaptation of *Stavrogin*. His modifications to the god-bearer scene followed a cultural trend that recast Dostoevsky's most conservative political work as a reflection on a contemporary crisis in religious faith and national destiny. But against these readings, Gorky continued to speak out against the Art Theater and the production itself: "In the newspapers they have been writing," said Gorky, "that the political element of *Devils* was removed from the adaptation, but, are there really no 'politics' in the scene of Stavrogin with Shatov?"[70] Gorky's frustrated questions and his objection to *Stavrogin* were generative of his own antipathy for Dostoevsky but should also be read as a rejection of the cultural hold of the religious-philosophical reception, which by this time had clearly eclipsed the established view among the revolutionary intelligentsia that Dostoevsky's moral vision was ultimately marred by its nationalism and exclusionary Orthodox sentiments.[71] For Gorky, the Art Theater, which had risen to prominence with its interpretation of his own plays, had gravitated toward the other shore on the political spectrum. Its Dostoevsky, reflecting the tremendous influence of the religious-philosophical cohort, looked for his politics not in a grotesque portrait of revolutionary turmoil but in a more usable, appropriate vision of his work on the brink of war and at the end of the Russian Empire as they knew it. For Nemirovich and the critics who were reconsidering the religious import of *Devils* in these years, the novel's tale of failed but still living promise must have resonated in uncertain and chaotic times. *Stavrogin* embodied and carefully reenacted the novel's longing for Orthodox community as a sort of mythic tragedy. The near erasure of the socialist background in the play shifted the novel's association with political reaction toward a new audience hoping for reform and a new page in Russian history. In his own way, Nemirovich had negotiated the same tension between respect for the author and rejection of his outmoded, dark corners: to be faithful to Dostoevsky, one needed to remake him.

Epilogue

Specters of Dostoevsky

In the months before the February Revolution in 1917, when Nikolai II abdicated the throne, two of Russia's most acclaimed writers wrote plays about two very different moments in Dostoevsky's life and work. In 1916, the Moscow Art Theater staged Dmitry Merezhkovsky's *There Will Be Happiness* (Budet radost'). Merezhkovsky had spent two decades promoting Dostoevsky's work as a blueprint for religious reawakening, and his play situated itself in the novelist's final period during the triumphant prophesies of *The Brothers Karamazov*. Meanwhile, his erstwhile literary foe, the talented playwright and prose writer Leonid Andreev's play *Beloved Specters* (Milye prizraki) began its run in Moscow and Petrograd in February 1917, just before the revolution.[1] His play fictionalized Dostoevsky's triumphant debut as a novelist and its immediate, ecstatic reception by Nikolai Nekrasov and Vissarion Belinsky (named favorably "Nezabytov," or Mr. Unforgettable, in Andreev's text). The names were changed, but many would have recognized the scene from Belinsky's historic exclamation about *Poor Folk*— "A new Gogol has appeared!"—which had already been enshrined in literary history.

It seems almost inevitable that two of Dostoevsky's most faithful literary descendants would turn to his body of work for answers about the future. Since Vladimir Soloviev's first efforts to privilege the universal spirit of Dostoevsky's religion and art, critics and theatrical adapters of the Russian Silver Age—from Merezhkovsky to Sergei Bulgakov, and Viacheslav Ivanov to Vladimir Nemirovich-Danchenko—had looked to the writer's novels, guided by a faith that the author's capacious religious idea was crystallized in his artistic word rather than what they perceived as his tendentious journalism and mistaken political views. I have called this decision to see two versions of Dostoevsky the "two Dostoevskys problem" and I have shown how critics' and adapters' faithful reading of Dostoevsky's novels owed something to a tension in modern criticism that separated the author from the text produced by that author. Silver Age critics wished to reconcile the author's body with his textual corpus; however, the dominant tendency in their readings was to elevate Dostoevsky's artistic word over the complex and often contradictory sum total of his life and work. The effect of doing this showed the tremendous power of the critic and the diminishing figure of the author. In their original plays, Merezhkovsky and Andreev represent a sort of final stage of the Silver Age's reckoning with Dostoevsky's prophetic stature in their cultural life. Of course, the different politics of both writers made their confrontation with the future of Dostoevsky distinct. Merezhkovsky laments the failure of Dostoevsky's prophesies by retreating to a resurrected figuration of the patriarchy. The filial protagonist of his play, a fictional remixing of Dostoevsky with a few of his most rebellious characters, dies by suicide; but his death reconciles his materialist father to his late son's spiritual insights. Andreev takes as his setting the deep past of Dostoevsky's career—before he garners any fame—seeking to frame the writer in the timeless yet hard-won promise of *Poor Folk*, his utopian socialist masterpiece of the 1840s.

A similar renegotiation of a utopian vision in the face of its collapse occurred in a later era when Marxists grappled with the end of communism in Europe and the proclamations of the triumph of liberal democracy exemplified by Francis Fukuyama's *End of History and the Last Man* (1992). Out of this debate arose Jacques Derrida's insistence that Marx would continue to haunt his disciples and their visions of a world they had hoped, and still hoped, to make, just as the opening of the "Communist Manifesto" once proclaimed: "A specter is haunting Europe—the specter of communism." What emerged was a "hauntology," a new state of being formed out of the still-present idea of Marxism amid its seeming historical failure. Jacques Derrida also isolated the temporal rupture in Karl Marx's hope and Europe's fear of spectral communism, which "had already been announced, with this name, some time ago, but it was not yet *there*."[2] In a sense, Merezhkovsky and Andreev were grappling with a similar dynamics of faithful disappointment when they wrote their own theatrical scenarios drawn from the two most promising polarities of Dostoevsky's life and work: the final proclamation of brotherhood in *The Brothers Karamazov* (Merezhkovsky) and the incipient genius of the writer of *Poor Folk* (Andreev). They could not look ahead to the future; as Derrida wrote in response to the question "whither Marxism?" "The future can only be for ghosts. And the past."[3] For Andreev and Merezhkovsky, the future was likewise spectral and their plays creatively conjured a union of author and text that their criticism could never manage.

Merezhkovsky's *There Will Be Happiness* employs the topos of generational conflict, made famous in Russian literature by Ivan Turgenev's *Fathers and Children*. But the play approaches this theme by reorganizing several key interventions in how *The Brothers Karamazov* itself had extended it, offering a glimpse into how Merezhkovsky envisioned the novel in the cultural sphere and social reality of 1916. One of the additions he makes is the incorporation of an incest theme, whose relationship to the Phaedra myth are made explicit in several metaliterary references to Racine and Euripides's versions (Merezhkovsky had translated several Greek tragedies in the 1890s and his rendering of Euripides's *Hippolytus* was staged in 1902). While in Dostoevsky's novel Dmitry and his father, Fyodor Pavlovich, become infatuated with the same woman during a dispute over the son's inheritance, in Merezhkovsky's play, the father-son rivalry plays out entirely within the family. The filial antagonist in *There Will Be Happiness* is named Fedor ("Fedya") Ivanovich, a self-proclaimed former "mystical anarchist" and decadent philosopher, who has been having an affair with the second wife of his materialist and agrarian socialist (populist) father, Ivan Sergeevich. In another important adjustment to the father-son theme in Dostoevsky's novel, Merezhkovsky gives Fedya characteristics of both Ivan and Dmitry Karamazov and names him after the Karamazov patriarch, Fedor Pavlovich. Making the association between Ivan and Fedya in the play even more obvious, the same actor who played both Ivan and Stavrogin in the Moscow Art Theater's productions of *The Brothers Karamazov* and *Devils*—Vasily Kachalov—played the role of Fedya. As is well known, Dostoevsky gave his own first name to the sensualist paterfamilias of *The Brothers Karamazov*, and so Merezhkovsky's portrait seems aimed at a reckoning with both the legacy of Fedor Pavlovich Karamazov and Fedor Mikhailovich Dostoevsky, who was after all the father of the

Silver Age cultural reawakening. But who is Merezhkovsky's Fedor Ivanovich and what does he believe?

As in Dostoevsky's portrayal of Raskolnikov and Ivan Karamazov,
Merezhkovsky conveys Fedor's ideas by making him the author of an
essay, "The Philosophy of Suicide." This article initiates an argument
between Fedor, an aspiring psychiatrist, and his father about whether
suicide can be eradicated by improving social conditions—a classic argument of utilitarian socialists of the father's generation. Fedor disagrees
because "the better people are set up the more deaths by suicide there
will be."[4] Providing further explanation, Fedor contends that ending
one's life is what distinguishes human beings from animals and that the
human being is a "natural suicide," preferring freedom (the right to end
one's life) to mere existence (the struggle to survive). While the only suicides practiced in their time are acts of despair, Fedor prophesies that in
the future, suicide will become a "victory over the fear of death," quoting the direct speech of suicidal proponent of self-deification, Aleksei
Kirillov, one of the theatrically unrepresentable figures in Nemirovich-
Danchenko's adaptation of *Devils*. "There will come a time when people
will die a free, an actually free death—from abundance, from luxury, from
power, from happiness."[5] Fedor may have been inspired by Kirillov, but
he makes an important revision by claiming that suicide is not about
the exercise of free will to become God but rather a person's free choice
to end life out of joy instead of fear. Fedor sees suicide as a way of *con-
firming* happiness: if a person takes her life, she is doing so because she
has achieved some pinnacle of pleasure or satiation. It is for that reason
he argues that suicides would actually increase if social welfare were
improved for the greatest number.

As the play continues, the father learns of his son's betrayal. Rather
than punishing his son and wife for their illicit affair, in a reversal of
the filial dynamics of forgiveness in *The Brothers Karamazov*, he blames
himself. His wife quickly arranges to restart her acting career and goes
off to play Phaedra on the stage. Fedya, on the other hand, chooses to
implement his ideas of self-annihilation and ends his life. In another
plot reversal of the classics, this Phaedra lives and her lover-stepson dies
by suicide. The reconciliation of father and son occurs only in death.
Fedya's grave is the setting of the final scene of the play and serves as a
metaphor for Dostoevsky's own mortality and its untold future meaning. Symbolically, his father has found a way to reconcile himself to his
son's despairing philosophy, one that affirms life and does not aban-
don hope.

Such direct references and extensions of Dostoevsky's heroes and other writers prompted one critic to write, "When you leave the theater, in your head resounds Pascal, Racine, Tiutchev, and Dostoevsky, Dostoevsky."[6] Casting the most radical variety of Dostoevsky's characters—the suicidal nihilist—in his own contemporary times, Merezhkovsky sought to make connections between the flawed younger generation of his idol's novels and his own youthful membership in the decadent movement, which in his mature thinking produced either aesthetes or atheists. At one point in the play, Fedor muses on his high-school flirtation with "A. M.—anarchist-mystics," who styled themselves as radicals and carried Browning revolvers, in the same speech quoting Merezhkovsky's own early decadent verse from his poem "Daring" (*Derznovenie*):

We stand for a new beauty
We will destroy all laws,
Cross all boundaries.[7]

We can read Fedor as a stand-in for the rebellious decadent current in Dostoevsky that spoke to the Silver Age generation. By reincarnating a simulacrum of Dostoevsky composed entirely of his rebel protagonists, in *There Will Be Happiness*, Merezhkovsky not only exorcizes his own youthful attachment to the radical ideas in the novels but also implicates the author as a bad father to his literary children. It took Merezhkovsky just over a decade, but he seemed to have finally been convinced of Andrei Belyi's stronger rejection of Dostoevsky that arose out of the 1906 jubilee commemorations. Merezhkovsky's play first conjures a composite of Dostoevsky's rebellious inheritance in the character of Fedor and then leads him to suicide, a symbolic destruction of Merezhkovsky's fascination with Dostoevsky's trespassing mystics, the writer's darkest ideological creations, and the ones that spoke seductively to the Silver Age critics' need for religious prophecy.

If *There Will Be Happiness* returns to Dostoevsky's final work, conjuring the author anew with the raw material of his own fictional creations, Andreev's *Beloved Specters* returns to a time when Dostoevsky was unknown, just a "former student," as he is described in the dramatis personae—the same way that Raskolnikov is described in *Crime and Punishment*. Andreev's version of Dostoevsky is named Mikhail Fedorovich Taezhnikov. (The first name and patronymic invert the author's own: Fedor Mikhailovich.) *Beloved Specters* begins at the lodgings of Taezhnikov, who rents a room with a family experiencing extreme poverty. The elder sister, Tanya, works as a prostitute to feed her family.

Anyone who has read *Poor Folk* would connect the hardship on display to one of Makar Devushkin's first letters to his beloved Varenka. Andreev's setting serves the purpose of identifying the young Dostoevsky with his first fictional creation of great acclaim, but his rendition of a fictional Dostoevsky is not as metatextually recognizable as Merezhkovsky's Fedor. Taezhnikov is Dostoevsky before he became Dostoevsky. Andreev's work is a sort of fictional prequel to Dostoevsky's life before he attained literary acclaim for *Poor Folk*, claiming of his portrait that "I imagined my own Dostoevsky . . . the way that he seemed to me at the moment he was working on *Poor Folk*. It is like a specter of Dostoevsky."[8] In one scene, following the acceptance of Taezhnikov's manuscript for publication, the character Monastyrskii (derived from the word for "monastery") quotes Pushkin's "Prophet," a poem that the actual Dostoevsky especially loved. But this version of Dostoevsky is terrified by the poem's articulation of the poet's power: " 'With your word burn the hearts of man'—you're especially struck by that, yes? No, my dear, this is a different matter. . . . Look at this line: 'Fulfill my will!' Brother, I am not a meek person; I'm even a daring person, but when I imagine this [*quietly and significantly*] 'fulfill *my will*,' I am terrified to the point of shaking and shivers run up my spine! Do you understand *whose* will this is?"[9] Andreev's fictionalized Dostoevsky anticipates the spiritual burden of becoming a writer. The necessity of taking on divine wisdom and will mingles with the writer's departure from the earthly inspiration for his God-given creation. The destruction of Taezhnikov's close-knit accidental family coincides with his rise to literary stardom. The play concludes with the tragic death of his landlady's daughter, Tanya, who has just recently been delivered from prostitution by a benefactor and is engaged to Monastyrskii. She arrives to the lodgings barely conscious, having just been crushed by horses (an homage to the death of Marmeladov in *Crime and Punishment*). Taezhnikov views her death as an emblem of his parasitic writerly existence: his divine gift rests on the stories of broken lives and broken families, which disappear and exist only as specters. "Time will pass, and all of this sadness and darkness will become a dear specter in my imagination," Taezhnikov says.[10] To the distraught Monastyrskii, Taezhnikov admits, "You see, I am a bit of a raven; I feed on dead flesh (*breaks into laughter*). Don't you understand? By dying, you see, they give me their soul, their life, and . . . their suffering! Oh, how many of these lives are inside of me!"[11] But the loss of rendering real lives into fictional phantoms deepens when he witnesses the death of Tanya, which he claims is *his* death. Lines from his final speech in the play—which are the last ones spoken before the curtain falls—resound like a requiem to the author's life as much as they represent the view of fiction as the repository of once-living phantoms:

> You see where she is lying there? That's not her, Egor [Monastyrskii]. That's me who died, yes, that is me who lies there. Tanya died, quiet Tanya died, and with her something very precious died within me. It seems to me that I myself have died. Who has remained—he who is now speaking to you and who is leaving here—this is not me anymore. This is a different, alien, and unknown person to me. Now I can predict something—and I say this to you, Monastyrskii: before me is a great and extraordinary life. There will be creation; there will be minutes of fiery inspiration, there will be intoxicated tears shed over life and the sufferings of people; there will be somebody's ecstasy, there will be loud shouts of greetings—but *this* has gone and will never return again. Who was this woman to me? I did not love her; she only flashed like a specter, like a speechless shadow . . . but with her my entire youth is leaving, my soul, my unknown happiness.[12]

Andreev thus suggests that Taezhnikov—or *his* Dostoevsky—dies so that his works can live. It is another way of insisting on the continued life of the text amid the limited and dead material of the writer's life.

Unlike Merezhkovsky's Fedor, Taezhnikov reads like a fresh take on Dostoevsky's life and work, framing his rise to fame as a time of both deep personal turmoil and transformation. What their plays have in common, however, is an impulse to rewrite not only Dostoevsky's plots and characters but also to rewrite *the author's life* as if to reforge its organic connection to the texts with the most utopian and liberationist potential. At the twilight of the revolution, both writers returned to Dostoevsky's novels by reorganizing their plots, reframing their characters, and offering their own creative, rather than critical, reflections on their idol's future. Dostoevsky is nowhere in their plays, but he is everywhere. He haunts the fresh ground of their creations at the same moment that both plays reimagine his plots and religious ideas for their era of disintegration, apocalypse, and revolution. Perhaps it was no longer possible to write critical essays like Merezhkovsky's "Prophet of the Russian Revolution" (1906) in 1916; critics were turning to their art to think through Dostoevsky's legacy and left unresolved what had become the impossible task of reconciling the author with his valued prophesies of a religious and cultural awakening. That critical task continues as this book concludes. Future readers might ask critics today whether the kind of reparative project wrought by Silver Age faithful reading is still capable of restoring this author's work to creative use. At present, one might say that Dostoevsky has been returned to the oppression, tyranny, and violence from which Silver Age critics had tried to wrest him.

Notes

Introduction

1. Yurii Aikhenval'd, "Literaturnye zametki. Po povodu novogo izdaniia sochinenii Dostoevskogo," *Russkaia mysl'* 9 (1907): 162–63.

2. Rosenshield has pointed out early signs of the nationalism displayed in Dostoevsky's *Writer's Diary* in his earlier journal, *Vremia*. See Gary Rosenshield, *The Ridiculous Jew: The Exploitation and Transformation of a Stereotype in Gogol, Turgenev, and Dostoevsky* (Stanford, CA: Stanford University Press, 2008), 143.

3. Obituary, *Peterburgskaia gazeta* 25, January 30, 1881, quoted in F. M. Dostoevskii, *Polnoe sobranie sochinenii*, vol. 15, ed. V. G. Bazanov et al. (Leningrad: Nauka, 1976), 501.

4. Konstantin Bal'mont, "Prizrak mezh liudei (Shelli, 1792–1822)," in *Gornye vershiny. Sbornik statei* (Moscow: Grif, 1904), 131.

5. Very recent examples of this critical turn include Patricia Stuelke, *The Ruse of Repair: US Neoliberal Empire and the Turn from Critique* (Durham, NC: Duke University Press, 2021); and Roy Ben-Shai, *Critique of Critique* (Stanford, CA: Stanford University Press, 2023).

6. Susan Stanford Friedman, "Both/And: Critique and Discovery in the Humanities," *PMLA* 132, no. 2 (2017): 345, https://doi.org/10.1632/pmla.2017.132.2.344.

7. Rita Felski, *The Limits of Critique* (Chicago: University of Chicago Press, 2015), 131.

8. See Friedman, "Both/And," 349; Patrick Jagoda, "Critique and Critical Making," *PMLA* 132, no. 2 (2017): 357, https://doi.org/10.1632/pmla.2017.132.2.356; and Diana Fuss, "But What about Love?," *PMLA* 132, no. 2 (2017): 354, https://doi.org/10.1632/pmla.2017.132.2.352.

9. Felski, *The Limits of Critique*, 151–52.

10. Paul Ricoeur, *Freud and Philosophy: An Essay on Interpretation*, trans. Denis Savage (New Haven, CT: Yale University Press, 1970), 33.

11. Ricoeur, *Freud and Philosophy*, 29.

12. Eve Kosofsky Sedgwick, "Paranoid Reading and Reparative Reading, or, You're So Paranoid, You Probably Think This Essay Is about You," in *Touching Feeling: Affect, Pedagogy, Performativity* (Durham, NC: Duke University Press, 2002), 150–51.

13. Galin Tihanov, *The Birth and Death of Literary Theory: Regimes of Relevance in Russia and Beyond* (Stanford, CA: Stanford University Press, 2019),

14. Roland Barthes, *Image–Music–Text*, trans. Stephen Heath (New York: Hill and Wang, 1977), 143.

15. Barthes, *Image–Music–Text*, 147.

16. Felski, *The Limits of Critique*, 54–55.

17. Joseph Frank, *The Mantle of the Prophet, 1871–1881*, vol. 5 in *Dostoevsky* (Princeton, NJ: Princeton University Press, 2002), xii.

18. Aileen Kelly, "The Two Dostoevskys," *New York Review of Books* 50, no. 5 (March 27, 2003): 23–25. Robin Miller reviewed Frank's final volume positively but noted that he had not engaged with recent American critics on *A Writer's Diary*. See Robin Feuer Miller, "Frank's Dostoevsky," *Slavic and East European Journal* 47, no. 3 (Autumn 2003): 471–77. Kate Holland has resisted the "two Dostoevskys" problem, presenting *A Writer's Diary* as a "creative laborator[y]" and linking it directly with the fiction. She treats it as a venue for his working out of "realist" and "utopian" visions of Russia's confrontation with modernity. See Kate Holland, "Dostoevsky's Journalism in the 1870s," in *Dostoevsky in Context*, ed. Deborah Martinsen and Olga Maiorova (Cambridge: Cambridge University Press, 2015), 288–94, https://doi.org/10.1017/CBO9781139236867.035. Finally, Sarah Hudspith has looked to Slavophile thought to understand problems of unity and fragmentation in Dostoevsky's art, thus bridging the conventional separation of his ideological and artistic practices. See Sarah Hudspith, *Dostoevsky and the Idea of Russianness: A New Perspective on Unity and Brotherhood* (London: Routledge, 2004).

19. Gary Saul Morson, "Dostoevsky's Anti-Semitism and the Critics: A Review Article," *Slavic and East European Journal* 27, no. 3 (Autumn 1983): 314.

20. Translated by and quoted in Ksana Blank, *Dostoevsky's Dialectics and the Problem of Sin* (Evanston, IL: Northwestern University Press, 2010), 11. The passage occurs in V. V. Rozanov, "Na lektsii o Dostoevskom," in *Vlastitel' dum: F. M. Dostoevskii v russkoi kritike kontsa XIX–nachala XX veka*, ed. N. Ashimbaeva (St. Petersburg: Khudozhestvennaia literatura, 1997), 261–62. His dialectical skill could be what prompted Bruce K. Ward to consider Dostoevsky a "suspicious" critic. See Bruce K. Ward, "Dostoevsky and the Hermeneutics of Suspicion," *Literature and Theology* 11, no. 3 (September 1997): 270–83.

21. Stephen Carter, *The Political and Social Thought of F. M. Dostoevsky* (New York: Garland, 1991), 8. See also Mikhail Bakhtin, *Problems of Dostoevsky's Poetics*, ed. and trans. Caryl Emerson (Minneapolis: University of Minnesota Press, 1984), 21.

22. Morson, "Dostoevsky's Anti-Semitism and the Critics," 309.

23. For a reading positioning Dostoevsky outside official Orthodoxy, see Nel Grillaert, "Orthodox Spirituality," in *Dostoevsky in Context*, ed. Deborah Martinsen and Olga Maiorova (Cambridge: Cambridge University Press, 2015), 189–93. https://doi.org/10.1017/CBO9781139236867.022.

24. Margaret Ziolkowski makes brief mention of the political dimension of his Christian faith. See Margaret Ziolkowski, "Dostoevsky and the Kenotic Tradition," in *Dostoevsky and the Christian Tradition*, ed. George Pattison and Diane Oenning Thompson (Cambridge: Cambridge University Press, 2001), 31–40.

25. Gary Saul Morson, "Conclusion: Reading Dostoevsky," in *The Cambridge Companion to Dostoevskii*, ed. W. J. Leatherbarrow (Cambridge: Cambridge University Press, 2002), 217.

26. A. L. Bem, *O Dostoevskom. Sborniki statei pod red. A. L. Bema. Praga, 1929/1933 /1936*, ed. I. L. Volgin (Moscow: Al'ma Mater/Akademicheskii proekt, 2019), 407.

27. For a summary of the different scholarly approaches to Dostoevsky's religion, see Malcolm V. Jones, *Dostoevsky and the Dynamics of Religious Experience* (London: Anthem, 2005), esp. 25–43. For muted treatment of his political views in post-Soviet Russian scholarship, see Carol Apollonio and Joseph Fitzpatrick, eds., *The New Russian Dostoevsky: Readings for the Twenty-First Century* (Bloomington, IN: Slavica, 2010). Steven Cassedy comes closest to handling the apparent disjuncture between the writer's religious morality and politics but ultimately advocates the relativist argument in a chapter titled "Belief Is Contextual." See Steven Cassedy, *Dostoevsky's Religion* (Stanford, CA: Stanford University Press, 2005).

28. Zakharov has diagnosed critics since Turgenev of suffering from what he calls the "Dostoevsky syndrome," which disables critics from perceiving Dostoevsky's artistic contributions to world literature and the art of the novel. His view assumes that most if not all negative criticism of Dostoevsky is "unhealthy," implying that appreciation of the novelist is "normal" because his artistic accomplishments are so wedded to its moral-religious ideas that it is a sign of pathology or even immorality to dispute them. See Vladimir Zakharov, "The Dostoevsky Syndrome," trans. Aura Young, in Apollonio and Fitzpatrick, *The New Russian Dostoevsky*, 9–24. The essay was first published in 1991.

29. Some view Dostoevsky's religion as the key to solving tensions in his legacy. Leonard G. Friesen claims that Dostoevsky's Orthodox heritage provides the ethical framework that resolves the "two Dostoevskys" problem. See Leonard G. Friesen, *Transcendent Love: Dostoevsky and the Search for a Global Ethic* (Notre Dame, IN: University of Notre Dame Press, 2016). Paul Contino has drawn on theology to explore the transformational poetics of *The Brothers Karamazov*. See Paul Contino *Dostoevsky's Incarnational Realism: Finding Christ among the Karamazovs* (Eugene, OR: Cascade, 2020).

30. Orest Miller, "Materialy dlia zhizneopisaniia F. M. Dostoevskogo," in *Biografiia, pis'ma i zametki iz zapisnoi knizhki F. M. Dostoevskogo*, ed. Orest Miller and Nikolai Strakhov (St. Petersburg: Tipografiia A. S. Suvorina, 1883), 3.

31. N. N. Bulich, *F. M. Dostoevskii i ego sochineniia (istoriko-literaturnye ocherki): rech' na akte Imperatorskogo Kazanskogo universiteta 5 noiabria 1881 g.* (Kazan': Tipografiia Imperatorskogo Universiteta, 1881), 9.

32. Nikolai Strakhov, "Vospominaniia o Fedore Mikhailoviche Dostoevskom," in *Biografiia, pis'ma i zametki*, 275. The most intimate descriptions in Strakhov's account are of the nature and frequency of Dostoevsky's epileptic attacks.

33. Some examples are K. A. Trutovskii, "Vospominaniia o Fedore Mikhailoviche Dostoevskom. Materialy dlia kharakteristiki russkikh pisatelei," *Russkoe obozrenie* 1 (1893): 212–17; and F. M. Dostoevskii, "Perepiska i zametki F. M. Dostoevskogo," *Severnyi vestnik* 11 (1891): 5–34. For a complete list of publications directly relevant to the life and work of Dostoevsky, see S. V. Belov, *F. M. Dostoevskii. Ukazatel' proizvedenii F. M. Dostoevskogo i literatury o nem na russkom iazyke, 1844–2004 gg.* (St. Petersburg: Rossiiskaia natsional'naia biblioteka, 2011).

34. Viktor Shklovsky, *Za i protiv. Zametki o Dostoevskom* (Moscow: Sovetskii pisatel', 1957), 256.

35. Interest in Dostoevsky's talent for psychopathology continued into the next decade, with studies such as R. A. Iantareva[-Vilkina], *Detskie tipy v proizvedeniiakh Dostoevskogo. Psikhologicheskie etiudy* (St. Petersburg: Gramotnost', 1895); and I. G. Orshanskii, "Istoriia odnogo ideinogo prestupleniia. 'Prestuplenie i Nakazanie' F. M. Dostoevskogo," *Severnyi vestnik* (1896); 10: 15–34; 11: 48–70.

36. V. Zelinskii, ed., "Predislovie," in *Istoriko-kriticheskii kommentarii k sochineniiam F. M. Dostoevskogo*, vol. 1 (Moscow: Tip. T. Malinskogo, 1885). A reviewer at *The Herald of Europe* found Zelinskii's approach of assembling diverse material confusing for the reader and complained that interspersing his own commentary in the midst of other critics' reviews indicated his intent to guide and influence the reader's opinion of Dostoevsky. A. V—n, "Review of *Istoriko-kriticheskii kommentarii . . .*," *Vestnik Evropy* 5 (1885): 408–10.

37. James L. Rice, *Dostoevsky and the Healing Art: An Essay in Literary and Medical History* (Ann Arbor, MI: Ardis, 1985), 208.

38. Vladimir Chizh, *Dostoevskii kak psikhopatolog. Ocherk* (Moscow: V Universitetskoi tipografii (M. Katkov), 1885), 2. Orshanskii seconded this observation when he wrote, "For understanding criminality and criminal psychology, Dostoevsky's work has enormous significance as the only document of its kind." Orshanskii, *Severnyi vestnik* 10 (1896), 16.

39. Vladimir Solov'ev, *Tri rechi v pamiat' Dostoevskogo (1881–1883 gg.)* (Moscow: V Universitetskoi tipografii na Strastnom bul'vare (M. Katkov), 1884), 18–19.

40. Solov'ev, *Tri rechi v pamiat' Dostoevskogo*, 19.

41. Sedgwick, "Paranoid Reading," 128.

42. Sedgwick, "Paranoid Reading," 128.

43. Carol Apollonio, *Dostoevsky's Secrets: Reading against the Grain* (Evanston, IL: Northwestern University Press, 2009), 7.

44. Apollonio, *Dostoevsky's Secrets*, 8.

45. Apollonio, *Dostoevsky's Secrets*, 7–8.

46. Sedgwick, "Paranoid Reading," 128.

47. Oksana Zabuzhko, "No Guilty People in the World? Rereading Russian Literature after Bucha," *Times Literary Supplement*, April 22, 2022.

48. Sedgwick, "Paranoid Reading," 126.

49. Elizabeth S. Anker and Rita Felski, eds., *Critique and Postcritique* (Durham, NC: Duke University Press, 2017), 18.

50. Anker and Felski, *Critique and Postcritique*, 20.

51. Bruno Latour, "Why Has Critique Run Out of Steam? From Matters of Fact to Matters of Concern," *Critical Inquiry* 30, no. 2 (Winter 2004): 246.

1. Adapting *The Idiot* and *Crime and Punishment*, 1890–1900

1. I. L. Volgin, *Poslednii god Dostoevskogo* (Moscow: Sovetskii pisatel', 1986), 414. Cited in Joseph Frank, *Dostoevsky*, vol. 5 (Princeton, NJ: Princeton University Press, 1976–2002), 741.

2. Volgin, *Poslednii god Dostoevskogo*, 414.

3. F. M. Dostoevskii, *Polnoe sobranie sochinenii*, vol. 7 (Leningrad: Nauka, 1973), 356–57. Princess V. D. Obolenskaia received the author's permission in 1872 to

attempt her own adaptation, but it was unrealized. For Dostoevsky's letter to her, see *Pss*, vol. 29, kn. 1, 225.

4. For an overview of the censor's objections to Dostoevsky's works in the two decades immediately following his death, see I. L. Volgin, "Dostoevskii i pravitel'stvennaia politika v oblasti prosveshcheniia (1881–1917)," in *Dostoevskii: Materialy i issledovaniia*, vol. 4, ed. G. M. Fridlender (Leningrad: Nauka, 1980), 192–206.

5. Sutugin seems to have had a special interest in adapting Dostoevsky. In 1910, Sutugin wrote an adaptation of *The Brothers Karamazov*, the same year that the Moscow Art Theater premiered its more famous adaptation. See Sergei Sutugin, *Brat'ia Karamazovy: Drama v 5 d. i 8 kart.* (St. Petersburg: Izdanie S. Rassokhina, 1910).

6. In those years plays by the most respected modern playwright, Nikolai Ostrovsky, ran about 520 times; Krylov's came close to that frequency at 510 times. Cf. I. Petrovskaia and V. Somina, *Teatral'nyi Peterburg: Nachalo XVIII veka–oktiabr' 1917 goda. Obozrenie-putevoditel'* (St. Petersburg: RIII, 1994), 192. In *Russia at Play*, McReynolds treats Krylov's role in the theater with greater nuance. See Louise McReynolds, *Russia at Play: Leisure Activities at the End of the Tsarist Era* (Ithaca, NY: Cornell University Press, 2003), 61–62.

7. Paul Davis, *The Lives and Times of Ebenezer Scrooge* (New Haven, CT: Yale University Press, 1990), 13.

8. Bruno Latour, *Reassembling the Social: An Introduction to Actor-Network-Theory* (Oxford: Oxford University Press, 2005).

9. Vasily Rozanov's review of this book appears in his *Sumerki prosveshcheniia: sbornik statei po voprosam obrazovaniia* (St. Petersburg: Tipografiia M. Merkusheva, 1899), 237–39.

10. S. Petrovskii, *Pamiati Imperatora Aleksandra III* (Moscow: S. Petrovskii, 1894), 317–19. Quoted in Richard Wortman, *Scenarios of Power: Myth and Ceremony in Russian Monarchy from Peter the Great to the Abdication of Nicholas II* (Princeton, NJ: Princeton University Press, 2006), 314.

11. Howard Marchitello, *Remediating Shakespeare in the Eighteenth and Nineteenth Centuries* (Cham, Switzerland: Palgrave Macmillan, 2019), 11.

12. For a brief summary of Stanislavsky's difficulties with the censor, see E. Anthony Swift, "Russia," in *The Frightful Stage: Political Censorship of the Theater in Nineteenth-Century Europe*, ed. Robert Justin Goldstein (New York: Berghahn, 2009), 144–45.

13. On Stanislavsky's production of *Foma*, see A. V. Arkhipova, "Iz stsenicheskoi istorii 'Sela Stepanchikova,'" in *Dostoevskii i ego vremia*, ed. V. G. Bazanov and G. M. Fridlender (Leningrad: Nauka, 1971), 308–12.

14. S. "Obshchestvo Iskusstva i Literatury," *Artist* 18 (December 1891): 127. Coming full circle, the Moscow Art Theater would later do an adaptation in 1917.

15. On the decree, see Murray Frame, *School for Citizens: Theatre and Civil Society in Imperial Russia* (New Haven, CT: Yale University Press, 2006), 74–106.

16. McReynolds, *Russia at Play*, 10.

17. Murray Frame, "'Freedom of the Theatres': The Abolition of the Russian Imperial Theatre Monopoly," *Slavonic and East European Review* 83, no. 2 (2005): 259.

18. On the popular theater during this time, see Gary Thurston, *The Popular Theatre Movement in Russia, 1862–1919* (Evanston, IL: Northwestern University Press, 1998); on censorship and the popular theater, see E. Anthony Swift, "Fighting the Germs of Disorder: The Censorship of Russian Popular Theater, 1888–1917," *Russian History* 18, no. 1 (Spring 1991): 1–49.

19. Marc Slonim, *Russian Theater: From the Empire to the Soviets* (Cleveland, OH: World, 1961), 83.

20. A. L. Volynskii, *Kniga velikogo gneva* (St. Petersburg: Trud, 1904), 222.

21. Petrovskaia and Somina, *Teatral'nyi Peterburg*, 193.

22. Volynskii, *Kniga velikogo gneva*, 223.

23. Volynskii, *Kniga velikogo gneva*, 224.

24. "Teatr. Tekushchii repertuar," *Severnyi vestnik* 3 (1895): 44.

25. Renata Kobetts Miller, "Nineteenth-Century Theatrical Adaptations of Novels: The Paradox of Ephemerality," in *The Oxford Handbook of Adaptation Studies*, ed. Thomas Leitch (Oxford: Oxford University Press, 2017), 56–57.

26. In his 1885 diary, Tsarevich Nikolai indicated that he had been reading Dostoevsky's *Devils*. It is unclear who gave him this book to read, but in the same year Pobedonostsev assumed charge of his legal studies. See Andrew M. Verner, *The Crisis of Russian Autocracy: Nicholas II and the 1905 Revolution* (Princeton, NJ: Princeton University Press, 1990), 20.

27. Robert F. Byrnes, *Pobedonostsev: His Life and Thought* (Bloomington: Indiana University Press, 1968), 251. Byrnes notes that Pobedonostsev wrote seventy-nine letters to E. M. Feoktistov, the director of press censorship between 1883 and 1896, with specific requests.

28. Letter to Alexander III, 1887, *Tainyi pravitel' Rossii: K. P. Pobedonostsev i ego korrespondenty*, ed. T. F. Prokopov (Moscow: Russkaia kniga, 2001), 214. Performances of Tolstoy's play were not permitted for educated audiences until 1895.

29. For more on Suvorin's stewardship of *Novoe vremia* with attention to these contemporary issues, see Effie Ambler, *The Career of Aleksei S. Suvorin: Russian Journalism and Politics, 1861–1881* (Detroit, MI: Wayne State University Press, 1972), 113–75.

30. Merezhkovsky accused Suvorin of cheapening the Pushkin jubilee of 1899 by commercializing the commemorations. D. S. Merezhkovskii, "Prazdnik Pushkina," *Mir iskusstva* 13–14 (1899): 11–20.

31. See James L. Rice, "Dostoevsky's Endgame: The Projected Sequel to 'The Brothers Karamazov,'" *Russian History* 33, no. 1 (2006): 45–62.

32. Frank, *Dostoevsky*, 5: 726–27. See also A. S. Suvorin, "O pokoinom," in *F. M. Dostoevskii v vospominaniiakh sovremennikov*, vol. 2, ed. K. Tiun'kin and M. Tiun'kina (Moscow: Khudozhestvennaia literatura, 1990), 465–73.

33. For an overview of some reviews of both productions, see A. V. Burmistrova, "Instsenirovki romanov Dostoevskogo (pervye opyty)," *Neizvestnyi Dostoevskii* 3 (2019): 96–115.

34. A. S. Suvorin, *Dnevnik A. S. Suvorina* (Moscow: Izd. L. D. Frenkel', 1923), 209.

35. A. S. Suvorin, *V ozhidanii veka XX. Malen'kie pis'ma 1889–1903 gg.* (Moscow: Algoritm, 2005), 641.

36. See Zhores Trofimov, ed., *V. N. Andreev-Burlak: pamiat' i nasledie* (Ul'ianovsk: Simbirskaia kniga, 1995), 249.

37. In 1891, "Marmeladov. Stsena iz romana F. M. Dostoevskogo: "Prestuplenie i Nakazanie," was listed as "unconditionally permitted for staging." See "Alfavitnyi spisok . . .," *Artist* 15 (1891): 116. For an extremely detailed account of Andreev-Burlak's reading of Dostoevsky, see A. Ninov, "Rozhdenie teatra Dostoevskogo," in *Dostoevskii i teatr: sbornik statei*, ed. A. A. Ninov (Leningrad, 1983), 200–13. Andreev-Burlak was a favorite among the "democratic stratum" of his 1880s audience (B. A. Gorin-Gorianov, *Aktery. Iz vospominanii* [Leningrad: Iskusstvo, 1947], 41; quoted in Ninov, "Rozhdenie teatra Dostoevskogo," 212).

38. For an example of the effect Dostoevsky's reading had on his audiences, see I. A. Vitiugova, "I. L. Leont'ev-Shcheglov i F. M. Dostoevskii," in *Dostoevskii. Materialy i issledovaniia*, vol. 11, ed. G. M. Fridlender (St. Petersburg: Nauka, 1994), 276–78. It was a well-known fact that Dostoevsky recited his own works beautifully. This fact was so generally acknowledged that by 1903 it was a cliché and a reviewer chastised the author of a recent memoir about Dostoevsky for even mentioning it at all. See Z. B., "Review of V. Mikulich [L. I. Veselitskaia]. 'Vstrecha so znamenitost'iu,'" *Novyi put'* 12 (1903): 209–11.

39. Ninov, "Rozhdenie teatra Dostoevskogo," 205.

40. V. L., "Khronika teatra i isskustva," *Teatr i iskusstvo* 41 (1899): 711.

41. Irina Paperno has noted two suicide epidemics in the pre-revolutionary period: the 1860s–1880s and again from 1906 to 1914. In the 1880s, she writes, "Suicide was now presented as an annual, seasonal epidemic." See Irina Paperno, *Suicide as a Cultural Institution in Dostoevsky's Russia* (Ithaca, NY: Cornell University Press, 1997), 77.

42. Irina Paperno, *Chernyshevsky and the Age of Realism: A Study in the Semiotics of Behavior* (Stanford, CA: Stanford University Press, 1988), 88.

43. V. P. Kupchenko, "F. Dostoevskii i M. Voloshin," in *Dostoevskii: materialy i issledovaniia*, vol. 8, ed. G. M. Fridlender (Leningrad: Nauka, 1988), 213–14.

44. S. Andreevskii, "Brat'ia Karamazovy. Kriticheskii etiud," *Russkii vestnik* 6 (1889): 121.

45. Aleksandr Kugel' [Staryi teatral], "Review of *Idiot*," *Teatr i iskusstvo* 45 (1899): 793.

46. R. Mech, "Zhiteiskie motivy," *Russkii listok* 280 (October 13, 1899): 2.

47. Prozaik, "Khronika teatra i iskusstva. Malyi teatr," *Teatr i iskusstvo* 41 (1899): 712.

48. Michael Holquist, *Dostoevsky and the Novel* (Princeton, NJ: Princeton University Press, 1977), 102.

49. "Ia. P. Pliushchevskii-Pliushchik," *Teatral'naia gazeta* 16 (1916): 7.

50. Petrovskaia and Somina, *Teatral'nyi Peterburg*, 206. The weekly *Teatr i iskusstvo* published the text of the play as an attachment in no. 38 (1900). In nos. 41–42 (1899) it featured illustrations of the production.

51. Osip Dymov, "Dramaticheskie elementy v romanakh Dostoevskogo," *Teatr i iskusstvo* 6 (1900): 120. The essay continued in no. 7 (1900): 138–39 and no. 8 (1900): 159–60.

52. Dymov, "Dramaticheskie elementy," *Teatr i iskusstvo* 6 (1900): 120.

53. Dymov, "Dramaticheskie elementy," *Teatr i iskusstvo* 6 (1900): 120.

54. Dymov, "Dramaticheskie elementy," *Teatr i iskusstvo* 8 (1900): 160.

55. Dymov, "Dramaticheskie elementy," *Teatr i iskusstvo* 7 (1900): 138.

56. Dymov, "Dramaticheskie elementy," *Teatr i iskusstvo* 7 (1900): 139.

57. Ia. A. Del'er, *Prestuplenie i nakazanie. Dramaticheskie stseny v 10 kartinakh, s epilogom. Po romanu F. M. Dostoevskogo* (St. Petersburg: Izd. zhurn. "Teatr i iskusstvo," 1899), 35.

58. See Pl. Krasnov, "Peredelki," *Teatral'naia Rossiia* 2–3 (1905): 28–31.

59. For an illustration of the set design of the Epilogue, see I. A. Suvorov, "Dekoratsiia epiloga," *Teatr i iskusstvo* 42 (1899): 734.

60. Aleksandr Kugel', "Teatral'nye zametki," *Teatr i iskusstvo* 41 (1899): 716.

61. Dymov, "Dramaticheskie elementy," *Teatr i iskusstvo* 8 (1900): 159.

62. For a brief summary of the production, see N. G. Zograf, *Malyi teatr v kontse XIX–nachale XX veka* (Moscow: Nauka, 1966), 232–34.

63. Alpatova's informative article on Komissarzhevsky's 1912 adaptation of *Idiot* for Nezlobin's theater does not address the political or social dimension of this production. See Irina Alpatova, "Vechnoe vo vremennom (o spektakle 'Idiot' v postanovke F. F. Komissarzhevskogo 1912 g.)," in *Dostoevskii i mirovaia kul'tura*, ed. K. A. Stepanian (Moscow: Klassika plius, 1997), 256.

64. These scripts were accessed at Sankt-peterburgskaia gosudarstvennaia teatral'naia biblioteka (SPbGTB), Otdel redkoi knigi, rukopisnykh, arkhivnykh i izobrazitel'nykh materialov (ORiRK): A. I. Leman, *Idiot. Drama v 4 deistviiakh. (Iz romana F. M. Dostoevskogo)* (1889), access number: 23145, rukopisnyi tekst, L 440; A. G. Kraseva, *Idiot. Drama v 5 deistviiakh i 7 kartinakh, peredelannaia dlia stseny iz romana Dostoevskogo* (1890), access number: 30435, rukopisnyi tekst, K 780; N. Sténson, *Rytsar' bednyi. Dramaticheskie stseny v 5 deistviiakh v 6 kartinakh. Soch. N. Sténson* (Peredelano iz romana F. M. Dostoevskogo) (1893), access number: 45455, rukopisnyi tekst, S 887; L. V. Platonov, *Kniaz' Myshkin. Drama v 5 deistviiakh. (Peredelka romana F. M. Dostoevskogo "Idiot")* (1895), access number: 40567, rukopisnyi tekst, P 375; N. Mirovich, *Rytsar' bednyi. Dramaticheskie stseny v 5 deistviiakh v 6 kartinakh. Soch. N. Sténson* (Peredelano iz romana F. M. Dostoevskogo) (1899), access number: 69562, rukopisnyi tekst, M 640.

65. See B. V. Varneke, *History of the Russian Theatre*, trans. Boris Brasol (New York: Hafner, 1971), 374–78. Ermolova was in her late forties. Some critics believed that she was not an ideal choice to play the twenty-five-year-old Nastasya Filippovna. For the play's Petersburg premiere on November 4 at the Aleksandrinka, Mariia Savina played the lead, with the young Vera Komissarzhevskaya in the role of Aglaia.

66. Aleksandr Kugel' and V. Filippov, eds., *Sto let Malomu teatru, 1824–1924* (Moscow: Russkoe teatral'noe obshchestvo, 1924), 10.

67. T. I. Ornatskaia and G. V. Stepanova, "Romany Dostoevskogo i dramaticheskaia tsenzura (60-e gody XIX v.–nachalo XX v.)," in *Dostoevskii. Materialy i issledovaniia*, vol. 1, ed. G. M. Fridlender (Leningrad: Nauka, 1974), 276.

68. "Teatr i muzyka," *Sankt-peterburgskaia viedomosti* 304 (November 6/18, 1899): 4.

69. Impressionist, "Teatr i muzyka," *Novosti i birzhevaia gazeta* 276 (October 6/18, 1899): 3.

70. Robin Feuer Miller, *Dostoevsky and* The Idiot: *Author, Narrator and Reader* (Cambridge, MA: Harvard University Press, 1981).

71. V. I. Nemirovich-Danchenko, *Tvorcheskoe nasledie v chetyrekh tomakh*, vol. 2 (Moscow: Izd. MAT, 2003), 19.

72. Ornatskaia and Stepanova, "Romany Dostoevskogo i dramaticheskaia tsenzura," 279.

73. V. Krylov and G. [sic] Sutugin, *Idiot. Drama v 5 deistviiakh, peredelannaia iz romana M. F. [sic] Dostoevskogo, Stsena*, vyp. 7 (1899), 83–84.

74. I–t., "Teatr i muzyka," *Russkaia viedomosti* 283 (October 13, 1899): 3.

75. Osip Dymov, "Review of *The Idiot*," *Teatr i iskusstvo* 46 (1899): 811. In Krylov's playscript, shortly after Nastasya Filippovna throws the packet of money into the fire at her party, Myshkin utters the lines, "Let the money burn. It's nothing. Just let the money burn; only harm comes from it . . ." Krylov and Sutugin, *Idiot*, 70.

76. Zinaida Gippius, "Dve dramy A. Tolstogo," *Mir iskusstva* 5 (1899): 34.

77. M. Iuzhnyi, "K postanovke tragedii 'Tsar′ Fedor Ioannovich,'" *Teatr i iskusstvo* 42 (1898): 748. Orlenev, who played Raskolnikov in Del′er's *Crime and Punishment*, had been offered the role by Krylov and Sutugin, but he declined, saying he was "afraid to replicate Tsar Fedor in Prince Myshkin, for they had so much in common." See P. N. Orlenev, *Zhizn′ i tvorchestvo russkogo aktera Pavla Orleneva opisannye im samim* (Moscow: Academia, 1931), 115. One reviewer even thought that Orlenev's Raskolnikov recalled Tsar Fedor. See N. B. "Teatral′noe ekho," *Peterburgskaia gazeta* 273 (October 5, 1899): 3.

78. Skeptik, "Vslukh," *Grazhdanin* 86 (November 7, 1899): 7. In the Aleksandrinka production, Myshkin was played by R. B. Apollonskii (1862–1928).

79. Robert Hollander, "The Apocalyptic Framework of Dostoevsky's *The Idiot*," *Mosaic* 6 (1974): 123–39.

80. M. Olikov, "Teatr i muzyka," *Russkii listok* 280 (October 13, 1899): 3.

81. Aleksandr Chepurov, *A. P. Chekhov i Aleksandrinskii teatr* (St. Petersburg: Baltiiskie sezony, 2006), 65.

82. Krylov and Sutugin, *Idiot*, 87.

83. Sergei Sutugin, "Mysli o teatre," *Teatr i iskusstvo* 4 (1902): 77.

84. Krylov and Sutugin, *Idiot*, 109–10.

85. Mamont Dal′skii, who played the role of Rogozhin in the Aleksandrinka's production of the play, was apparently so perfect for the part that they removed it from the repertoire when he left the theater. Petrovskaia and Somina, *Teatral′nyi Peterburg*, 184.

86. Krylov and Sutugin, *Idiot*, 111.

87. Burmistrova notes the cribbing of Mitya's lines but not the others identified by me. Burmistrova, "Instsenirovki romanov Dostoevskogo," 110.

88. Re., "Khronika," *Teatr i iskusstvo* 42 (1899): 734.

89. –in., "Pis′ma o sovremennom iskusstve," *Russkaia mysl′* 11 (1899): 204.

90. Novyi, "Teatr i muzyka," *Russkoe slovo* 282 (October 13, 1899): 3.

91. Skeptik, "Vslukh," 8.

92. A. F., "Teatr i muzyka. 'Idiot,'" *Novosti i birzhevaia gazeta* 305 (November 5/17, 1899): 3.

93. Vita Brevis, "Idiot," *Russkii listok* 280 (October 13, 1899): 2.

94. –in, "Pis′ma o sovremennom iskusstve," 204.

2. Rozanov, Merezhkovsky, and the Conjuring of Authorial Fictions, 1899–1903

1. A. L. Volynskii, "Tragediia krasoty. 'Idiot,'" in *Dostoevskii* (St. Petersburg: Obshchestvennaia pol'za, 1909), 24. The essay is dated November–December 1899.

2. Dmitrii Filosofov, "O 'lzhi' Gor'kogo," *Novyi put'* 6 (1903): 215.

3. Zinaida Gippius [Anton Krainyi], "Kharakternoe priznanie," *Novyi put'* 2 (1903): 201. For the original review, see "The Muscovite Genius," *New York Times*, December 6, 1902.

4. A. L. Volynskii, "Sovremennaia russkaia belletristika," in *Kniga velikogo gneva* (St. Petersburg: Trud, 1904), 174.

5. D. S. Merezhkovskii, "'Ottsy i deti' russkogo liberalizma," *Mir iskusstva* 3 (1901): 127.

6. D. S. Merezhkovskii, "Avtobiograficheskaia zametka," in *Polnoe sobranie sochineniia*, vol. 23 (Moscow: Tipografiia I. D. Sytina, 1914), 111. In the same document, Merezhkovsky seems to respond to Dostoevsky's criticism from the perspective of a more confident and self-aware writer: "I am often accused of 'schematism,' or of the 'bookish' quality (*knizhnosti*) of my religious thought. This is untrue, or maybe it comes from the weakness of my literary gift. I can say honestly: everything that I say and think about religious questions comes not from books, nor from other people's thoughts (*chuzhye mysli*), but from my own life. I lived through (*perezhil*) all of this" (114).

7. Merezhkovskii, "Avtobiograficheskaia zametka," 111.

8. On the significance of Merezhkovsky to the reception of both Tolstoy and Dostoevsky, see Chloë Kitzinger, *Mimetic Lives: Tolstoy, Dostoevsky, and Character in the Novel* (Evanston, IL: Northwestern University Press, 2021), 67–68.

9. Merezhkovsky's choice of the word *dukh*, or "spirit," carries with it the sense of historical destiny reminiscent of Hegel's theory of national genius. It is significant that the word appears associated with Dostoevsky, who for Merezhkovsky represents the true future destiny of Russian spirituality.

10. It would later occupy four volumes (nine through twelve) of a total of twenty-four in the 1914 edition of his collected works. For an analysis of the work, see E. A. Andrushchenko, "Iz chego 'sdelana' kniga 'L. Tolstoi i Dostoevskii,'" in *Vlastelin "chuzhogo": tekstologiia i problemy poetiki D. S. Merezhkovskogo* (Moscow: Vodolei, 2012), 80.

11. In contrast to this trend, Mondry has discussed Rozanov's fascination with Tolstoy's "physical Russianness." See Henrietta Mondry, *Vasily Rozanov and the Body of Russian Literature* (Bloomington, IN: Slavica, 2010), 118.

12. On the history of physical anthropology in Russia, see Marina Mogilner, *Homo Imperii: A History of Physical Anthropology in Russia* (Lincoln: University of Nebraska Press, 2013). On the understanding of race in the nineteenth century, see Vera Tolz, "Constructing Race, Ethnicity, and Nationhood in Imperial Russia: Issues and Misconceptions," in *Ideologies of Race: Imperial Russia and the Soviet Union in Global Context*, ed. David Rainbow (Montreal: McGill-Queens University Press, 2019), 29–58.

13. When Rozanov published seditious antisemitic articles during the Beilis affair, his colleagues firmly rebuked him, and Merezhkovsky succeeded in

expelling him from the second instantiation of the Religious-Philosophical Meetings in 1914. On this period, see Laura Engelstein, *Slavophile Empire: Imperial Russia's Illiberal Path* (Ithaca, NY: Cornell University Press, 2009), 198–200. On their entire stormy and often ambivalent relationship, but only from Rozanov's perspective, see A. N. Nikoliukin, *Rozanov* (Moscow: Molodaia gvardiia, 2018), 358–89.

14. Eugene M. Avrutin, *Jews and the Imperial State: Identification Politics in Tsarist Russia* (Ithaca, NY: Cornell University Press, 2010), 10–11. On state policies and antisemitism during this period, see Hans Rogger, *Jewish Policies and Right-Wing Politics in Imperial Russia* (Berkeley: University of California Press, 1986); and John D. Klier, *Imperial Russia's Jewish Question* (Cambridge: Cambridge University Press, 1995).

15. On these issues, see Ann Laura Stoler, "Racial Histories and Their Regimes of Truth," *Political Power and Social Theory* 11 (1997): 183–206; and Nancy Leys Stepan, "Race and Gender: The Role of Analogy in Science," in *The Anatomy of Racism*, ed. David Theo Goldberg (Minneapolis: University of Minnesota Press, 1990), 38–57.

16. For more on Rozanov's later period, see Laura Engelstein, *The Keys to Happiness: Sex and the Search for Happiness in Fin-de-Siècle Russia* (Ithaca, NY: Cornell University Press, 1992): 299–333; Harriet Murav, "The Predatory Jew and Russian Vitalism: Dostoevsky, Rozanov, and Babel," in *Ritual Murder in Russia, Eastern Europe, and Beyond*, ed. Eugene M. Avrutin et al. (Bloomington: Indiana University Press, 2017), 151–57; Olga Matich, *Erotic Utopia: The Decadent Imagination in Russia's Fin de Siècle* (Madison: University of Wisconsin Press, 2005), 236–73; Edith Clowes, *Fiction's Overcoat: Russian Literary Culture and the Question of Philosophy* (Ithaca, NY: Cornell University Press, 2018), 155–81; and Mondry, *Vasily Rozanov*.

17. Mondry, *Vasily Rozanov*, 79–100.

18. V. V. Rozanov, "Mesto khristianstva v istorii," in *Religiia i kul'tura* (St. Petersburg: Tipografiia M. Merkusheva, 1901), 5. This argument is likely inspired by Renan. See Ernest Renan, *History of the People of Israel Till the Time of King David* (London: Chapman and Hall, 1888), 41.

19. Quoted in E. F. Gollerbakh, *V. V. Rozanov: zhizn' i tvorchestvo* (St. Petersburg: Poliarnaia Zvezda, 1922), 29.

20. For a concise overview of the historical use of these terms in Russia, see Vera Tolz [Tol'ts], "Diskursy o *rase*: imperskaia Rossiia i Zapad v sravnenii," in *"Poniatiia o Rossii": k istoricheskoi semantike imperskogo perioda*, vol. 2, ed. I. A. Miller et al. (Moscow: NLO, 2012), 146–93.

21. V. V. Rozanov, "Legenda o Velikom inkvizitore F. M. Dostoevskogo," *Russkii vestnik* 1–4 (1891). It appeared in book form in 1894.

22. Rozanov's biographer Fateev dates Rozanov's growing critique of Christianity to around 1897, when he left this circle. See V. A. Fateev, *V. V. Rozanov: zhizn', tvorchestvo, lichnost'* (Leningrad: Khudozhestvennaia literatura, 1991), 63.

23. On Rozanov's interest in ancient Egypt, see Adam Ure, *Vasilii Rozanov and the Creation: The Edenic Vision and the Rejection of Eschatology* (London: Continuum, 2011): 103–32. See also Lada Panova, *Russkii Egipet: Aleksandriiskaia poetika Mikhaila Kuzmina*, vol. 1 (Moscow: Progress-Pleiada, 2006), 141.

24. Apart from the connection to Egypt, there is some basis for Rozanov's interpretation here. Dostoevsky was known to have been influenced by the philosopher Nikolai Fedorov's (1829–1903) theories about the resurrection of the dead. On Fedorov, see Svetlana Semenova, *Nikolai Fedorov: Tvorchestvo zhizni* (Moscow: Sovetskii pisatel', 1990).

25. Andrei Belyi [Boris Bugaev], "Na perevale," *Vesy* 1 (1906): 69.

26. Svidrigailov appears in Rozanov's essay on *The Legend of the Grand Inquisitor*, but without Semitic spiritual characteristics (48–49); see also V. V. Rozanov, "Iz zagadok chelovesheskoi prirody," in *V mire neiasnogo i nereshennogo* (St. Petersburg: Tipografiia M. Merkusheva, 1901), 15.

27. Dostoevskii, *Pss*, vol. 6, 221. My translation.

28. For the most recent of these, see Donna Orwin, "Achilles in *Crime and Punishment*," in *Dostoevsky Beyond Dostoevsky: Science, Religion, Philosophy*, ed. Svetlana Evdokimova and Vladimir Golstein (Boston: Academic Studies, 2019), 367–78.

29. V. V. Rozanov, "O drevne-egipetskoi krasote," *Mir iskusstva* 16–17 (1899): 29. This passage has been wonderfully analyzed by Mondry with special attention to what Semiticization here says about Rozanov's early fondness for Jews and the closeness he felt to his idol, Dostoevsky. See Mondry, *Vasily Rozanov*, 97–98.

30. V. V. Rozanov, "Iz vostochnykh motivov," in *Sobranie sochineniia*, vol. 10, *Vo dvore iazychnikov*, ed. A. N. Nikoliukin (Moscow: Respublika, 1999), 185. First published as "Zvezdy," *Mir iskusstva* 7–8 (1901): 69–78.

31. Rozanov, "Iz vostochnykh motivov," 186.

32. See V. V. Rozanov, "Kontsy i nachala, 'bozhestvennoe' i 'demonicheskoe,' bogi i demony (Po povodu glavnogo siuzheta Lermontova)," *Mir iskusstva* 8 (1902): 122–37.

33. Zinaida Gippius, "Khleb zhizni," *Mir iskusstva* 11–12 (1901): 331. Elsewhere, Gippius wrote contemptuously of Rozanov's defense of practices of the Jewish faith, especially the ritual bath known as the mikvah. She wrote, "Rozanov's religious thirst must be great if he resolves to quench it even at such a stream," likening him to the Eternal Jew. Zinaida Gippius [A. Krainyi], "Vechnyi zhid," *Novyi put'* 9 (1903): 243. In the minutes of the Religious-Philosophical Meetings published in *Novyi put'*, Merezhkovsky asked provocatively, "I'm interested to know—who is this eternal Rozanov for? For Christ or against Christ?" See "Zapiski religioznykh-filosofskikh sobranii v S.-Peterburge. Zasedanie XVI. (Okonchanie prenii o brake)," *Novyi put'* 10 (1903): 383. Gippius devoted an entire chapter to Rozanov in her memoirs. See Zinaida Gippius, *Stikhotvoreniia. Zhivye litsa*, ed. N. A. Bogomolov (Moscow: Khudozhestvennaia literatura, 1991), 314–60.

34. Zinaida Gippius [A. Krainyi], "Byt i sobytiia," *Novyi put'* 9 (1904): 280.

35. M. Iu. Koreneva, ed., "Pis'ma D. S. Merezhkovskogo k P. P. Pertsovu," *Russkaia literatura* 2 (1991): 164.

36. L. Sh. [Lev Shestov], "Dostoevskii i Nitshe. (Filosofiia tragedii.). Predislovie," *Mir iskusstva* 2 (1902): 69–79.

37. Most personal of all, Volynsky had had a romantic relationship with Gippius, Merezhkovsky's spouse.

38. A. L. Volynskii, *Tsarstvo Karamazovykh. N. S. Leskov. Zametki.* (St. Petersburg: Tipografiia M. M. Stasiulevicha, 1901), 203.

39. A. L. Volynskii, *Bor'ba za idealizm* (St. Petersburg: Tipografiia M. Merkusheva, 1900), iii.

40. A. L. Volynskii, "O simvolizme i simvolistakh. (Polemicheskaia zametka)," in *Bor'ba za idealizm*, 482.

41. Volynskii, "Sovremennaia russkaia belletristika," 172. An essay with the same name but different content appears in *Bor'ba za idealizm*.

42. Volynskii, "Sovremennaia russkaia belletristika," 174.

43. See Robert Louis Jackson, *Dostoevsky's Quest for Form* (New Haven, CT: Yale University Press, 1966).

44. Volynskii, "Sovremennaia russkaia belletristika," 175.

45. Volynskii, "Sovremennaia russkaia belletristika," 173.

46. V. V. Rozanov, "A. L. Volynskii. F. M. Dostoevskii," *Kriticheskoe obozrenie* 5 (1909): 40.

47. Volynskii, *Kniga velikogo gneva*, 378.

48. Volynskii, *Kniga velikogo gneva*, 378–79.

49. Volynskii, *Kniga velikogo gneva*, 379.

50. See P. Pertsov, "Venetsianskaia shkola zhivopisi," *Novyi put'* 9 (1903): 24. Pertsov describes the prophet as "the true biblical patriarch" and "the shepherd of the peoples."

51. D. S. Merezhkovskii, *O prichinakh upadka i o novykh techeniiakh sovremennoi russkoi literatury* (St. Peterburg: Tipo-Litografiia B. M. Vol'fa, 1893), 33.

52. Merezhkovskii, *O prichinakh upadka*, 33.

53. M. Iu. Koreneva, ed., "Pis'ma D. S. Merezhkovskogo k P. P. Pertsovu (pt. 2)," *Russkaia literatura* 3 (1991): 142–43. The phrase "about that" could also refer to Myshkin's direct speech in *The Idiot*. See Dostoevskii, *Pss*, vol. 8, 184, 221.

54. D. S. Merezhkovskii, "Lev Tolstoi i Dostoevskii. Zakliuchenie," *Mir iskusstva* 2 (1902): 121. This installment of the book was later revised and became the introduction of the second volume of the completed book.

55. D. S. Merezhkovskii, "O novom religioznom deistvii (otkrytoe pis'mo N. A. Berdiaevu)," *Voprosy zhizni* 10–11 (1905): 361.

56. Koreneva, "Pis'ma D. S. Merezhkovskogo k P. P. Pertsovu (pt. 2)," 147.

57. V. V. Rozanov, "Pis'mo v redaktsiiu," *Mir iskusstva* 15–16 (1900): 64. This letter appeared around the same time as a longer, more nuanced review in *Novoe vremia* of Merezhkovsky's book, which could be the origin of the latter's developing tendency to frame Tolstoy as "Semitic." Merezhkovsky was not entirely alone in framing Tolstoy as culturally aligned with the Judaic tradition. In 1903, Sergei Bulgakov briefly acknowledged Tolstoy's affinity with the prophets of Judaism and isolated two kinds of idealism in Russia: an ethical one (Tolstoy, Socrates, Kant) and a platonic one (Plato, Soloviev, Hegel, Dostoevsky). By this distinction, Bulgakov is tending toward Merezhkovsky's strategy of aligning Tolstoy with nonreligious, rational forms of knowledge and arguing for Dostoevsky's fundamentally spiritual life philosophy. Cf. S. N. Bulgakov, *Ot marksizma k idealizmu. Sbornik statei (1896–1903)* (St. Petersburg: Obshchestvennaia pol'za, 1903), xix–xx.

58. The lecture was later published as part of *L. Tolstoi and Dostoevskii* with a different chapter heading: D. S. Merezhkovskii, "Khristianstvo L. Tolstogo," *Mir iskusstva* 6 (1901): 289–318. For Merezhkovsky's response to the blowback, see Merezhkovskii, "'Ottsy i deti' russkogo liberalizma."

59. V. V. Rozanov, "Seriia nedorazumenii," *Novoe vremia* 8970, February 16, 1901.

60. A giant *bogatyr* from Russian folk epics, who finds a heavy saddlebag and, failing to lift it, sinks into the earth.

61. V. V. Rozanov, "Novaia rabota o Tolstom i Dostoevskom," in Nikoliukin, *Sobranie sochineniia*, vol. 27, *Iudaizm, Stat'i i ocherki, 1898–1901* (1999), 494.

62. See D. S. Merezhkovskii, "Glava vtoraia. L. Tolstoi i Dostoevskii, kak khudozhniki," *Mir iskusstva* 17–18 (1900): 71–84.

63. D. S. Merezhkovskii, *L. Tolstoi i Dostoevskii*, ed. E. A. Andrushchenko (Moscow: Nauka, 2000), 130. All translations are mine.

64. In nineteenth-century usage, *plemia* (tribe) was employed interchangeably with the more recent term *rasa* (race). For a discussion of terminology and epistemologies of race in Russia, see Karl Hall, "'Rasovye priznaki koreniatsia glubzhe v prirode chelovecheskogo organizma': neulovimoe poniatie *rasy* v Rossiiskoi imperii," trans. V. S. Dubinaia, in *"Poniatiia o Rossii"*, vol. 2, 194–258.

65. V. V. Rozanov, "Malen'kaia istoricheskaia popravka," in Nikoliukin, *Ss*, vol. 10, 151.

66. Tolstoy was an outspoken advocate for the Jews. He had studied Arabic and Turkic languages at university in Kazan, and toward the end of his life he became more interested in Buddhism. Merezhkovsky's strategy may have been to racially identify Tolstoy with peoples and worldviews with which Tolstoy himself was sympathetic.

67. Volynskii, "Tragediia krasoty. 'Idiot,'" in *Dostoevskii*, 24.

68. Merezhkovskii, *L. Tolstoi i Dostoevskii*, 210.

69. Merezhkovskii, *L. Tolstoi i Dostoevskii*, 346, 378, 424.

70. The phrase "consuming fire" also appears in Deuteronomy 4:24 and Isaiah 33:14.

71. Merezhkovsky makes direct reference to the Book of Deuteronomy in the first reference to this biblical verse. See Merezhkovskii, *L. Tolstoi i Dostoevskii*, 83.

72. Merezhkovskii, *L. Tolstoi i Dostoevskii*, 465.

73. Merezhkovskii, *L. Tolstoi i Dostoevskii*, 474. By *"zhidovstvuiushchii,"* Merezhkovsky refers to the so-called Judaizing heresy of fifteenth-century Novgorod. It is used elsewhere in the book (see also Merezhkovskii, *L. Tolstoi i Dostoevskii*, 28, 148). For a summary of this heresy and its relationship to modern antisemitism, see Charles J. Halperin, "Judaizers and the Image of the Jew in Medieval Russia: A Polemic Revisited and a Question Posed," *Canadian-American Slavic Studies* 9 (1975): 141–55.

74. Maksim Gor'kii, *Kniga o russkikh liudiakh* (Moscow: Vagrius, 2000), 483. Quoted and translated in Inessa Medzhibovskaia, ed., "Tolstoy's Jewish Problems," in *Tolstoy and His Problems: Views from the Twenty-First Century* (Evanston, IL: Northwestern University Press, 2019), 133–34. Thank you to Susan McReynolds for pointing this out to me.

75. See D. S. Merezhkovskii, "Zheltolitsye pozitivisty," *Vestnik inostrannoi literatury* 3 (1895): 71–84. On the interrelationship of Jewish and Asian stereotypes, see Henrietta Mondry, *"Petersburg* and Contemporary Racial Thought," in *A Reader's Guide to Andrei Bely's* Petersburg, ed. Leonid Livak (Madison: University of Wisconsin Press, 2019), 134–35. On this period's apocalyptic anti-Asianism, see Susanna

Soojung Lim, "Pan-Mongolians at Twilight: East Asia and Race in Russian Modernism, 1890–1921," in *Race and Racism in Modern East Asia: Western and Eastern Constructions*, ed. Rotem Kowner and Walter Demel (Leiden: Brill, 2013), 154–75.

76. Merezhkovskii, *L. Tolstoi i Dostoevskii*, 317.

77. Stepan, "Race and Gender," 47.

78. Klier, *Imperial Russia's Jewish Question*, 396–403.

79. Merezhkovskii, *L. Tolstoi i Dostoevskii*, 133.

80. Made explicit in the references to Eroshka's Old Testament faith. See Merezhkovskii, *L. Tolstoi i Dostoevskii*, 315, 349.

81. N. M. Mikhailovskii, "Literatura i zhizn'," *Russkoe bogatstvo* 8 (1902): 99. Rozanov defended Merezhkovsky's assault on Tolstoy, vouching for his friend's private reverence for the novelist. See V. V. Rozanov, "Zametka o Merezhkovskom," in Nikoliukin, *Sobranie sochineniia*, vol. 7, *Legenda o velikom inkvizitore* (1996), 446–47. Merezhkovsky's novel *Peter and Alexis* includes many allusions to Jews. See D. S. Merezhkovskii, *Antikhrist: Petr i Aleksei* (St. Petersburg: Izd. M. B. Pirozhkova, 1905). Jewish characteristics are attributed to the new Western-style wigs adopted in Peter's Russia (75) and are associated with Peter himself in his guise as the Antichrist (57–60, 427, 468). These examples link Westernization with Jewishness as threats to native Russianness and authentic faith.

82. N. M. Mikhailovskii, "Literatura i zhizn'," *Russkoe bogatstvo* 9 (1902): 46. Another reviewer objected only to the irreverence and "pettiness" shown to Tolstoy in Merezhkovsky's book. See A. B., "Kriticheskie zametki," *Mir Bozhii* 11 (1901): 1–14.

83. Mikhailovskii, "Literatura i zhizn'," *Russkoe bogatstvo* 9 (1902): 49–50.

84. V. V. Rozanov, "Tema nashego vremeni," in Nikoliukin, *Sobranie sochineniia*, vol. 10, *Vo dvore iazychnikov* (1999), 167.

85. Rozanov, "Tema nashego vremeni," 168.

86. V. V. Rozanov, "Sredi inoiazychnykh. (D. S. Merezhkovskii)," *Mir iskusstva* 7–8 (1903): 70.

87. V. V. Rozanov, *Mimoletnoe. 1915 god*, in Nikoliukin, *Sobranie sochineniia*, vol. 2, *Mimoletnoe* (1994), 49.

88. Koreneva, "Pis'ma D. S. Merezhkovskogo k P. P. Pertsovu (pt. 2)," 133.

89. Koreneva, "Pis'ma D. S. Merezhkovskogo k P. P. Pertsovu (pt. 2)," 136. Dixon's comprehensive essay surveys Rozanov's own reception of Peter as a historical figure despite his ties to the conservative camp and his ideological Slavophilism; I suspect Rozanov's positive reception of Peter is a result of Merezhkovsky's influence. See Simon Dixon, "Rozanov's Peter," in *Word and Image in Russian History*, ed. Maria di Salvo, Daniel H. Kaiser, and Valerie A. Kivelson (Boston: Academic Studies, 2019), 172–90.

3. Idealist Critics and the Reign of Character over Author, 1901–1905

1. Konstantin Bal'mont, "O russkikh poetakh," in *Gornye vershiny. Sbornik statei* (Moscow: Grif, 1904), 61.

2. See also his 1906 lecture on the twenty-fifth anniversary of Dostoevsky's death: S. N. Bulgakov, "Venets ternovyi (Pamiati F. M. Dostoevskogo)," *Svoboda i kul'tura* 1 (1906): 17–36.

3. Vladimir Zakharov, "Paradoksy priznaniia: problema 'traditsii Dostoevskogo' v kul'ture XX veka," in *Dostoevsky and the Twentieth Century: The Ljubljana Papers*, ed. Malcolm V. Jones (Nottingham, UK: Astra, 1993), 21.

4. P. I. Novgorodtsev, "Foreword to the Russian Edition," in *Problems of Idealism: Essays in Russian Social Philosophy*, ed. and trans. Randall A. Poole (New Haven, CT: Yale University Press, 2003), 83.

5. Novgorodtsev, "Foreword to the Russian Edition," 83.

6. Glinka's work on Dostoevsky paralleled Bulgakov's investigations. See Volzhskii [A. S. Glinka], *Dva ocherka ob Uspenskom i Dostoevskom* (St. Petersburg: Tipografiia M. M. Stasiulevicha, 1902), as well as his longer essay, "Religiozno-nravstvennaia problema u Dostoevskogo," *Mir Bozhii* 6: 161–78; 7: 109–32; 8: 137–60 (1905). See also A. I. Reznichenko, "'Zhizn' i tvorchestvo F. M. Dostoevskogo' A. S. Glinka-Volzhskogo: iz istorii odnogo 'nesbyvshegosia sobytiia,'" in *F. M. Dostoevskii i kul'tura Serebrianogo veka: traditsii, traktovki, transformatsii*, ed. Elena Takho-Godi et al. (Moscow: Vodolei, 2012), 249–66.

7. Vladimir Lenin, who was among their main opponents, referred to Bulgakov and his colleagues as "legal Marxists." I avoid that moniker and call them instead "idealists." For a history of their activity as "legal Marxists," see Richard Kindersley, *The First Russian Revisionists: A Study of "Legal Marxism" in Russia* (Oxford: Clarendon, 1962).

8. S. N. Bulgakov, "Ivan Karamazov kak filosofskii tip," in *Ot marksizma k idealizmu. Sbornik statei (1896–1903)* (St. Petersburg: Obshchestvennaia pol'za, 1903), 85.

9. For a history of the group, see Randall A. Poole, *The Moscow Psychological Society and the Neo-Idealist Development of Russian Liberalism, 1885–1922* (PhD dissertation, University of Notre Dame, 1996).

10. Randall A. Poole, "The Neo-Idealist Reception of Kant in the Moscow Philosophical Society," *Journal of the History of Ideas* 60, no. 2 (April 1999): 320. See also Leszek Kołakowski, *The Alienation of Reason: A History of Positivist Thought* (Garden City, NY: Doubleday, 1968).

11. Bulgakov, "Ivan Karamazov kak filosofskii tip," 108.

12. Volzhskii [A. S. Glinka], "Avtobiograficheskie zapiski," in *Ss v trekh knigakh*, kn. 1, ed. Anna Reznichenko (Moscow: Modest Kolerov, 2005), 729.

13. D. S. Merezhkovskii, "Vse protiv vsekh," *Zolotoe runo* 1 (1906): 93–94.

14. Nikolai Berdiaev [Nicholas Berdyaev], *Dream and Reality: An Essay in Autobiography*, trans. Katherine Lampert (New York: Macmillan, 1951), 67. See also Donald A. Lowrie, *Rebellious Prophet: A Life of Nicolai Berdyaev* (Westport, CT: Greenwood, 1974), 25.

15. F. M. Dostoevskii, *Polnoe sobranie sochinenii*, vol. 27, ed. G. M. Fridlender et al. (Leningrad: Nauka, 1972–90), 24. This passage is quoted in S. N. Bulgakov, "Vasnetsov, Dostoevskii, Vl. Solov'ev, Tolstoi. (Paralleli)," in *Literaturnoe delo. Sbornik* (St. Petersburg: Tipografiia A. E. Kolpinskogo, 1902), 138; and Volzhskii [A. S. Glinka], "Torzhestvuiushchii amoralizm (Po povodu 'Russkogo Fausta' A. Lunacharskogo)," *Voprosy filosofii i psikhologii*, kn. 4, no. 64 (1902): 897–98.

16. Berdiaev uses Ivan's words as an epigraph in "O novom russkom idealizme," first published in 1904 and later included in *Sub specie aeternitatis. Opyty*

filosofskie, sotsial'nye i literaturnye (1900–1906 g.) (St. Petersburg: Izdanie M. V. Pirozhkova, 1907).

17. V. V. Rozanov, *Legenda o velikom inkvizitore F. M. Dostoevskogo. Opyt kriticheskogo kommentariia* (St. Petersburg: Tipo-litografiia i notopechatnia S. M. Nikolaeva, 1894), 11.

18. Nikolai Grot, "Eshche o zadachakh zhurnala," *Voprosy filosofii i psikhologii*, no. 2, kn. 6 (1891): v–vi. Grot's fondness for Dostoevsky was noted in memoir accounts of him published after his death. See D. V. Viktorov, "Pamiati N. Ia. Grota kak professora," in *Nikolai Iakovlevich Grot: v ocherkakh, vospominaniiakh i pis'makh tovarishchei i uchenikov, druzei i pochitatelei* (St. Petersburg: Tipografiia Ministerstva Putei Soobshcheniia, 1911), 182.

19. Vladimir Solov'ev, "Russkii natsional'nyi ideal (Po povodu stat'i N. Ia Grota v 'Voprosakh Filosofii i Psikhologii')," in *Sobranie sochinenii*, vol. 5 (St. Petersburg: Obshchestvennaia pol'za, 1901), 382.

20. Solov'ev, "Russkii natsional'nyi ideal," 382.

21. Solov'ev, "Russkii natsional'nyi ideal," 383.

22. Bulgakov, "Ivan Karamazov kak filosofskii tip," 106.

23. S. N. Bulgakov, "Chto daet sovremennomu soznaniiu filosofiia Vl. Solov'eva" (pt. 2 of 2), *Voprosy filosofii i psikhologii*, kn. 2, no. 67 (1903): 156–61. The distinction between right and left Slavophilism was likely nurtured by Soloviev as part of his own break with conservative Slavophilism and his writings on nationalism. We see the same understanding without reference to Dostoevsky in Nikolai Berdiaev, "Filosofiia i zhizn'," *Novyi put'* 12 (1904): 323–33.

24. Shestov later noted Berdiaev's remarkable tolerance for writers ordinarily unexamined because of their feared rightist tendencies (such as Leontiev, to whom Berdiaev dedicated an important essay). See L. Sh. [Lev Shestov], "Pokhvala gluposti," in *Fakely*, kn. 2, ed. Georgii Chulkov (St. Petersburg: Izdanie D. K. Tikhomirova, 1907), 146.

25. Dostoevskii, *Pss*, vol. 26, 147.

26. Berdiaev, "O novom russkom idealizme," 158.

27. Dmitrii Filosofov, "Propoved' idealizma," *Novyi put'* 10 (1903): 177–84.

28. Liza Knapp, *The Annihilation of Inertia: Dostoevsky and Metaphysics* (Evanston, IL: Northwestern University Press, 1996), 7–8.

29. Joseph Frank, *Dostoevsky*, vol. 5 (Princeton, NJ: Princeton University Press, 1976–2002), 427.

30. For a summary of the immediate critical reception of the novel, see Dostoevskii, *Pss*, vol. 15, 487–512; see also V. B. Smirnov, *F. M. Dostoevskii i russkaia demokraticheskaia zhurnalistika 70–80-kh godov* (Volgograd: Izdatel'stvo Volgogradskogo gos. universiteta, 1996).

31. This interpretation of Ivan as Dostoevsky's mouthpiece was settled privately by the author himself. In a letter to his editor Liubimov in May 1879, Dostoevsky wrote about book 5, "That is *his* language, *his* words, *his* pathos, *and not mine*" (*Pss*, vol. 2, 45). However, later on, his daughter wrote that "according to stories spread in the family, my father depicted himself in Ivan Karamazov." Liubov' Dostoevskaia, *Dostoevskii v izobrazhenii ego docheri*, trans. L. Ia. Krukovskaia, ed. A. G. Gornfel'd (Moscow: Gosudarstvennoe izdatel'stvo, 1922), 18. For a summary of the critical tradition that identified Ivan's views with the

Grand Inquisitor (and with the author himself), see Robert Belknap, *The Genesis of* The Brothers Karamazov (Evanston, IL: Northwestern University Press, 1990), 127–57.

32. Dostoevskii, *Pss*, vol. 1, 63. There is a mistake in Joseph Frank's rendering of this passage. Frank pluralizes "my hero" and so his English translation confusingly shifts the focus from Ivan. See Frank, *Dostoevsky*, 5: 428. This mistake carries over in Joseph Frank, *Dostoevsky: A Writer in His Time* (Princeton, NJ: Princeton University Press, 2009), 789.

33. Dostoevskii, *Pss*, vol. 1, 63.

34. In a letter to Dostoevsky, Pobedonostsev expressed his fear that "The Grand Inquisitor" was too convincing. K. P. Pobedonostsev to F. M. Dostoevskii, Petergof, August 16, 1879, in L. Averbakh, ed., *Literaturnoe nasledstvo*, vol. 15 (Moscow: Zhurnal'no-gazetnoe ob"edinenie, 1934), 139–40.

35. The essay was written prior to Dostoevsky's death and published with a brief concluding note acknowledging the writer's recent passing.

36. S. Vengerov, "Dostoevskii i prichiny ego populiarnosti v poslednie gody," in *Otklik. Literaturnyi sbornik. V pol'zu studentov i slushatel'nits vysshikh zhenskikh kursov goroda SPb* (St. Petersburg: Tipografiia A. S. Suvorina, 1881), 279.

37. L. E. Obolenskii [N. N.], "Literaturnye tipy," *Svet* 9 (1879): 96–105.

38. Dostoevskii, *Pss*, vol. 15, 492.

39. Rozanov, *Legenda o velikom inkvizitore F. M. Dostoevskogo*, 172–73.

40. B. A. Filippov, ed., *Konstantin Leont'ev. Pis'ma k Vasiliiu Rozanovu* (London: Nina Karsov, 1981), 39.

41. K. Leont'ev, *Nashi novye khristiane. F. M. Dostoevskii i gr. Lev Tolstoi* (Moscow: Tipografiia E. I. Pogodinoi, 1882), 30. See also Glenn Cronin, *Disenchanted Wanderer: The Apocalyptic Vision of Konstantin Leontiev* (Ithaca, NY: Cornell University Press, 2021), 154–56.

42. Soloviev's short response to Leontiev provides a good summary of his understanding of the legitimate Christian foundations of Dostoevsky's "universal brotherhood." See Vladimir Solov'ev, "Prilozhenie. Zametka v zashchitu Dostoevskogo ot obvineniia v 'novom' khristianstve," in *Tri rechi v pamiat' Dostoevskogo (1881–1883 gg.)* (Moscow: V Universitetskoi tipografii na Strastnom bul'vare (M. Katkov), 1884).

43. Shestov and Merezhkovsky wrote nuanced comparative studies of Nietzsche and Dostoevsky (examined in chapter 2), paving the way for Marxist critiques, such as M. Kheisin, "Dostoevskii i Nittsshe," *Mir Bozhii* 5 (1903): 119–41. Minei Leont'evich Kheisin (1871–1924) was a contributor to Lenin's illegal newspaper *Iskra*.

44. The lecture was soon afterward published in the Philosophical Society's journal, *Questions of Philosophy and Psychology*. We find similar titles elsewhere in Bulgakov's writings, such as "The Spiritual Drama of Alexander Herzen" (1902) and "Karl Marx as a Religious Type" (1907), each of which sought to subject the epistemological development of a thinker to diagnostic criteria of belief.

45. Catherine Evtuhov, *The Cross and the Sickle: Sergei Bulgakov and the Fate of Russian Religious Philosophy* (Ithaca, NY: Cornell University Press, 1997), 49; see also 49–50 and 60–64.

46. Bulgakov, "Ivan Karamazov kak filosofskii tip," 84–85.

47. Vanessa Rampton, *Liberal Ideas in Tsarist Russia: From Catherine the Great to the Russian Revolution* (Cambridge: Cambridge University Press, 2020), 92.

48. A. Lunacharskii, "O g. Volzhskom i ego idealakh," *Obrazovanie* 5 (1904): 111.

49. Filosofov, "Propoved' idealizma," 178.

50. A. B. "Kriticheskie zametki," *Mir Bozhii* 2 (1903): 4.

51. N. K. Krupskaia, *Vospominaniia o Lenine* (Moscow: Partizdat, 1933), 48. This meeting is summarized in Richard Pipes, *Struve: Liberal on the Left, 1870–1905*, vol. 1 (Cambridge, MA: Harvard University Press, 1970), 313.

52. Bulgakov, "Ivan Karamazov kak filosofskii tip," 109.

53. Regula M. Zwahlen, "Sergei Bulgakov's Intellectual Journey, 1900–1922," in *The Oxford Handbook of Russian Religious Thought*, ed. Caryl Emerson, George Pattison, and Randall A. Poole (Oxford: Oxford University Press, 2020), 280. On Bulgakov's liberal approach to Orthodoxy, see Regula M. Zwahlen, "Sergii Bulgakov's Reinvention of Theocracy for a Democratic Age," *Journal of Orthodox Christian Studies* 3, no. 2 (2020): 175–94. See also Berdiaev's letter to Struve, dated September 29, 1901, in M. A. Kolerov, ed., *Iznutri: Pis'ma Berdiaeva, Bulgakova, Novgorodtseva i Franka k Struve* (Moscow: Izdanie knizhnogo magazina 'Tsiolkovskii,' 2018), 40. For a summary of the beginnings of Russian revisionism, see Shmuel Galai, *The Liberation Movement in Russia 1900–1905* (Cambridge: Cambridge University Press, 1973), 74–83. Reflecting his focus on moral concerns, Bulgakov several years later defined political economy as the "ethics of economic life." See S. N. Bulgakov, "Ob ekonomicheskom ideale," *Nauchnoe slovo* 5 (1903): 103.

54. Evtuhov, *The Cross and the Sickle*, 31. See also George F. Putnam, *Russian Alternatives to Marxism* (Knoxville: University of Tennessee Press, 1977), 47.

55. Even as late as his 1931 essay, "Russian Religious Psychology and Communistic Atheism," Berdiaev claimed that Russian atheism is a fundamentally religious psychology typified by Ivan Karamazov. See Nikolai Berdiaev, *The Russian Revolution*, trans. D. B. (London: Sheed & Ward, 1933), 14.

56. Albert Camus, *Notebooks: 1935–1942*, vol. 1, trans. Philip Thody (New York: Knopf, 1963), 225.

57. S. N. Bulgakov, "O realisticheskom mirovozzrenie," *Voprosy filosofii i psikhologii*, kn. 3, no. 73 (May–June 1904): 391.

58. Nikolai Berdiaev, "O realizme. (Vmesto predisloviia)," in *Sub specie aeternitatis*, 4.

59. See Ruth Coates, "Feuerbach, Kant, Dostoevskii: The Evolution of 'Heroism' and 'Asceticism' in Bulgakov's Work to 1909," in *Landmarks Revisited: The Vekhi Symposium One Hundred Years On*, ed. Robin Aizlewood and Ruth Coates (Boston: Academic Studies, 2013), 292.

60. Bulgakov considered theodicy an inevitable stage in all individual philosophical development. See Bulgakov, "Ivan Karamazov kak filosofskii tip," 98. He makes a similar point in "Ob ekonomicheskom ideale," 113.

61. Bulgakov, "Ivan Karamazov kak filosofskii tip," 105.

62. It is maybe unsurprising that Bulgakov would help found the brief "Christian socialism" movement when he left the liberation coalition toward

the end of 1905. His work on Ivan may have helped lead him to synthesize these two oppositional ideologies. For a summary of his activity in this period, see Rowan Williams, ed., *Sergii Bulgakov: Towards a Russian Political Theology* (Edinburgh: T&T Clark, 1999), 6–8.

63. Dostoevskii, *Pss*, vol. 14, 214.

64. Nikolai Berdiaev, "Eticheskaia problema v svete filosofskogo idealizma," in *Problemy idealizma: sbornik statei*, ed. P. I. Novgorodtsev (Moscow: Izd. Moskovskogo psikhologicheskogo obshchestva, 1903), 94.

65. Berdiaev, "Eticheskaia problema v svete filosofskogo idealizma," 130. See also Nikolai Berdiaev, "The Ethical Problem in the Light of Philosophical Idealism," in *Problems of Idealism*, ed. and trans. Randall A. Poole (New Haven, CT: Yale University Press, 2003), 196.

66. Dostoevskii, *Pss*, vol. 10, 201.

67. A. L. Volynskii, *Tsarstvo Karamazovykh. N. S. Leskov. Zametki* (St. Petersburg: Tipografiia M. M. Stasiulevicha, 1901), 125. Quoted in Volzhskii [A. S. Glinka], *Dva ocherka ob Uspenskom i Dostoevskom* (St. Petersburg: Tipografiia M. M. Stasiulevicha, 1902), 155.

68. Volzhskii [A. S. Glinka], "Religiozno-nravstvennaia problema u Dostoevskogo. (Okonchanie)," *Mir Bozhii* 8 (1905): 160.

69. M. Tsebrikova, "Dvoistvennoe tvorchestvo," *Slovo* 2 (1881): 23. Miller reads this encounter as the possible initiation of Ivan's perverse conversion back to God; see Robin Feuer Miller, *Dostoevsky's Unfinished Journey* (New Haven, CT: Yale University Press, 2007), 163–70.

70. Tsebrikova, "Dvoistvennoe tvorchestvo," 22.

71. See A. Dolinin, "Dostoevskii sredi Petrashevtsev," in *Zven'ia: Sborniki materialov i dokumentov po istorii literatury, iskusstva, i obshchestvennoi mysli xix veka*, vyp. 6, ed. Vlad. Bonch-Bruevich (Moscow: Academia, 1936), 522–23.

72. Vladimir Solov'ev, "Referat V. S. Solov'eva, chitannyi v zasedanii Moskovskogo Psikhologicheskogo Obshchestva, 19-ogo oktiabria 1891 goda," *Voprosy filosofii i psikhologii*, no. 56 (1901): 151.

73. Dostoevskii, *Pss*, vol. 30, bk. 1, 66.

74. Bulgakov, "O realisticheskom mirovozzrenie," 382.

75. Bulgakov, "O realisticheskom mirovozzrenie," 383.

76. S. N. Bulgakov, "Dushevnaia drama Gertsena," in *Ot marksizma k idealizmu*, 174.

77. Bulgakov, "Dushevnaia drama Gertsena," 194.

78. Berdiaev, "O novom russkom idealizme,"153.

79. A. Lunacharskii, "Russkii Faust," *Voprosy filosofii i psikhologii*, kn. 3, no. 63 (1902): 788.

80. In his investigation into the psychological basis of belief, the psychologist Pavel Sokolov considered *Faust* a tragedy of humanity, which proved that human beings rely on faith to cope with barriers to absolute knowledge. See P. Sokolov, "Vera (Psikhologicheskii etiud)," *Voprosy filosofii i psikhologii*, kn. 2–4, no. 62: 909–33; no. 63: 1158–94; no. 64: 1305–62 (1902). Lunacharsky disagreed with this interpretation in his response to Bulgakov, claiming "Faust is not an epistemological tragedy, but a tragedy of all human life in its totality." Lunacharskii, "Russkii Faust," 793. Volzhskii responded to Lunacharsky

on behalf of Bulgakov. See Volzhskii [A. S. Glinka], "Torzhestvuiushchii amoralizm."

81. Lunacharskii, "Russkii Faust," 787. Berdiaev responded to another critic, M. B. Ratner, who likewise claimed that idealism had nothing to do with theodicy. See S. Z., "Zapiski o filosofskikh preniiakh. (Mezhdu N. A. Berdiaevym i M. B. Ratnerom)," *Novyi put'* 3 (1904): 222–23. Lunacharsky would later write his own version of the Faust myth. See A. Lunacharskii, *Faust i gorod. Drama dlia chteniia* (Petrograd: Narkompros, 1918).

82. Johann Wolfgang von Goethe, *Faust: A Tragedy*, trans. Walter Arndt (New York: Norton, 2001), 12. See also Bulgakov, "Ivan Karamazov kak filosofskii tip," 106.

83. Lunacharskii, "Russkii Faust," 787.

84. S. Z. "Filosofskie vozzreniia Vladimira Solov'eva. Otchet o lektsii prof. S. N. Bulgakova v g. Kieve i stenograficheskaia zapis' prenii," *Novyi put'* 3 (1904): 94.

85. S. Z. "Filosofskie vozzreniia Vladimira Solov'eva," 94.

86. S. Z. "Filosofskie vozzreniia Vladimira Solov'eva," 97.

87. This was in large part a response to a collection that set out to portray the idealists as dreamers, detached from political reality. See S. Dorovatovskii and A. Charushinkov, eds., *Ocherki realisticheskogo mirovozreniia: Sbornik statei po filosofii, obshchestvennoi nauke i zhizni*, 2nd ed. (St. Petersburg: Tip. Montvida, 1905). The same sort of debate—between "idealist" and "realist" modes of inquiry—would take place among Symbolists a few years later; see Viacheslav Ivanov, "Dve stikhii v sovremennom simvolizme," *Zolotoe runo* 3–4: 86–94; 5: 44–55 (1908).

88. S. N. Bulgakov, "Chekhov kak myslitel'," *Novyi put'* 10 (1904): 39.

89. S. N. Bulgakov, "Chekhov kak myslitel'. (pt. 2)," *Novyi put'* 11 (1904): 138–39.

90. Bulgakov, "Ivan Karamazov kak filosofskii tip," 96. This concern over the survival of an individual in rebellion is raised by Volzhskii as well.

91. Terence Emmons, "The Statutes of the Union of Liberation," *Russian Review* 33, no. 1 (January 1974): 83.

92. To my knowledge, Struve never referred to Dostoevsky in his many critical essays on Marxism. Pipes believed that for Struve religion was a personal matter, rather than one with application to politics and society (as his colleagues Bulgakov and Berdiaev clearly thought). Lesser-known supporters of Bulgakov and Berdiaev defended their views but rarely if ever appealed to Dostoevsky's authority. See as an example G. Markelov, "Idealizm i marksizm," *Mir Bozhii* 5 (1902): 225–41.

93. The compiler notes that these lines, and the larger passage to which they belong, were underlined by Struve. See "N. A. Berdiaev. Pis'ma k P. B. i N. A. Struve (1899–1905)," in *Iznutri*, 22.

94. Poole, "The Neo-Idealist Reception of Kant in the Moscow Philosophical Society," 323.

95. Randall A. Poole, "Editor's Introduction: Philosophy and Politics in the Russian Liberation Movement," in *Problems of Idealism*, 4.

96. On Soloviev's reading of Dostoevsky, see Marina Kostalevsky, *Dostoevsky and Soloviev: The Art of Integral Vision* (New Haven, CT: Yale University Press, 1997); and Judith Deutsch Kornblatt and Gary Rosenshield, "Vladimir

Solovyov: Confronting Dostoevsky on the Jewish and Christian Questions," *Journal of the American Academy of Religion* 68, no. 1 (March 2000): 69–98.

97. For a summary of idealist views of selfhood, see Rampton, *Liberal Ideas in Tsarist Russia*, 74–76.

98. Andreevich, *Opyt filosofii russkoi literatury*, 2nd ed. (St. Petersburg: Znanie, [1905] 1909), 274.

99. Williams, *Sergii Bulgakov*, 7.

100. See Leonid Grossman, "Dostoevskii i pravitel′stvennye krugi 1870-kh godov," in *Literaturnoe nasledstvo*, vol. 15, ed. Averbakh, 83–123.

101. Mikhail Bakhtin, *Problems of Dostoevsky's Poetics*, ed. and trans. Caryl Emerson (Minneapolis: University of Minnesota Press, 1984), 7.

102. Mikhail Bakhtin, *Art and Answerability: Early Philosophical Essays by M. M. Bakhtin*, ed. Michael Holquist and Vadim Liapunov, trans. Vadim Liapunov, supplement trans. Kenneth Brostrom (Austin: University of Texas Press, 1990), 147.

103. Bakhtin, *Art and Answerability*, 141.

104. Bakhtin, *Art and Answerability*, 145.

105. Bialik has noted that the three final issues of the *New Path* had the character of "a journal within the journal of the Merezhkovskys," signaling the more political focus of *Voprosy zhizni*. See I. V. Koretskaia, "*Novyi put′*. *Voprosy zhizni*," in *Literaturnyi protsess i russkaia zhurnalistika kontsa xix–nachala xx veka*, vol. 2, ed. B. A. Bialik (Moscow: Nauka, 1982), 229.

106. Dmitrii Filosofov, "Iskusstvo i zhizn′," *Novyi put′* 7 (1904): 235. Andrei Belyi echoed this in sharper terms in "'Idealisty' i '*Novyi put′*,'" *Vesy* 11 (1904): 66–67.

107. Filosofov, "Iskusstvo i zhizn′," 236.

108. Nikolai Berdiaev, "Filosofiia i zhizn′. (Dnevnik publitsista)," *Novyi put′* 11 (1904): 367.

109. S. N. Bulgakov, "Bez plana. 'Idealizm' i obshchestvennye programy. (pt. 2 of 3)," *Novyi put′* 11 (1904): 360. See also Bulgakov, "O realisticheskom mirovozzrenie."

110. Bulgakov, "O realisticheskom mirovozzrenie," 403.

4. Symbolist Critics and the Death of the Author, 1905–1910

1. On Merezhkovsky's changing politics during this time, see C. H. Bedford, "Dmitry Merezhkovsky, the Intelligentsia, and the Revolution of 1905," *Canadian Slavonic Papers* 3 (1958): 27–42.

2. D. S. Merezhkovskii, "Prorok russkoi revoliutsii. K iubileiu Dostoevskogo (pt. 2 of 2)," *Vesy* 3–4 (1906): 27. On January 9, 1905 (O.S.), the police assaulted, arrested, or murdered members of an assembly of St. Petersburg workers led by a priest on their way to petition Nicholas II with labor grievances and calls for social reform. When Merezhkovsky's essay appeared in *Vesy* (*Libra*), stronger phrasing had been removed for publication. Ellipsis replaced the omitted words "how a father's love responded to a child's plea: the murder of the people, infanticide." For this text, from the archival draft where it appears, see E. A. Andrushchenko, "Ulovka D. S. Merezhkovskogo: kakuiu stat′iu kritik pisal dlia A. G. Dostoevskaia," *Neizvestnyi Dostoevskii* 8, no. 2 (2021): 163.

3. V. I. Sakharov, "Dostoevskii, simvolisty i Aleksandr Blok," in *Dostoevskii: materialy i issledovaniia*, vol. 6, ed. G. M. Fridlender (Leningrad: Nauka, 1985), 170–71.

4. "Vesti otovsiudu," *Zolotoe runo* 11–12 (1906): 149.

5. Georgii Chulkov is best known for *Kak rabotal Dostoevskii* (How Dostoevsky Worked) (Moscow: Sovetskii pisatel', 1939), but he also produced the unpublished *Life of Dostoevsky* and a novel about the Petrashevsky circle, *Peterburgskie mechtateli*. Following the revolution he published numerous articles under his pseudonym, Boris Kremnev, including "Dostoevskii i sud'ba Rossii," in *Ogni. Literaturnyi al'manakh* (Moscow: Izdanie G. N. Sementsova, 1918), 133–48.

6. A small indication of Rozanov's influence on Chulkov is in the latter's essay "The Distances Are Getting Brighter," where Svidrigailov's mystical insights are framed as Dostoevsky's own. See Georgii Chulkov, "Svetleiut dali," *Vesy* 3 (1904): 14.

7. V. V. Rozanov, "Poslesloviia k Kommentariiu 'Legendy o velikom inkvizitore' F. M. Dostoevskogo," *Zolotoe runo* 11–12 (1906): 99.

8. Rozanov, "Poslesloviia k Kommentariiu," 97.

9. Rozanov, "Poslesloviia k Kommentariiu," 98.

10. Michel Foucault, "What Is an Author?," in *Textual Strategies: Perspectives in Post-Structuralist Criticism*, ed. and trans. José V. Harari (Ithaca, NY: Cornell University Press, 1979), 159.

11. Foucault, "What Is an Author?," 147–48.

12. For an account of Anna Dostoevskaia's supervision of her husband's complete works, see Raffaella Vassena, "Populiarnyi Dostoevskii: nachalo massovogo rasprostraneniia tvorcheskogo naslediia, 1881–1906," *Russian Literature* 111–112 (2020): 1–34. On Dostoevskaia's role in this and other publications and memorialization projects, see Irina Andrianova, "Dostoyevsky's First Bibliographer," *Slavic & East European Information Resources* 17, no. 1–2 (2016): 4–15.

13. A. G. Gornfel'd, *Knigi i liudi. Literaturnye besedy* (St. Petersburg: Zhizn', 1908), 264.

14. A. G. Dostoevskaia, *Bibliograficheskii ukazatel' sochinenii i proizvedenii iskusstva, otnosiashchikhsia k zhizni i deiatel'nosti F. M. Dostoevskogo, sobrannykh v 'Muzee pamiati F. M. Dostoevskogo' v Moskovskom Istoricheskom Muzee Imeni Imperatora Aleksandra III. 1846–1903* (St. Petersburg: Tip. P. F. Panteleeva, 1906), 291–92.

15. F. M. Dostoevskii, *Polnoe sobranie sochinenii F. M. Dostoevskogo. Iubileinoe (shestoe) izdanie*, vol. 8 (St. Petersburg: Tip. P. F. Panteleeva, 1905), 597.

16. On their time in Paris, see A. L. Sobolev, "Merezhkovskie v Parizhe (1906–1908)," *Litsa. Biograficheskii al'manakh*, vol. 1 (1992): 319–71.

17. They became friendly with some revolutionary terrorists while there. See Zinaida Gippius, *Dmitrii Merezhkovskii* (Paris: YMCA, 1951), 160–61.

18. See D. Mérejkowsky, Z. Hippius, Dm. Philosophoff, *Le tsar et la révolution* (Paris: Société du Mercure de France, 1907), where the essay was published as "Religion et révolution." According to Gippius, on the day all three authors were scheduled to deliver the lectures published in this volume there was a commotion and the police were summoned. Merezhkovsky finally delivered his lecture on February 21, 1907, in the Salle d'Orient. Nearly one thousand people attended. Gippius, *Dmitrii Merezhkovskii*, 170.

19. On Merezhkovsky's changing views on Dostoevsky, see E. A. Andrushchenko, "Dostoevskii i Merezhkovskii (po arkhivym nakhodkam)," in *Dostoevskii i russkoe zarubezh'e XX veka*, ed. Zhan-Fillipp Zhakkar i Ul'rikh Shmid (St. Petersburg: Dmitrii Bulanin, 2008), 40–49; V. A. Keldysh, "F. M. Dostoevskii v kritike Merezhkovskogo," in *D. S. Merezhkovskii: mysl' i slovo*, ed. V. A. Keldysh, I. V. Koretskaia, and M. A. Nikitina (Moscow: Nasledie, 1999), 207–23; and Temira Pakhmuss, "Dostoevskii v proizvedeniiakh Merezhkovskogo perioda emigratsii," *Novyi zhurnal*, kn. 184–185 (1991): 270–74.

20. Ivanov offered a slightly more forceful version of this point in 1907 when he remarked that "true talent in [revolutionary] epochs necessarily serves revolution, even if it seems to others and even to itself to be its opponent." Viacheslav Ivanov, "On the Joyful Craft and the Joy of the Spirit," in *Selected Essays*, ed. Michael Wachtel, trans. and notes by Robert Bird (Evanston, IL: Northwestern University Press, 2001), 116. I will use Bird's translations of Ivanov unless otherwise noted.

21. See Andrushchenko, "Ulovka D. S. Merezhkovskogo."

22. Merezhkovskii to A. G. Dostoevskaia, September 15/28, 1906, in *Polnoe sobranie sochinenii F. M. Dostoevskogo*, vol. 1. For his original letter, see E. A. Andrushchenko and L. G. Frizman, "Zapisnye knizhki i pis'ma D. S. Merezhkovskogo," *Russkaia rech'* 5 (1993): 31–32.

23. N. N. Mostovskaia, "Dostoevskii v dnevnikakh S. I. Smirnovoi (Sazonovoi)," in *Dostoevskii. Materialy i issledovaniia*, vol. 4, ed. G. M. Fridlender (Leningrad: Nauka, 1980), 273.

24. Andrushchenko and Frizman, "Zapisnye knizhki i pis'ma D. S. Merezhkovskogo," 30.

25. Andrushchenko and Frizman, "Zapisnye knizhki i pis'ma D. S. Merezhkovskogo," 31.

26. Dostoevskii, *Polnoe sobranie sochinenii*, vol. 27, 64. See also D. S. Merezhkovskii, "Prorok russkoi revoliutsii. K iubileiu Dostoevskogo," *Vesy* 2 (1906): 30–31. I have capitalized "Church," since the Soviet edition sets it lowercase.

27. Merezhkovskii, "Prorok russkoi revoliutsii," *Vesy* 2 (1906): 30.

28. Merezhkovskii, "Prorok russkoi revoliutsii," *Vesy* 2 (1906): 25.

29. See Adam Weiner, *By Authors Possessed: The Demonic Novel in Russia* (Evanston, IL: Northwestern University Press, 1998), 132–33; W. J. Leatherbarrow, ed., *Dostoevsky's* The Devils: *A Critical Companion* (Evanston, IL: Northwestern University Press, 1999), 52; and Craig Cravens, "The Strange Relationship of Stavrogin and Stepan Trofimovich as Told by Anton Lavrent'evich G-v," *Slavic Review* 59, no. 4 (Winter 2000): 794.

30. Leatherbarrow, *Dostoevsky's* The Devils, 22; Steven Cassedy, *Dostoevsky's Religion* (Stanford, CA: Stanford University Press, 2005), 57–59.

31. Dostoevskii, *Polnoe sobranie sochinenii*, vol. 29, 30. Quoted and translated by Joseph Frank, *Dostoevsky: The Miraculous Years, 1865–1871* (Princeton, NJ: Princeton University Press, 1995), 354.

32. Cravens, "The Strange Relationship," 792.

33. Frank, *Dostoevsky: The Miraculous Years*, 438.

34. See Susanne Fusso, "Maidens in Childbirth: The Sistine Madonna in Dostoevskii's *Devils*," *Slavic Review* 54, no. 2 (Summer 1995): 261–75.

35. Merezhkovskii, "Prorok russkoi revoliutsii," *Vesy* 3–4 (1906): 28. "Klystovstvo" refers to the religious sect known as "Flagellants." Elsewhere in the essay, Merezhkovsky defines *klystovstvo* as "unvanquished, unconscious, pre-Christian paganism." Merezhkovskii, "Prorok russkoi revoliutsii," *Vesy* 3–4 (1906): 34.

36. Merezhkovskii, "Prorok russkoi revoliutsii," *Vesy* 3–4 (1906): 20.

37. Merezhkovskii, "Prorok russkoi revoliutsii," *Vesy* 3–4 (1906): 42.

38. Merezhkovskii, "Prorok russkoi revoliutsii," *Vesy* 3–4 (1906): 42.

39. See also D. S. Merezhkovskii, "Revoliutsiia i religiia," *Russkaia mysl'* 2: 64–85; 3: 17–34 (1907).

40. Merezhkovskii, "Prorok russkoi revoliutsii," *Vesy* 2 (1906): 29.

41. Merezhkovskii, "Prorok russkoi revoliutsii," *Vesy* 2 (1906): 29.

42. Merezhkovskii, "Prorok russkoi revoliutsii," *Vesy* 3–4 (1906): 35.

43. Dostoevskii, *Polnoe sobranie sochinenii*, vol. 14, 234.

44. Roland Barthes, "The Death of the Author," in *Image–Music–Text*, trans. Stephen Heath (New York: Hill and Wang, 1977), 147.

45. Merezhkovskii, "Prorok russkoi revoliutsii," *Vesy* 3–4 (1906): 45. The final words are a quotation from *The Brothers Karamazov*, Dostoevskii, *Polnoe sobranie sochinenii*, vol. 27, 61.

46. S. N. Bulgakov, "Neotlozhnaia zadacha," *Voprosy zhizni* 9 (1905): 352.

47. Dostoevskii, *Polnoe sobranie sochinenii*, vol. 27, 62.

48. Dostoevskii, *Polnoe sobranie sochinenii*, vol. 27, 18–19.

49. S. N. Bulgakov, "Ocherk o F. M. Dostoevskom. Chrez chetvert veka (1881–1906)," in Dostoevskii, *Polnoe sobranie sochinenii F. M. Dostoevskogo*, vol. 1, xxviii.

50. Bulgakov, "Ocherk o F. M. Dostoevskom," xvii.

51. Gippius, *Dmitrii Merezhkovskii*, 182. Bulgakov said as much early in 1905. See S. N. Bulgakov, "Bez plana," *Voprosy zhizni* 3 (1905): 395–401.

52. Chulkov did not consider Bulgakov's political adaptation of Christian socialism a separate phenomenon from Orthodoxy itself. He wrote in the second installment of "Torches," "The 'Christian Brotherhood of Struggle' has effectively broken with the official church, but it still continues to dream of an ideal Orthodox Church, of the kind that it ought to be, per their opinion." Georgii Chulkov, "Ob utverzhdenii lichnosti," in *Fakely*, kn. 2 (St. Petersburg: Fakely, 1907), 13.

53. Bulgakov, "Ocherk o F. M. Dostoevskom," xxiv.

54. Bulgakov, "Ocherk o F. M. Dostoevskom," xxiv.

55. Bulgakov, "Ocherk o F. M. Dostoevskom," xxvi.

56. S. N. Bulgakov, "Venets ternovyi (Pamiati F. M. Dostoevskogo)," *Svoboda i kul'tura* 1 (1906): 31. First delivered in Kiev on February 25, 1906. He commits a similar hypothetical fallacy in Bulgakov, "Ocherk o F. M. Dostoevskom," xxxii–xxxiii. Tsushima was a brutal defeat suffered by the Russian fleet in the Russo-Japanese War.

57. Bulgakov, "Ocherk o F. M. Dostoevskom," xxvi.

58. Volzhskii, "Literaturnyi otdel," *Kriticheskoe obozrenie* 1 (1907): 28.

59. L. Sh. [Lev Shestov], "Pokhvala gluposti," in Chulkov, *Fakely*, kn. 2, 157.

60. Konstantin Bal'mont, "Nashe literaturnoe segodnia. Zametka," *Zolotoe runo* 11–12 (1907): 61.

61. See Andrei Belyi, "Dostoevskii. Po povodu 25-letiia so dnia smerti," *Zolotoe runo* 2 (1906): 89–90; Andrei Belyi, "Nastoiashchee i budushchee russkoi literatury. II," *Vesy* 3 (1909): 71–82; Andrei Belyi, "Mirovaia Ekteniia. (Po povodu trilogii Merezhkovskogo)," *Zolotoe runo* 3 (1906): 72–83. On Dostoevsky's literary influence on Belyi, see A. V. Lavrov, "Dostoevskii v tvorcheskom soznanii Andreia Belogo (1900-e gody)," in *Andrei Belyi. Problemy tvorchestva*, ed. St. Lesnevskii and Al. Mikhailov (Moscow: Sovetskii pisatel', 1988), 131–50.

62. Andrei Belyi [Boris Bugaev], "Na perevale," *Vesy* 1 (1906): 70.

63. Belyi, "Na perevale," 71.

64. Andrei Belyi, "A. L. Volynskii. Dostoevskii," *Zolotoe runo* 2 (1906): 129.

65. Andrei Belyi, "Ibsen i Dostoevskii," *Vesy* 1 (1906): 49.

66. Belyi, "Ibsen i Dostoevskii," 53.

67. Belyi, "A. L. Volynskii. Dostoevskii," 128.

68. Belyi, "Ibsen i Dostoevskii," 54.

69. Aleksandr Blok, "Bezvremen'e," *Zolotoe runo* 11–12 (1906): 107.

70. Blok, "Bezvremen'e," 112.

71. A. A. Kholikov, " 'Boria, Boria, mal'chik moi liubimyi, edinstvennyi . . .' Pis'ma D. S. Merezhkovskogo Andreiu Belomu," *Voprosy literatury* 1 (2006): 164.

72. Kholikov, " 'Boria, Boria, mal'chik moi liubimyi, edinstvennyi,' " 164.

73. On the polemic, see Avril Pyman, *A History of Russian Symbolism* (Cambridge: Cambridge University Press, 1994), 282–84; Bernice Glatzer Rosenthal, "The Transmutation of Symbolist Ethos: Mystical Anarchism and the Revolution of 1905," *Slavic Review* 36, no. 4 (December 1977): 608–27; and Bernice Glatzer Rosenthal, "From Decadence to Religion: Ivanov and Merezhkovskij," in *Cultura e memoria: Atti del terzo Simposio Internazionale dedicato a Vjačeslav Ivanov*, ed. Fausto Malcovati (Florence, 1988): 144–46. On internal disagreements, see G. V. Obatnin, ed., "Neopublikovannye materialy Viach. Ivanova po povodu polemiki o 'misticheskom anarkhizme,' " in *Litsa. Biograficheskii al'manakh*, vol. 3, ed. A. V. Lavrov (Moscow: Feniks, 1993): 466–77; and James West, *Russian Symbolism: A Study of Viacheslav Ivanov and the Russian Symbolist Aesthetic* (London: Methuen, 1970), 121–26.

74. But the Merezhkovskys likely served as direct influences on Chulkov's project. See for example, Georgii Chulkov, "Review of *Severnye tsvety*," *Voprosy zhizni* 6 (1905): 258.

75. For more on plans for the "Torches" theater, see Iu. E. Galanina, "V. E. Meierkhol'd na bashne Viach. Ivanova," in *Bashnia Viacheslava Ivanova i kul'tura serebriannogo veka*, ed. V. E. Bagno and A. B. Shishkin (St. Petersburg: Filolologicheskii fakul'tet S.-Peterburgskogo universiteta, 2006), 187–205.

76. Meyerhold to Briusov, January 6, 1906, in V. E. Meierkhol'd, *Perepiska, 1896–1939*, ed. V. P. Korshunova and M. M. Sitkovetskaia (Moscow: Iskusstvo, 1976), 59. Corroborated in Ivanov's letter to Zamiatnina, in N. A. Bogomolov, ed., *Kuzmin: stat'i i materialy* (Moscow: NLO, 1995), 69. Cited in Galanina, "V. E. Meierkhol'd na bashne Viach. Ivanova," 197.

77. Chulkov found Orthodoxy later in life after his earlier years of radicalism. See I. V. Leont'ev, " '. . . Nichto ne mozhet zamenit' religiiu' (Sokrovennye pis'ma Georgiia Chulkova)," *Zvezda* 3 (1995): 116–25.

78. Quoted in Georgii Chulkov, *Gody stranstvii* (Moscow: Ellis Lak, 1999), 63.

79. Dmitrii Filosofov, "Misticheskii anarkhizm. Dekadentstvo, obshchestvennost' i misticheskii anarkhizm," *Zolotoe runo* 10 (1906): 62.

80. See also Viacheslav Ivanov, "Lik i lichiny Rossii. K issledovaniiu ideologii Dostoevskogo," *Russkaia mysl'* 1 (1917): 16–43, and much later, Viacheslav Ivanov, *Freedom and the Tragic Life: A Study in Dostoevsky* (New York: Noonday, 1952). A recent volume provides a detailed and informative history of Ivanov's writing on Dostoevsky; see Viacheslav Ivanov, *Dostoevskii: tragediia, mif, mistika*, eds. A. B. Shishkin and O. L. Fetisen'ko (St. Petersburg: Pushkinskii dom, 2021).

81. Viacheslav Ivanov, "Dostoevskii i roman-tragediia. Printsip mirosozertsaniia," *Russkaia mysl'* 6 (1911): 9. The first part was published in *Russkaia mysl'* 5 (1911): 46–61.

82. Ivanov's Russian literary debut was the publication of his extensive essays on the Dionysian cult. See Viacheslav Ivanov, "Ellinskaia religiia stradaiushchego boga," *Novyi put'* 1: 110–34; 2: 48–78; 3: 38–61; 5: 28–40; 8: 17–26; 9: 47–70 (1904); and Viacheslav Ivanov, "Religiia Dionisa. Ee proiskhozhdenie i vliianie," *Voprosy zhizni* 6: 185–220; 7: 122–48 (1905).

83. On how Orthodox rite influenced the aesthetics and form of Symbolist poetry, see Martha Kelly, *Unorthodox Beauty: Russian Modernism and Its New Religious Aesthetic* (Evanston, IL: Northwestern University Press, 2016).

84. Viacheslav Ivanov, "The Symbolics of Aesthetic Principles," in *Selected Essays*, 6. This essay was originally titled "O niskhozhdenii," *Vesy* 5 (1905): 26–36.

85. Ivanov, "The Symbolics of Aesthetic Principles," 8.

86. The concept of theomachy so permeated the discourse of Symbolist criticism that it deserves its own book.

87. Viacheslav Ivanov, "Krizis individualizma," *Voprosy zhizni* 9 (1905): 49. My translation. In *The Rebel*, Camus wrote of Ivan, "One can live in a state of rebellion only by pursuing it to the bitter end. What is the bitter end of metaphysical rebellion? Metaphysical revolution. The master of the world, after his legitimacy has been contested, must be overthrown. Man must occupy his place." Albert Camus, *The Rebel: An Essay on Man in Revolt*, trans. Anthony Bower (New York: Vintage, 1991), 59.

88. Georgii Chulkov, "Teatr i muzyka," *Nasha zhizn'* 353, January 25/February 8, 1906. For mention of theomachy, see also Georgii Chulkov, "Teatr i muzyka," *Tovarishch* 239, April 11/24, 1907.

89. Viacheslav Ivanov, "Ideia nepriiatiia mira i misticheskii anarkhizm," in Georgii Chulkov, *O misticheskom anarkhizme* (St. Petersburg: Fakely, 1906), 10. A *poema* is a narrative poem in verse. In the Russian poetic tradition, it is analogous to the epic.

90. Ivanov, "Ideia nepriiatiia mira," 10. All translations of this essay are mine.

91. Ivanov, "On the Joyful Craft and the Joy of the Spirit," 126.

92. Ivanov, "Ideia nepriiatiia mira," 12.

93. Viacheslav Ivanov, "Nepriiatie mira," in *Fakely*, kn. 1, 51.

94. Thanks to Johannes Haubold, who provided helpful historical background about this term.

95. Chulkov also uses this term as a synonym for mystical anarchism in his essay, "Pokryvalo Izidy," *Zolotoe runo* 5 (1908): 72.

96. The prototypical icon that carried this name was first located in Constantinople; there is also a famous exemplar of this icon genre in Smolensk, about which Ivanov may have known.

97. Ivanov, "Ideia nepriiatiia mira," 15–16.

98. Ivanov, "Ideia nepriiatiia mira," 10.

99. Ivanov, "Ideia nepriiatiia mira," 9.

100. See for instance, Konst Erberg, "Bezvlastie," *Zolotoe runo* 4 (1907): 46–63.

101. Chulkov, *O misticheskom anarkhizme*, 77. Ivanov quotes this passage in "Ideia nepriiatiia mira," 15. Ivanov renders the Hebrew as "God, God, why have you left me?"

102. Andrei Belyi, "O propovednikakh, gastronomakh, misticheskikh anarkhistakh, i t.d.," *Zolotoe runo* 1 (1907): 63. See also Andrei Belyi, "Georgii Chulkov. O misticheskom anarkhizme," *Zolotoe runo* 7–9 (1906): 174.

103. For a summary of the disagreements that precipitated the end of *Novyi put'*, see M. A. Kolerov, *Ne mir, no mech: russkaia religiozno-filosofskaia pechat' ot 'Problema idealizma' do 'Vekh,' 1902–1909* (St. Petersburg: Izd. Aleteiia, 1996), 85–89.

104. Quoted in Kolerov, *Ne mir, no mech*, 111.

105. Quoted in Kolerov, *Ne mir, no mech*, 112.

106. D. S. Merezhkovskii, "Griadushchii kham," *Poliarnaia zvezda* 3 (1905): 188.

107. Merezhkovskii, "Griadushchii kham," 188.

108. I'm using Avrahm Yarmolinsky's translation of Gorky's character's name from Maksim Gor'kii, *Best Short Stories of Maxim Gorki*, trans. Avrahm Yarmolinsky (New York: Grayson, 1947).

109. See Viacheslav Ivanov, "Doklad 'Evangel'skii smysl slova "Zemlia."' Pis'ma. Avtobiografiia (1926)," publication and commentary by G. V. Obatnin, in *Ezhegodnik rukopisnogo otdela Pushkinskogo doma na 1991 god*, ed. T. S. Tsar'kova (St. Petersburg: Akademicheskii proekt, 1994), 161–62.

110. This point is echoed in Dmitrii Filosofov, "Igra v religiiu," *Russkaia mysl'* 4 (1908): 150.

111. D. S. Merezhkovskii, "V obez'ian'ikh lapakh. O Leonide Andreeve," *Russkaia mysl'* 1 (1908): 97–98. Merezhkovsky is paraphrasing Proverbs 1:31.

112. Merezhkovskii, "V obez'ian'ikh lapakh," 98.

113. Their debate is brilliantly summarized in N. V. Skvortsova, "Aleksandr Blok v stat'e Andreiia Belogo 'Khimery,'" in *Blokovskii sbornik*, vyp. 657, ed. Z. G. Mints (Tartu: Uchenye zapiski Tartuskogo gosudarstvennogo universiteta, 1985), 88–95.

114. Viacheslav Ivanov, "Ancient Terror: On Leon Bakst's Painting *Terror Antiquus*," in *Selected Essays*, 150. For the first publication of this passage, see Ivanov, "Drevnii uzhas," *Zolotoe runo* 4 (1909): 56.

115. Sergei Gorodetskii, "Blizhaishaia zadacha russkoi literatury," *Zolotoe runo* 4 (1909): 75.

116. Merezhkovskii, "Prorok russkoi revoliutsii," *Vesy* 3–4 (1906): 29.

5. The Moscow Art Theater's Rewriting of *Devils*, 1910–1914

1. I. N. Solov'eva, *Nemirovich-Danchenko* (Moscow: Iskusstvo, 1979), 304.

2. Solus, "Moskovskii khudozhestvennyi teatr. 'Nikolai Stavrogin,' Otryvki iz romana F. M. Dostoevskogo 'Besy,'" *Birzhevye vedomosti*, April 8, 1914.

3. Maksim Gor'kii, "O 'Karamazovshchine,'" *Russkoe slovo*, September 22, 1913. On the polemic, see O. A. Radishcheva and E. A. Shingareva, eds.,

Moskovskii khudozhestvennyi teatr v russkoi teatral'noi kritike, 1906–1918 (Moscow: Artist. Rezhisser. Teatr, 2007); Robert Louis Jackson, *Dialogues with Dostoevsky: The Overwhelming Questions* (Stanford, CA: Stanford University Press, 1993), 121–33; Nicholas Rzhevsky, *The Modern Russian Theater: A Literary and Cultural History* (Armonk, NY: M. E. Sharpe, 2009), 34–35; and Aileen Kelly, *Toward Another Shore: Russian Thinkers Between Necessity and Chance* (New Haven, CT: Yale University Press, 1998), 153.

4. V. I. Nemirovich-Danchenko, "Otkrytoe pis'mo M. Gor'komu," *Russkoe slovo* 221, October 26, 1913.

5. See Sharon Marie Carnicke, *Stanislavsky in Focus: An Acting Master for the Twenty-First Century*, 2nd ed. (London: Routledge, 2009), 33; and Julia Listengarten, "Stanislavsky and the Avant-Garde," in *The Routledge Companion to Stanislavsky*, ed. R. Andrew White (London: Routledge, 2014), 73.

6. Rebecca B. Gauss, *Lear's Daughters: The Studios of the Moscow Art Theatre, 1905–1927* (New York: Peter Lang, 1999), 2.

7. Igor' Grabar', "Teatr i khudozhniki," *Vesy* 4 (1908): 94.

8. Osip Dymov, "Four Pillars of Russian Art," Papers of Ossip Dymow, YIVO Institute for Jewish Research, RG 469, folder 50, Vignettes (Portraits) (from: "This I Remember"), 14.

9. Volzhskii, "Literaturnyi otdel," *Kriticheskoe obozrenie* 1 (1907): 27–28.

10. These sources are held at the Moscow Art Theater's library at the theater's museum on Kamergerskii pereulok. They were accessed in summer 2017.

11. "Teatr i muzyka. Instsenirovannye 'Besy.' (Beseda s Vl. I. Nemirovichem-Danchenko)," *Russkoe slovo*, August 17, 1913 (O.S.).

12. See Vladimir Seduro, *Dostoevsky in Russian and World Theatre* (North Quincy, MA: Christopher Publishing, 1977); and Alexander Burry, *Multi-Mediated Dostoevsky: Transposing Novels into Opera, Film, and Drama* (Evanston, IL: Northwestern University Press, 2011).

13. Linda Hutcheon, *A Theory of Adaptation* (New York: Routledge, 2006), 9.

14. For plot summaries, see I. N. Solov'eva, "Nikolai Stavrogin," in *Moskovskii khudozhestvennyi teatr 100 let*, vol. 1, ed. I. N. Solov'eva and O. V. Egoshina (Moscow: Izd. MKhT, 1998), 74–76; Seduro, *Dostoevsky in Russian and World Theatre*.

15. On his dramaturgy, see I. I. Korzov, *Dramaturgiia Vl. I. Nemirovicha-Danchenko* (Kiev: Izdatel'stvo Kievskogo universiteta, 1971).

16. Marc Slonim, *Russian Theater: From the Empire to the Soviets* (Cleveland, OH: World, 1961), 107.

17. Abalkin has argued that the revival of the Art Theater's *Brothers Karamazov* in 1960, seventeen years after Nemirovich's death, managed to avoid "Dostoevshchina" (Dostoevskyism) and fulfill the accomplishments of the 1910 production. See N. A. Abalkin, *Khudozhnik i revoliutsiia: tvorchestvo Vl. I. Nemirovicha-Danchenko v sovetskie gody* (Moscow: Iskusstvo, 1982), 239.

18. L. M. Freidkina, *Dni i gody Vl. I. Nemirovicha-Danchenko: letopis' zhizni i tvorchestva* (Moscow: Vserossiiskoe teatral'noe obshchestvo, 1962), 35–36; Solov'eva, *Nemirovich-Danchenko*, 286.

19. Solov'eva, "Nikolai Stavrogin," 76.

20. Yet another adaptation of *Devils* by the dramatist I. I. Smirnov was completed in 1908 but was never staged and the playscript went unpublished.

It covers the revolutionary drama but amazingly does not dramatize (or deliver by récit) Stavrogin's suicide. See I. I. Smirnov, *Besy (Nikolai Stavrogin). Stseny iz romana F. M. Dostoevskogo v 6 kartinakh*. 1908. SPbGTB. ORiRK. Access number: 35302; litograficheskii tekst: S 506.

21. Osip Dymov, "Peterburgskie teatry," *Zolotoe runo* 10 (1906): 80.

22. "Khronika," *Obozrenie teatrov* 171 (August 18, 1907), 7–8; 193 (September 18, 1907), 14.

23. V. Sh., "Besy," *Novoe vremia*, October 1, 1907.

24. Aleksandr Kugel', "Teatral'nye zametki," *Teatr i iskusstvo* 40 (1907): 656.

25. V. P. Burenin, "Zhurnalistika. Nechto o 'novykh tipakh' v romane g. Dostoevskogo 'Besy' . . .," *Sankt-peterburgskie vedomosti* 250 (October 11, 1871) (N.S.).

26. V. P. Burenin and M. A. Suvorin, *Besy. Stseny iz romana F. M. Dostoevskogo. V 5 deistviakh* (St. Peterburg: Zhurnal Teatra Literaturno-khudozhestvennogo obshchestva, 1908), 37–50.

27. Georgii Chulkov, "Teatr i muzyka. Malyi teatr. Stseny iz romana F. M. Dostoevskogo 'Besy,'" *Tovarishch*, October 2, 1907 (O.S.).

28. Chulkov, "Teatr i muzyka."

29. Murray Frame, *School for Citizens: Theatre and Civil Society in Imperial Russia* (New Haven, CT: Yale University Press, 2006), 183–84.

30. For an essential guide to late imperial and Soviet adaptations, see S. V. Belov, *F. M. Dostoevskii i teatr, 1846–1977. Bibliograficheskii ukazatel'* (Leningrad: Leningradskii gosudarstvennyi institut teatra, muzyki i kinematografii, 1980).

31. E. Anthony Swift, *Popular Theater and Society in Tsarist Russia* (Berkeley: University of California Press, 2002), 115–20.

32. Nikolai Berdiaev, "Stavrogin," *Russkaia mysl'* 5 (1914): 80–89.

33. Viacheslav Ivanov, "Dostoevskii i roman-tragediia," *Russkaia mysl'* 6 (1911): 17.

34. Viacheslav Ivanov, "Viach. Ivanov o F. M. Dostoevskom," published by D. V. Ivanov and A. B. Shishkin, introduction by A. T. Kazarian, in *Viacheslav Ivanov: Arkhivnye materialy i issledovaniia*, ed. L. A. Gogotishvili and A. T. Kazarian (Moscow: Russkie slovari, 1999), 65.

35. Victor Terras, *Reading Dostoevsky* (Madison: University of Wisconsin Press, 1998), 99.

36. S. N. Bulgakov, "Ocherk o F. M. Dostoevskom," in F. M. Dostoevskii, *Polnoe sobranie sochinenii F. M. Dostoevskogo. Iubileinoe (shestoe) izdanie*, vol. 1 (St. Petersburg: Tip. P. F. Panteleeva, 1904), xl.

37. Ivanov, "Viach. Ivanov o F. M. Dostoevskom," 67.

38. Volynskii had claimed a few years earlier that Dostoevsky's Stavrogin was his take on the decadent type, a new "psychological phenomenon," which had only just appeared in Europe. This interpretation of Stavrogin is at odds with the religious potential accorded to him by Ivanov. See A. L. Volynskii, *Kniga velikogo gneva* (St. Petersburg: Trud, 1904), 47.

39. N. F. Budanova, "O nekotorykh istochnikakh nravstvenno-filosofskoi problematiki romana 'Besy,'" in *Dostoevskii: materialy i issledovannia*, vol. 8, ed. G. M. Fridlender (Leningrad: Nauka, 1988): 93.

40. Burry, *Multi-Mediated Dostoevsky*, 25; Hutcheon, *A Theory of Adaptation*, 9.

41. Burry, *Multi-Mediated Dostoevsky*, 34.

42. Nick Worrall, *The Moscow Art Theatre* (London: Routledge, 1996), 202.

43. Following more closely the novel's plot as a whole, Burenin and Suvorin begin their scenario with this scene.

44. Some of his sketches for *Stavrogin* have been published most recently in N. Ashimbaeva and B. Tikhomirov, eds., *Teatr Dostoevskogo v rabotakh khudozhnikov stseny. S.-Peterburg–Moscow XX vek* (St. Petersburg: Kuznechnyi pereulok, 2015), 59–67.

45. M. Dobuzhinskii, "O khudozhestvennom teatre," *Novyi Zhurnal* 5 (1943): 54.

46. Worrall, *The Moscow Art Theatre*, 202.

47. Rzhevsky, *The Modern Russian Theater*, 38.

48. A. P. Gusarova, *Mstislav Dobuzhinskii: Zhivopis'. Grafika. Teatr. Al'bom* (Moscow: Izobrazitel'noe iskusstvo, 1982), 156–57.

49. V. I. Nemirovich-Danchenko, *Tvorcheskoe nasledie v chetyrekh tomakh*, vol. 2 (Moscow: Izd. MAT, 2003), 339.

50. A constant source of stress in Nemirovich's letters is Ivan Moskvin, an actor who had taken a leave of absence due, it seems, to his deteriorating mental health.

51. Nemirovich-Danchenko, *Tvorcheskoe nasledie*, 344.

52. Nemirovich hoped that Lilina (the stage name of Mar'ia Petrovna Perevostchikova), who played Mar'ia Timofeevna in *Stavrogin*, would play Marie Shatova in "Shatov and Kirillov." She was Stanislavsky's wife.

53. Nemirovich-Danchenko, *Tvorcheskoe nasledie*, 342.

54. Nemirovich-Danchenko, *Tvorcheskoe nasledie*, 339.

55. S. N. Bulgakov, "Russkaia tragediia," *Russkaia mysl'* 4 (1914): 17.

56. Nemirovich-Danchenko, *Tvorcheskoe nasledie*, 345.

57. V. I. Nemirovich-Danchenko, Ekzempliar 1; "Nikolai Stavrogin," otryvki iz romana F. M. Dostoevskogo "Besy" [pervyi variant teksta]; Instsenirovka [Vl. Iv. Nemirovicha-Danchenko.] [1913, okolo 17 avgusta]–[1913, sentiabria, 3]. Moskovskii khudozhestvennyi teatr, BRCh ˜ 661; MM ˜ 661.

58. Aleksandr Kugel' [Homo novus], "Zametki," *Teatr i iskusstvo* 18 (1914): 407.

59. Bulgakov, "Russkaia tragediia," 17.

60. Sulerzhitsky likely engaged Kachalov and Massalitinov in the "System," which he and Stanislavsky had been developing at their new Studio, founded in 1912 at MAT.

61. V. I. Nemirovich-Danchenko, *My Life in the Russian Theatre*, trans. John Cournos (New York: Theatre Arts, 1968), 270.

62. V. I. Nemirovich-Danchenko, "Nikolai Stavrogin, otryvki iz romana F. M. Dostoevskogo 'Besy,'" Dnevnik repetitsii. Sezon 1913–1914 goda, 1913, avgust, 16–1913, oktiabria, 31. Muzei MKhAT, RCh˜95, MM˜95, F1 44/46.

63. F. M. Dostoevskii, *Besy, Polnoe sobranie sochinenii*, vol. 10, 197. These translations from *Devils* are my own.

64. Following this omitted statement is a longer comment from Shatov summarizing Stavrogin's view that Catholicism is not Christianity and that the West had given itself over to the Antichrist.

65. This omission is closely related to a thought expressed by Dostoevsky in a letter from 1854, which suggests that the author and Stavrogin shared the same kind of faith. See Dostoevskii, *Polnoe sobranie sochinenii*, vol. 28, bk. 1, 176.

66. Dostoevskii, *Besy, Polnoe sobranie sochinenii*, 10: 196–98.

67. Dostoevskii, *Besy, Polnoe sobranie sochinenii*, 10: 199–200.

68. Marina Kostalevsky, *Dostoevsky and Soloviev: The Art of Integral Vision* (New Haven, CT: Yale University Press, 1997), 32.

69. Sergei Iablonovskii, "Budi! Budi!," *Rampa i zhizn'* 4 (January 24, 1916): 5–6.

70. M. Nir, "Beseda s M. Gor'kim," *Teatr* 1459 (1914): 7–8.

71. D. Tal'nikov [D. L. Shpital'nikov], "Besovskoe navazhdenie," *Sovremennyi mir* 11 (1913): 209; quoted in Vladimir Zakharov, "The Dostoevsky Syndrome," in *The New Russian Dostoevsky: Readings for the Twenty-First Century*, ed. Carol Apollonio and Joseph Fitzpatrick (Bloomington, IN: Slavica, 2010), 14.

Epilogue

1. Merezhkovsky had fiercely attacked Andreev in D. S. Merezhkovskii, "V obez'ian'ikh lapakh. O Leonide Andreeve," *Russkaia mysl'* 1 (1908): 75–98.

2. Jacques Derrida, *Specters of Marx*, trans. Peggy Kamuf (London: Routledge, 1994), 46.

3. Derrida, *Specters of Marx*, 45.

4. D. S. Merezhkovskii, *Budet radost'* (Petrograd: Izd. Ogni, 1916), 21.

5. Merezhkovskii, *Budet radost'*, 24.

6. V. Malakhieva-Mirovich, "Novaia p'esa D. S. Merezhkovskogo," *Russkaia mysl'* 3 (1916): 24–25.

7. Merezhkovskii, *Budet radost'*, 42.

8. Leonid Andreev, *Sobranie sochinenii v shesti tomakh*, vol. 6, ed. V. A. Aleksandrov and V. N. Chuvakov (Moscow: Khudozhestvennaia literatura, 1996), 610. Quoted in commentary by Iu. N. Chirva and V. N. Chuvakov.

9. Andreev, *Sobranie sochinenii*, vol. 6, 356.

10. Andreev, *Sobranie sochinenii*, vol. 6, 357.

11. Andreev, *Sobranie sochinenii*, vol. 6, 370.

12. Andreev, *Sobranie sochinenii*, vol. 6, 371.

BIBLIOGRAPHY

-in. "Pis'ma o sovremennom iskusstve." *Russkaia mysl'* 11 (1899): 201–10.

Abalkin, N. A. *Khudozhnik i revoliutsiia: tvorchestvo Vl. I. Nemirovicha-Danchenko v sovetskie gody.* Moscow: Iskusstvo, 1982.

Aikhenval'd, Yurii. "Literaturnye zametki. Po povodu novogo izdaniia sochinenii Dostoevskogo." *Russkaia mysl'* 9 (1907): 162-77.

"Alfavitnyi spisok dramaticheskim sochineniiam, rassmotrennym dramaticheskoiu tsenzuroiu i bezuslovno dozvolennym k predstavleniiu." *Artist* 15 (1891): 115-18.

Alpatova, Irina. "Vechnoe vo vremennom (o spektakle 'Idiot' v postanovke F. F. Komissarzhevskogo 1912 g.)." In *Dostoevskii i mirovaia kul'tura*, edited by K. A. Stepanian, 256-57. Moscow: Klassika plius, 1997.

Ambler, Effie. *The Career of Aleksei S. Suvorin: Russian Journalism and Politics, 1861–1881.* Detroit, MI: Wayne State University Press, 1972.

Andreev, Leonid. *Sobranie sochinenii v shesti tomakh*, vol. 6, edited by V. A. Aleksandrov and V. N. Chuvakov. Moscow: Khudozhestvennaia literatura, 1996.

Andreevich. *Opyt filosofii russkoi literatury*, 2nd ed. St. Petersburg: Znanie, 1909.

Andreevskii, S. "Brat'ia Karamazovy. Kriticheskii etiud." *Russkii vestnik* 6 (1889): 120-63.

Andrianova, Irina. "Dostoyevsky's First Bibliographer." *Slavic & East European Information Resources* 17, no. 1-2 (2016): 4-15.

Andrushchenko, E. A. "Dostoevskii i Merezhkovskii (po arkhivym nakhodkam)." In *Dostoevskii i russkoe zarubezh'e XX veka*, edited by Zhan-Fillipp Zhakkar i Ul'rikh Shmid, 40-49. St. Petersburg: Dmitrii Bulanin, 2008.

Andrushchenko, E. A. "Iz chego 'sdelana' kniga 'L. Tolstoi i Dostoevskii.'" In *Vlastelin "chuzhogo": tekstologiia i problemy poetiki D. S. Merezhkovskogo.* Moscow: Vodolei, 2012.

Andrushchenko, E. A. "Ulovka D. S. Merezhkovskogo: kakuiu stat'iu kritik pisal dlia A. G. Dostoevskaia." *Neizvestnyi Dostoevskii* 8, no. 2 (2021): 157-73.

Andrushchenko, E. A., and L. G. Frizman. "Zapisnye knizhki i pis'ma D. S. Merezhkovskogo." *Russkaia rech'* 5 (1993): 25-40.

Anker, Elizabeth S., and Rita Felski, eds. *Critique and Postcritique.* Durham, NC: Duke University Press, 2017.

Apollonio, Carol. *Dostoevsky's Secrets: Reading against the Grain.* Evanston, IL: Northwestern University Press, 2009.

Apollonio, Carol, and Joseph Fitzpatrick, eds. *The New Russian Dostoevsky: Readings for the Twenty-First Century.* Bloomington, IN: Slavica, 2010.

Arkhipova, A. V. "Iz stsenicheskoi istorii 'Sela Stepanchikova.'" In *Dostoevskii i ego vremia*, edited by V. G. Bazanov and G. M. Fridlender, 307–21. Leningrad: Nauka, 1971.

Ashimbaeva, N., and B. Tikhomirov, eds. *Teatr Dostoevskogo v rabotakh khudozhnikov stseny: S.-Peterburg–Moscow XX vek*. St. Petersburg: Kuznechnyi pereulok, 2015.

Averbakh, L., ed. *Literaturnoe nasledstvo*, vol. 15. Moscow: Zhurnal'no-gazetnoe ob''edinenie, 1934.

Avrutin, Eugene M. *Jews and the Imperial State: Identification Politics in Tsarist Russia*. Ithaca, NY: Cornell University Press, 2010.

B., A. "Kriticheskie zametki." *Mir Bozhii* 11 (1901): 1–14.

B., A. "Kriticheskie zametki." *Mir Bozhii* 2 (1903): 1–12.

B., N. "Teatral'noe ekho." *Peterburgskaia gazeta* 273 (October 5, 1899): 3.

B., Z. "Review of V. Mikulich [L. I. Veselitskaia]. 'Vstrecha so znamenitost'iu.'" *Novyi put'* 12 (1903): 209–11.

Bakhtin, Mikhail. *Art and Answerability: Early Philosophical Essays by M. M. Bakhtin*, edited by Michael Holquist and Vadim Liapunov and translated by Vadim Liapunov. Supplement translation by Kenneth Brostrom. Austin: University of Texas Press, 1990.

Bakhtin, Mikhail. *Problems of Dostoevsky's Poetics*, edited and translated by Caryl Emerson. Minneapolis: University of Minnesota Press, 1984.

Bal'mont, Konstantin. *Gornye vershiny. Sbornik statei*. Moscow: Grif, 1904.

Bal'mont, Konstantin. "Nashe literaturnoe segodnia. Zametka." *Zolotoe runo* 11–12 (1907): 60–63.

Bal'mont, Konstantin. "O russkikh poetakh." In *Gornye vershiny*, 59–74.

Bal'mont, Konstantin. "Prizrak mezh liudei (Shelli, 1792–1822)." In *Gornye vershiny*, 130–36.

Barthes, Roland. *Image–Music–Text*, translated by Stephen Heath. New York: Hill and Wang, 1977.

Bedford, C. H. "Dmitry Merezhkovsky, the Intelligentsia, and the Revolution of 1905." *Canadian Slavonic Papers* 3 (1958): 27–42.

Belknap, Robert. *The Genesis of* The Brothers Karamazov. Evanston, IL: Northwestern University Press, 1990.

Belov, S. V. *F. M. Dostoevskii. Ukazatel' proizvedenii F. M. Dostoevskogo i literatury o nem na russkom iazyke, 1844–2004 gg*. St. Petersburg: Rossiiskaia natsional'naia biblioteka, 2011.

Belov, S. V. *F. M. Dostoevskii i teatr, 1846–1977. Bibliograficheskii ukazatel'*. Leningrad: Leningradskii gosudarstvennyi institut teatra, muzyki i kinematografii, 1980.

Belyi, Andrei. "A. L. Volynskii. Dostoevskii." *Zolotoe runo* 2 (1906): 127–30.

Belyi, Andrei. "Dostoevskii. Po povodu 25-letiia so dnia smerti." *Zolotoe runo* 2 (1906): 89–90.

Belyi, Andrei. "Georgii Chulkov. O misticheskom anarkhizme." *Zolotoe runo* 7–9 (1906): 174–75.

Belyi, Andrei. "Ibsen i Dostoevskii." *Vesy* 1 (1906): 47–54.

Belyi, Andrei. "'Idealisty' i '*Novyi put'*.'" *Vesy* 11 (1904): 66–67.

Belyi, Andrei. "Mirovaia Ekteniia. (Po povodu trilogii Merezhkovskogo)." *Zolotoe runo* 3 (1906): 72–83.

Belyi, Andrei [Boris Bugaev]. "Na perevale." *Vesy* 1 (1906): 68–71.

Belyi, Andrei. "Nastoiashchee i budushchee russkoi literatury. II." *Vesy* 3 (1909): 71–82.

Belyi, Andrei. "O propovednikakh, gastronomakh, misticheskikh anarkhist-akh, i t.d." *Zolotoe runo* 1 (1907): 61–64.

Bem, A. L. *O Dostoevskom. Sborniki statei pod red. A. L. Bema. Praga, 1929/1933/1936*, edited by I. L. Volgin. Moscow: Al'ma Mater/Akademicheskii proekt, 2019.

Ben-Shai, Roy. *Critique of Critique*. Stanford, CA: Stanford University Press, 2023.

Berdiaev, Nikolai [Nicholas Berdyaev]. *Dream and Reality: An Essay in Autobiography*, translated by Katherine Lampert. New York: Macmillan, 1951.

Berdiaev, Nikolai. "The Ethical Problem in the Light of Philosophical Ideal-ism." In *Problems of Idealism*, edited and translated by Randall A. Poole, 161–97. New Haven, CT: Yale University Press, 2003.

Berdiaev, Nikolai. "Eticheskaia problema v svete filosofskogo idealizma." In *Problemy idealizma: sbornik statei*, edited by P. I. Novgorodtsev, 91–136. Moscow: Izd. Moskovskogo psikhologicheskogo obshchestva, 1903.

Berdiaev, Nikolai. "Filosofiia i zhizn'." *Novyi put'* 12 (1904): 323–33.

Berdiaev, Nikolai. "Filosofiia i zhizn'. (Dnevnik publitsista)." *Novyi put'* 11 (1904): 362–75.

Berdiaev, Nikolai. "O novom russkom idealizme." In *Sub specie aeternitatis. Opyty filosofskie, sotsial'nye i literaturnye (1900–1906 g.)*, 152–90. St. Petersburg: Izdanie M. V. Pirozhkova, 1907.

Berdiaev, Nikolai. "O realizme. (Vmesto predisloviia)." In *Sub specie aeternitatis*, 1–4.

Berdiaev, Nikolai. "Russian Religious Psychology and Communistic Atheism." In *The Russian Revolution*, translated by D. B. London: Sheed & Ward, 1933.

Berdiaev, Nikolai. "Stavrogin." *Russkaia mysl'* 5 (1914): 80–89.

Berdiaev, Nikolai. *Sub specie aeternitatis. Opyty filosofskie, sotsial'nye i literaturnye (1900–1906 g.)*. St. Petersburg: Izdanie M. V. Pirozhkova, 1907.

Blank, Ksana. *Dostoevsky's Dialectics and the Problem of Sin*. Evanston, IL: North-western University Press, 2010.

Blok, Aleksandr. "Bezvremen'e." *Zolotoe runo* 11–12 (1906): 107–14.

Bogomolov, N. A., ed. *Kuzmin: stat'i i materialy*. Moscow: NLO, 1995.

Budanova, N. F. "O nekotorykh istochnikakh nravstvenno-filosofskoi probl-ematiki romana 'Besy.'" In *Dostoevskii: materialy i issledovannia*, vol. 8, edited by G. M. Fridlender, 93–106. Leningrad: Nauka, 1988.

Bulgakov, S. N. "Bez plana. 'Idealizm' i obshchestvennye programy. (pt. 2 of 3)." *Novyi put'* 11 (1904): 342–60.

Bulgakov, S. N. "Bez plana." *Voprosy zhizni* 3 (1905): 388–414.

Bulgakov, S. N. "Chekhov kak myslitel'." *Novyi put'* 10: 32–54; 11: 138–52 (1904).

Bulgakov, S. N. "Chto daet sovremennomu soznaniiu filosofiia Vl. Solov'eva" (pt. 2 of 2). *Voprosy filosofii i psikhologii*, kn. 2, no. 67 (1903): 125–66.

Bulgakov, S. N. "Dushevnaia drama Gertsena." In *Ot marksizma k idealizmu*, 162–94.

Bulgakov, S. N. "Ivan Karamazov kak filosofskii tip." In *Ot marksizma k idealizmu*, 83–112.

Bulgakov, S. N. "Neotlozhnaia zadacha." *Voprosy zhizni* 9 (1905): 332–60.

Bulgakov, S. N. "Ob ekonomicheskom ideale." *Nauchnoe slovo* 5 (1903): 102–25.

Bulgakov, S. N. "Ocherk o F. M. Dostoevskom. Chrez chetvert veka (1881–1906)." In F. M. Dostoevskii, *Polnoe sobranie sochinenii F. M. Dostoevskogo. Iubileinoe (shestoe) izdanie*, vol. 1, iii–xl. St. Petersburg: Tip. P. F. Panteleeva, 1904.

Bulgakov, S. N. "O realisticheskom mirovozzrenie." *Voprosy filosofii i psikhologii*, kn. 3, no. 73 (May–June 1904): 380–403.

Bulgakov, S. N. *Ot marksizma k idealizmu. Sbornik statei (1896–1903)*. St. Petersburg: Obshchestvennaia pol'za, 1903.

Bulgakov, S. N. "Russkaia tragediia." *Russkaia mysl'* 4 (1914): 1–26.

Bulgakov, S. N. "Vasnetsov, Dostoevskii, Vl. Solov'ev, Tolstoi. (Paralleli)." In *Literaturnoe delo. Sbornik*, 119–39. St. Petersburg: Tipografiia A. E. Kolpinskogo, 1902.

Bulgakov, S. N. "Venets ternovyi (Pamiati F. M. Dostoevskogo)." *Svoboda i kul'tura* 1 (1906): 17–36.

Bulich, N. N. *F. M. Dostoevskii i ego sochineniia (istoriko-literaturnye ocherki): rech' na akte Imperatorskogo Kazanskogo universiteta 5 noiabria 1881 g.* Kazan': Tipografiia Imperatorskogo Universiteta, 1881.

Burenin, V. P. [Z.]. "Zhurnalistika. Nechto o 'novykh tipakh' v romane g. Dostoevskogo 'Besy' …," *Sankt-peterburgskie vedomosti* 250 (October 11, 1871) (N.S.).

Burenin, V. P., and M. A. Suvorin. *Besy. Stseny iz romana F. M. Dostoevskogo. V 5 deistviakh*. St. Peterburg: Zhurnal Teatra Literaturno-khudozhestvennogo obshchestva, 1908.

Burenin, V. P., and M. A. Suvorin. *Besy [tekst]: Stseny iz romana v 5 d.* (tsenz. 1908), SPbGTB, ORiRK, Access number: 17035.

Burmistrova, A. V. "Instsenirovki romanov Dostoevskogo (pervye opyty)." *Neizvestnyi Dostoevskii* 3 (2019): 96–115.

Burry, Alexander. *Multi-Mediated Dostoevsky: Transposing Novels into Opera, Film, and Drama*. Evanston, IL: Northwestern University Press, 2011.

Byrnes, Robert F. *Pobedonostsev: His Life and Thought*. Bloomington: Indiana University Press, 1968.

Carnicke, Sharon Marie. *Stanislavsky in Focus: An Acting Master for the Twenty-First Century*, 2nd ed. London: Routledge, 2009.

Carter, Stephen. *The Political and Social Thought of F. M. Dostoevsky*. New York: Garland, 1991.

Cassedy, Steven. *Dostoevsky's Religion*. Stanford, CA: Stanford University Press, 2005.

Chepurov, Aleksandr. *A. P. Chekhov i Aleksandrinskii teatr*. St. Petersburg: Baltiiskie sezony, 2006.

Chizh, Vladimir. *Dostoevskii kak psikhopatolog. Ocherk*. Moscow: V Universitetskoi tipografii (M. Katkov), 1885.

Chulkov, Georgii [Boris Kremnev], ed. "Dostoevskii i sud'ba Rossii." In *Ogni. Literaturnyi al'manakh*, 133–48. Moscow: Izdanie G. N. Sementsova, 1918.

Chulkov, Georgii, ed. *Fakely*. Kn. 1. St. Petersburg: Tipografiia Montvida, 1906.

Chulkov, Georgii, ed. *Fakely*. Kn. 2. St. Petersburg: Izdanie D. K. Tikhomirova, 1907.

Chulkov, Georgii. *Gody stranstvii*. Moscow: Ellis Lak, 1999.

Chulkov, Georgii. *Kak rabotal Dostoevskii*. Moscow: Sovetskii pisatel', 1939.

Chulkov, Georgii. *O misticheskom anarkhizme*. St. Petersburg: Fakely, 1906.

Chulkov, Georgii. "Ob utverzhdenii lichnosti." In *Fakely*, kn. 2, 3–25. St. Petersburg: Fakely, 1907.

Chulkov, Georgii. "Pokryvalo Izidy." *Zolotoe runo* 5 (1908): 66–72.

Chulkov, Georgii. "Review of *Severnye tsvety*." *Voprosy zhizni* 6 (1905): 253–58.

Chulkov, Georgii. "Svetleiut dali." *Vesy* 3 (1904): 13–16.

Chulkov, Georgii. "Teatr i muzyka." *Nasha zhizn'* 353, January 25/February 8, 1906.

Chulkov, Georgii. "Teatr i muzyka." *Tovarishch* 239, April 11/24, 1907.

Chulkov, Georgii. [Tch.]. "Teatr i muzyka. Malyi teatr. Stseny iz romana F. M. Dostoevskogo 'Besy.'" *Tovarishch*, October 2, 1907 (O.S.).

Clowes, Edith. *Fiction's Overcoat: Russian Literary Culture and the Question of Philosophy*. Ithaca, NY: Cornell University Press, 2018.

Coates, Ruth. "Feuerbach, Kant, Dostoevskii: The Evolution of 'Heroism' and 'Asceticism' in Bulgakov's Work to 1909." In *Landmarks Revisited: The Vekhi Symposium One Hundred Years On*, edited by Robin Aizlewood and Ruth Coates, 287–307. Boston: Academic Studies, 2013.

Contino, Paul. *Dostoevsky's Incarnational Realism: Finding Christ among the Karamazovs*. Eugene, OR: Cascade, 2020.

Cravens, Craig. "The Strange Relationship of Stavrogin and Stepan Trofimovich as Told by Anton Lavrent'evich G-v." *Slavic Review* 59, no. 4 (Winter 2000): 782–801.

Cronin, Glenn. *Disenchanted Wanderer: The Apocalyptic Vision of Konstantin Leontiev*. Ithaca, NY: Cornell University Press, 2021.

Camus, Albert. *Notebooks: 1935–1942*, vol. 1, translated by Philip Thody. New York: Knopf, 1963.

Camus, Albert. *The Rebel: An Essay on Man in Revolt*, translated by Anthony Bower. New York: Vintage, 1991.

Davis, Paul. *The Lives and Times of Ebenezer Scrooge*. New Haven, CT: Yale University Press, 1990.

Del'er, Ia. A. *Prestuplenie i nakazanie. Dramaticheskie stseny v 10 kartinakh, s epilogom. Po romanu F. M. Dostoevskogo*. St. Petersburg: Izd. zhurn. "Teatr i iskusstvo," 1899. Printed in *Teatr i iskusstvo* 38 (1900).

Derrida, Jacques. *Specters of Marx*, translated by Peggy Kamuf. London: Routledge, 1994.

Dixon, Simon. "Rozanov's Peter." In *Word and Image in Russian History*, edited by Maria di Salvo, Daniel H. Kaiser, and Valerie A. Kivelson, 172–90. Boston: Academic Studies, 2019.

Dobuzhinskii, M. "O khudozhestvennom teatre." *Novyi Zhurnal* 5 (1943): 23–62.

Dolinin, A. "Dostoevskii sredi Petrashevtsev." In *Zven'ia: Sborniki materialov i dokumentov po istorii literatury, iskusstva, i obshchestvennoi mysli xix veka*, vyp. 6, edited by Vlad. Bonch-Bruevich, 512–45. Moscow: Academia, 1936.

Dorovatovskii, S., and A. Charushinkov, eds. *Ocherki realisticheskogo mirovozreniia: Sbornik statei po filosofii, obshchestvennoi nauke i zhizni*, 2nd ed. St. Petersburg: Tip. Montvida, 1905.

Dostoevskaia, A. G. *Bibliograficheskii ukazatel' sochinenii i proizvedenii iskusstva, otnosiashchikhsia k zhizni i deiatel'nosti F. M. Dostoevskogo, sobrannykh v 'Muzee pamiati F. M. Dostoevskogo' v Moskovskom Istoricheskom Muzee Imeni Imperatora Aleksandra III. 1846–1903.* St. Petersburg: Tip. P. F. Panteleeva, 1906.

Dostoevskii, F. M. "Perepiska i zametki F. M. Dostoevskogo." *Severnyi vestnik* 11 (1891): 5–34.

Dostoevskii, F. M. *Polnoe sobranie sochinenii,* edited by G. M. Fridlender et al. 30 volumes. Leningrad: Nauka, 1972–90.

Dostoevskii, F. M. *Polnoe sobranie sochinenii F. M. Dostoevskogo. Iubileinoe (shestoe) izdanie.* Vols. 1–14. St. Petersburg: Tip. P. F. Panteleeva, 1904–1906.

Dostoevskaia, Liubov'. *Dostoevskii v izobrazhenii ego docheri,* translated by L. Ia. Krukovskaia and edited by A. G. Gornfel'd. Moscow: Gosudarstvennoe izdatel'stvo, 1922.

Dymov, Osip. "Dramaticheskie elementy v romanakh Dostoevskogo." *Teatr i iskusstvo* 6 (1900): 118–20; 7 (1900): 138–39; 8 (1900): 159–60.

Dymov, Osip. "Four Pillars of Russian Art." Papers of Ossip Dymow. YIVO Institute for Jewish Research. RG 469, folder 50, Vignettes (Portraits) (from: "This I Remember").

Dymov, Osip. "Peterburgskie teatry." *Zolotoe runo* 10 (1906): 79–80.

Dymov, Osip. "Review of *The Idiot.*" *Teatr i iskusstvo* 46 (1899): 810–11.

Emmons, Terence. "The Statutes of the Union of Liberation." *Russian Review* 33, no. 1 (January 1974): 80–85.

Engelstein, Laura. *The Keys to Happiness: Sex and the Search for Happiness in Fin-de-Siècle Russia.* Ithaca, NY: Cornell University Press, 1992.

Engelstein, Laura. *Slavophile Empire: Imperial Russia's Illiberal Path.* Ithaca, NY: Cornell University Press, 2009.

Erberg, Konst. "Bezvlastie." *Zolotoe runo* 4 (1907): 46–63.

Evtuhov, Catherine. *The Cross and the Sickle: Sergei Bulgakov and the Fate of Russian Religious Philosophy.* Ithaca, NY: Cornell University Press, 1997.

F., A. "Teatr i muzyka. 'Idiot.'" *Novosti i birzhevaia gazeta* 305 (November 5/17, 1899).

Fateev, V. A. *V. V. Rozanov: zhizn', tvorchestvo, lichnost'.* Leningrad: Khudozhestvennaia literatura, 1991.

Felski, Rita. *The Limits of Critique.* Chicago: University of Chicago Press, 2015.

Filippov, B. A., ed. *Konstantin Leont'ev. Pis'ma k Vasiliiu Rozanovu.* London: Nina Karsov, 1981.

Filosofov, Dmitrii. "Igra v religiiu." *Russkaia mysl'* 4 (1908): 138–50.

Filosofov, Dmitrii. "Iskusstvo i zhizn'." *Novyi put'* 7 (1904): 208–37.

Filosofov, Dmitrii. "O 'lzhi' Gor'kogo." *Novyi put'* 6 (1903): 212–17.

Filosofov, Dmitrii. "Misticheskii anarkhizm. Dekadentstvo, obshchestvennost' i misticheskii anarkhizm." *Zolotoe runo* 10 (1906): 58–65.

Filosofov, Dmitrii. "Propoved' idealizma." *Novyi put'* 10 (1903): 177–84.

Foucault, Michel. "What Is an Author?" In *Textual Strategies: Perspectives in Post-Structuralist Criticism,* edited and translated by José V. Harari, 141–60. Ithaca, NY: Cornell University Press, 1979.

Frame, Murray. "'Freedom of the Theatres': The Abolition of the Russian Imperial Theatre Monopoly." *Slavonic and East European Review* 83, no. 2 (2005): 254–89.

Frame, Murray. *School for Citizens: Theatre and Civil Society in Imperial Russia*. New Haven, CT: Yale University Press, 2006.

Frank, Joseph. *Dostoevsky*. 5 volumes. Princeton, NJ: Princeton University Press, 1976–2002.

Frank, Joseph. *Dostoevsky: A Writer in His Time*. Princeton, NJ: Princeton University Press, 2009.

Freidkina, L. M. *Dni i gody Vl. I. Nemirovicha-Danchenko: letopis' zhizni i tvorchestva*. Moscow: Vserossiiskoe teatral'noe obshchestvo, 1962.

Friedman, Susan Stanford. "Both/And: Critique and Discovery in the Humanities." *PMLA* 132, no. 2 (2017): 344–51. https://doi.org/10.1632/pmla.2017.132.2.344.

Friesen, Leonard G. *Transcendent Love: Dostoevsky and the Search for a Global Ethic*. Notre Dame, IN: University of Notre Dame Press, 2016.

Fuss, Diana. "But What about Love?" *PMLA* 132, no. 2 (2017): 352–55. https://doi.org/10.1632/pmla.2017.132.2.352.

Fusso, Susanne. "Maidens in Childbirth: The Sistine Madonna in Dostoevskii's *Devils*." *Slavic Review* 54, no. 2 (Summer 1995): 261–75.

Galai, Shmuel. *The Liberation Movement in Russia 1900–1905*. Cambridge: Cambridge University Press, 1973.

Galanina, Iu. E. "V. E. Meierkhol'd na bashne Viach. Ivanova." In *Bashnia Viacheslava Ivanova i kul'tura serebriannogo veka*, edited by V. E. Bagno and A. B. Shishkin, 187–205. St. Petersburg: Filolologicheskii fakul'tet S.-Peterburgskogo universiteta, 2006.

Gauss, Rebecca B. *Lear's Daughters: The Studios of the Moscow Art Theatre, 1905–1927*. New York: Peter Lang, 1999.

Gippius, Zinaida [A. Krainyi]. "Byt i sobytiia." *Novyi put'* 9 (1904): 280–92.

Gippius, Zinaida [Gippius-Merezhkovskaia]. *Dmitrii Merezhkovskii*. Paris: YMCA, 1951.

Gippius, Zinaida. "Dve dramy A. Tolstogo." *Mir iskusstva* 5 (1899): 34–35.

Gippius, Zinaida [Anton Krainyi]. "Kharakternoe priznanie." *Novyi put'* 2 (1903): 201.

Gippius, Zinaida. "Khleb zhizni." *Mir iskusstva* 11–12 (1901): 323–34.

Gippius, Zinaida [A. Krainyi]. "Vechnyi zhid." *Novyi put'* 9 (1903): 241–44.

Gippius, Zinaida. *Stikhotvoreniia. Zhivye litsa*, edited by N. A. Bogomolov. Moscow: Khudozhestvennaia literatura, 1991.

Goethe, Johann Wolfgang von. *Faust: A Tragedy*, translated by Walter Arndt. New York: Norton, 2001.

Gollerbakh, E. F. *V. V. Rozanov: zhizn' i tvorchestvo*. St. Petersburg: Poliarnaia Zvezda, 1922.

Gorin-Gorianov, B. A. *Aktery. Iz vospominanii*. Leningrad: Iskusstvo, 1947.

Gornfel'd, A. G. *Knigi i liudi. Literaturnye besedy*. St. Petersburg: Zhizn', 1908.

Gorodetskii, Sergei. "Blizhaishaia zadacha russkoi literatury." *Zolotoe runo* 4 (1909): 66–81.

Gor'kii, Maksim [Maxim Gorki]. *Best Short Stories of Maxim Gorki*, translated by Avrahm Yarmolinsky. New York: Grayson, 1947.

Gor'kii, Maksim. *Kniga o russkikh liudiakh*. Moscow: Vagrius, 2000.

Gor'kii, Maksim. "O 'Karamazovshchine.'" *Russkoe slovo*, September 22, 1913.

Grabar', Igor'. "Teatr i khudozhniki." *Vesy* 4 (1908): 92–95.

Grossman, Leonid. "Dostoevskii i pravitel'stvennye krugi 1870-kh godov." In Averbakh, *Literaturnoe nasledstvo*, vol. 15, 83–123.

Grillaert, Nel. "Orthodox Spirituality." In *Dostoevsky in Context*, edited by Deborah Martinsen and Olga Maiorova, 189–93. Cambridge: Cambridge University Press, 2015. https://doi.org/10.1017/CBO9781139236867.022.

Grot, Nikolai. "Eshche o zadachakh zhurnala." *Voprosy filosofii i psikhologii*, no. 2, kn. 6 (1891): i–vi.

Gusarova, A. P. *Mstislav Dobuzhinskii: Zhivopis'. Grafika. Teatr. Al'bom.* Moscow: Izobrazitel'noe iskusstvo, 1982.

Hall, Karl. "'Rasovye priznaki koreniatsia glubzhe v prirode chelovecheskogo organizma:' neulovimoe poniatie *rasy* v Rossiiskoi imperii," translated by V. S. Dubinaia. In Miller et al., *"Poniatiia o Rossii": k istoricheskoi semantike imperskogo perioda*, vol. 2, edited by I. A. Miller et al., 194–258. Moscow: NLO, 2012.

Halperin, Charles J. "Judaizers and the Image of the Jew in Medieval Russia: A Polemic Revisited and a Question Posed." *Canadian-American Slavic Studies* 9 (1975): 141–55.

Holland, Kate. "Dostoevsky's Journalism in the 1870s." In *Dostoevsky in Context*, edited by Deborah Martinsen and Olga Maiorova, 288–94. Cambridge: Cambridge University Press, 2015. https://doi.org/10.1017/CBO9781139236867.035.

Hollander, Robert. "The Apocalyptic Framework of Dostoevsky's *The Idiot*." *Mosaic* 6 (1974): 123–39.

Holquist, Michael. *Dostoevsky and the Novel.* Princeton, NJ: Princeton University Press, 1977.

Hudspith, Sarah. *Dostoevsky and the Idea of Russianness: A New Perspective on Unity and Brotherhood.* London: Routledge, 2004.

Hutcheon, Linda. *A Theory of Adaptation.* New York: Routledge, 2006.

"Ia. P. Pliushchevskii-Pliushchik." *Teatral'naia gazeta* 16 (1916): 7.

Iablonovskii, Sergei. "Budi! Budi!" *Rampa i zhizn'* 4 (January 24, 1916): 5–6.

Iantareva[-Vilkina], R. A. *Detskie tipy v proizvedeniiakh Dostoevskogo. Psikhologicheskie etiudy.* St. Petersburg: Gramotnost', 1895.

Impressionist. "Teatr i muzyka." *Novosti i birzhevaia gazeta* 276 (October 6/18, 1899).

Ivanov, Viacheslav. "Ancient Terror: On Leon Bakst's Painting *Terror Antiquus*." In Bird and Wachtel, *Selected Essays*, 144–62.

Ivanov, Viacheslav. "Doklad 'Evangel'skii smysl slova "Zemlia,"' Pis'ma. Avtobiografiia (1926)." Publication and commentary by G. V. Obatnin. In *Ezhegodnik rukopisnogo otdela Pushkinskogo doma na 1991 god*, edited by T. S. Tsar'kova, 142–70. St. Petersburg: Akademicheskii proekt, 1994.

Ivanov, Viacheslav. "Dostoevskii i roman-tragediia." *Russkaia mysl'* 5: 46–61; 6 (1911): 1–17.

Ivanov, Viacheslav. *Dostoevskii: tragediia, mif, mistika*, edited by A. B. Shishkin and O. L. Fetisen'ko. St. Petersburg: Pushkinskii dom, 2021.

Ivanov, Viacheslav. "Drevnii uzhas: Po povodu kartiny L. Baksta 'Terror Antiquus.'" *Zolotoe runo* 4 (1909): 51–65.

Ivanov, Viacheslav. "Dve stikhii v sovremennom simvolizme." *Zolotoe runo* 3–4: 86–94; 5: 44–55 (1908).

Ivanov, Viacheslav. "Ellinskaia religiia stradaiushchego boga." *Novyi put'* 1: 110–34; 2: 48–78; 3: 38–61; 5: 28–40; 8: 17–26; 9: 47–70 (1904).

Ivanov, Viacheslav. *Freedom and the Tragic Life: A Study in Dostoevsky*. New York: Noonday, 1952.

Ivanov, Viacheslav. "Ideia nepriiatiia mira i misticheskii anarkhizm." In Chulkov, *O misticheskom anarkhizme*.

Ivanov, Viacheslav. "Krizis individualizma." *Voprosy zhizni* 9 (1905): 47–60.

Ivanov, Viacheslav. "Lik i lichiny Rossii. K issledovaniiu ideologii Dostoevskogo." *Russkaia mysl'* 1 (1917): 16–43.

Ivanov, Viacheslav. "O niskhozhdenii." *Vesy* 5 (1905): 26–36.

Ivanov, Viacheslav. "On the Joyful Craft and the Joy of the Spirit." In *Selected Essays*, edited by Michael Wachtel, translation and notes by Robert Bird, 113–27 (Evanston, IL: Northwestern University Press, 2001).

Ivanov, Viacheslav. "Nepriiatie mira." In *Fakely*, kn. 1, 51.

Ivanov, Viacheslav. "Religiia Dionisa. Ee proiskhozhdenie i vliianie." *Voprosy zhizni* 6: 185–220; 7: 122–48 (1905).

Ivanov, Viacheslav. *Selected Essays*, translation and notes by Robert Bird and edited by Michael Wachtel. Evanston, IL: Northwestern University Press, 2001.

Ivanov, Viacheslav. "The Symbolics of Aesthetic Principles." In Bird and Wachtel, *Selected Essays*, 5–12.

Ivanov, Viacheslav. "Viach. Ivanov o F. M. Dostoevskom." Published by D. V. Ivanov and A. B. Shishkin with an introduction by A. T. Kazarian. In *Viacheslav Ivanov: Arkhivnye materialy i issledovaniia*, edited by L. A. Gogotishvili and A. T. Kazarian. Moscow: Russkie slovari, 1999.

Iuzhnyi, M. "K postanovke tragedii 'Tsar' Fedor Ioannovich.'" *Teatr i iskusstvo* 42 (1898): 745–48.

I-t. "Teatr i muzyka." *Russkaia viedomosti* 283 (October 13, 1899).

Jackson, Robert Louis. *Dialogues with Dostoevsky: The Overwhelming Questions*. Stanford, CA: Stanford University Press, 1993.

Jackson, Robert Louis. *Dostoevsky's Quest for Form*. New Haven, CT: Yale University Press, 1966.

Jagoda, Patrick. "Critique and Critical Making." *PMLA* 132, no. 2 (2017): 356–63. https://doi.org/10.1632/pmla.2017.132.2.356.

Jones, Malcolm V. *Dostoevsky and the Dynamics of Religious Experience*. London: Anthem, 2005.

Keldysh, V. A. "F. M. Dostoevskii v kritike Merezhkovskogo." In *D. S. Merezhkovskii: mysl' i slovo*, edited by V. A. Keldysh, I. V. Koretskaia, and M. A. Nikitina, 207–23. Moscow: Nasledie, 1999.

Kelly, Aileen. *Toward Another Shore: Russian Thinkers Between Necessity and Chance*. New Haven, CT: Yale University Press, 1998.

Kelly, Aileen. "The Two Dostoevskys." *New York Review of Books* 50, no. 5 (March 27, 2003): 23–25.

Kelly, Martha. *Unorthodox Beauty: Russian Modernism and Its New Religious Aesthetic*. Evanston, IL: Northwestern University Press, 2016.

Kheisin, M. "Dostoevskii i Nittsshe." *Mir Bozhii* 5 (1903): 119–41.

Kholikov, A. A. "'Boria, Boria, mal'chik moi liubimyi, edinstvennyi . . .' Pis'ma D. S. Merezhkovskogo Andreiu Belomu." *Voprosy literatury* 1 (2006): 135–85.

"Khronika." *Obozrenie teatrov* 171 (August 18, 1907), 7–8; 193 (September 18, 1907), 14.

Kindersley, Richard. *The First Russian Revisionists: A Study of "Legal Marxism" in Russia.* Oxford: Clarendon, 1962.

Kitzinger, Chloë. *Mimetic Lives: Tolstoy, Dostoevsky, and Character in the Novel.* Evanston, IL: Northwestern University Press, 2021.

Klier, John D. *Imperial Russia's Jewish Question.* Cambridge: Cambridge University Press, 1995.

Knapp, Liza. *The Annihilation of Inertia: Dostoevsky and Metaphysics.* Evanston, IL: Northwestern University Press, 1996.

Kołakowski, Leszek. *The Alienation of Reason: A History of Positivist Thought.* Garden City, NY: Doubleday, 1968.

Kolerov, M. A. *Ne mir, no mech: russkaia religiozno-filosofskaia pechat' ot 'Problema idealizma' do 'Vekh,' 1902–1909.* St. Petersburg: Izd. Aleteiia, 1996.

Kolerov, M. A., ed. *Iznutri: Pis'ma Berdiaeva, Bulgakova, Novgorodtseva i Franka k Struve.* Moscow: Izdanie knizhnogo magazina 'Tsiolkovskii,' 2018.

Koreneva, M. Iu, ed. "Pis'ma D. S. Merezhkovskogo k P. P. Pertsovu." *Russkaia literatura* 2 (1991): 156–81; 3 (1991): 132–59.

Koretskaia, I. V. "*Novyi put'. Voprosy zhizni.*" In *Literaturnyi protsess i russkaia zhurnalistika kontsa xix–nachala xx veka*, vol. 2, edited by B. A. Bialik, 179–233. Moscow: Nauka, 1982.

Kornblatt, Judith Deutsch, and Gary Rosenshield. "Vladimir Solovyov: Confronting Dostoevsky on the Jewish and Christian Questions." *Journal of the American Academy of Religion* 68, no. 1 (March 2000): 69–98.

Korzov, I. I. *Dramaturgiia Vl. I. Nemirovicha-Danchenko.* Kiev: Izdatel'stvo Kievskogo universiteta, 1971.

Kostalevsky, Marina. *Dostoevsky and Soloviev: The Art of Integral Vision.* New Haven, CT: Yale University Press, 1997.

Kraseva, A. G. *Idiot. Drama v 5 deistviiakh i 7 kartinakh, peredelannaia dlia stseny iz romana Dostoevskogo.* 1890. SPbGTB. ORiRK. Access number: 30435, rukopisnyi tekst, K 780.

Krasnov, Pl. "Peredelki." *Teatral'naia Rossiia* 2–3 (1905): 28–31.

Krupskaia, N. K. *Vospominaniia o Lenine.* Moscow: Partizdat, 1933.

Krylov, V., and G. [sic] Sutugin. *Idiot. Drama v 5 deistviiakh, peredelannaia iz romana M. F. [sic] Dostoevskogo. Stsena*, vyp. 7 (1899).

Kugel', Aleksandr [Homo novus]. "Zametki." *Teatr i iskusstvo* 18 (1914): 407–09.

Kugel', Aleksandr [Staryi teatral]. "Review of *Idiot.*" *Teatr i iskusstvo* 45 (1899): 793–94.

Kugel', Aleksandr. "Teatral'nye zametki." *Teatr i iskusstvo* 41 (1899): 715–17.

Kugel', Aleksandr. "Teatral'nye zametki." *Teatr i iskusstvo* 40 (1907): 654–66.

Kugel', Aleksandr, and V. Filippov, eds. *Sto let Malomu teatru, 1824–1924.* Moscow: Russkoe teatral'noe obshchestvo, 1924.

Kupchenko, V. P. "F. Dostoevskii i M. Voloshin." In *Dostoevskii: materialy i issledovaniia*, vol. 8, edited by G. M. Fridlender, 203–17. Leningrad: Nauka, 1988.

Latour, Bruno. *Reassembling the Social: An Introduction to Actor-Network-Theory.* Oxford: Oxford University Press, 2005.

Latour, Bruno. "Why Has Critique Run Out of Steam? From Matters of Fact to Matters of Concern." *Critical Inquiry* 30, no. 2 (Winter 2004): 225–48.

Lavrov, A. V. "Dostoevskii v tvorcheskom soznanii Andreia Belogo (1900-e gody)." In *Andrei Belyi. Problemy tvorchestva*, edited by St. Lesnevskii and Al. Mikhailov, 131–50. Moscow: Sovetskii pisatel', 1988.

Leatherbarrow, W. J., ed. *Dostoevsky's* The Devils: *A Critical Companion.* Evanston, IL: Northwestern University Press, 1999.

Leman, A. I. *Idiot. Drama v 4 deistviakh. (Iz romana F. M. Dostoevskogo)* (unpublished manuscript). 1889. SPbGTB. ORiRK. Access number: 23145, rukopisnyi tekst, L 440.

Leont'ev, K. *Nashi novye khristiane. F. M. Dostoevskii i gr. Lev Tolstoi.* Moscow: Tipografiia E. I. Pogodinoi, 1882.

Leont'ev, I. V. "' . . . Nichto ne mozhet zamenit' religiiu' (Sokrovennye pis'ma Georgiia Chulkova)." *Zvezda* 3 (1995): 116–25.

Lim, Susanna Soojung. "Pan-Mongolians at Twilight: East Asia and Race in Russian Modernism, 1890–1921." In *Race and Racism in Modern East Asia: Western and Eastern Constructions*, edited by Rotem Kowner and Walter Demel, 154–75. Leiden: Brill, 2013.

Listengarten, Julia. "Stanislavsky and the Avant-Garde." In *The Routledge Companion to Stanislavsky*, edited by R. Andrew White, 67–81. London: Routledge, 2014.

Lowrie, Donald A. *Rebellious Prophet: A Life of Nicolai Berdyaev.* Westport, CT: Greenwood, 1974.

Lunacharskii, A. *Faust i gorod. Drama dlia chteniia.* Petrograd: Narkompros, 1918.

Lunacharskii, A. "O g. Volzhskom i ego idealakh." *Obrazovanie* 5 (1904): 110–22.

Lunacharskii, A. "Russkii Faust." *Voprosy filosofii i psikhologii*, kn. 3, no. 63 (1902): 783–95.

Malakhieva-Mirovich, V. "Novaia p'esa D. S. Merezhkovskogo," *Russkaia mysl'* 3 (1916): 24–27.

Marchitello, Howard. *Remediating Shakespeare in the Eighteenth and Nineteenth Centuries.* Cham, Switzerland: Palgrave Macmillan, 2019.

Markelov, G. "Idealizm i marksizm." *Mir Bozhii* 5 (1902): 225–41.

Martinsen, Deborah, and Olga Maiorova, eds. *Dostoevsky in Context.* Cambridge: Cambridge University Press, 2015.

Matich, Olga. *Erotic Utopia: The Decadent Imagination in Russia's Fin de Siècle.* Madison: University of Wisconsin Press, 2005.

McReynolds, Louise. *Russia at Play: Leisure Activities at the End of the Tsarist Era.* Ithaca, NY: Cornell University Press, 2003.

Mech, R. "Zhiteiskie motivy." *Russkii listok* 280 (October 13, 1899): 2.

Medzhibovskaia, Inessa, ed. "Tolstoy's Jewish Problems." In *Tolstoy and His Problems: Views from the Twenty-First Century.* Evanston, IL: Northwestern University Press, 2019.

Meierkhol'd, V. E. *Perepiska, 1896–1939*, edited by V. P. Korshunova and M. M. Sitkovetskaia. Moscow: Iskusstvo, 1976.

Merezhkovskii, D. S. *Antikhrist: Petr i Aleksei*. St. Petersburg: Izd. M. B. Pirozh-kova, 1905.

Merezhkovskii, D. S. "Avtobiograficheskaia zametka." In *Polnoe sobranie sochine-niia*, vol. 23. Moscow: Tipografiia I. D. Sytina, 1914.

Merezhkovskii, D. S. *Budet radost'*. Petrograd: Izd. Ogni, 1916.

Merezhkovskii, D. S. "Glava vtoraia. L. Tolstoi i Dostoevskii, kak khudozh-niki." *Mir iskusstva* 17–18 (1900): 71–84.

Merezhkovskii, D. S. "Griadushchii kham." *Poliarnaia zvezda* 3 (1905): 185–92.

Merezhkovskii, D. S. "Khristianstvo L. Tolstogo." *Mir iskusstva* 6 (1901): 289–318.

Merezhkovskii, D. S. *L. Tolstoi i Dostoevskii*, edited by E. A. Andrushchenko. Mos-cow: Nauka, 2000.

Merezhkovskii, D. S. "Lev Tolstoi i Dostoevskii. Zakliuchenie." *Mir iskusstva* 2 (1902): 89–132.

Merezhkovskii, D. S. "O novom religioznom deistvii (otkrytoe pis'mo N. A. Berdiaevu)." *Voprosy zhizni* 10–11 (1905): 358–76.

Merezhkovskii, D. S. "'Ottsy i deti' russkogo liberalizma." *Mir iskusstva* 3 (1901): 126–28.

Merezhkovskii, D. S. *O prichinakh upadka i o novykh techeniiakh sovremennoi russkoi literatury*. St. Petersburg: Tipo-Litografiia B. M. Vol'fa, 1893.

Merezhkovskii, D. S. "Prazdnik Pushkina." *Mir iskusstva* 13–14 (1899): 11–20.

Merezhkovskii, D. S. "Prorok russkoi revoliutsii. K iubileiu Dostoevskogo." *Vesy* 2: 27–45; 3–4: 19–47 (1906).

Merezhkovskii, D. S. "Revoliutsiia i religiia." *Russkaia mysl'* 2: 64–85; 3: 17–34 (1907).

Merezhkovskii, D. S. "V obez'ian'ikh lapakh. O Leonide Andreeve." *Russkaia mysl'* 1 (1908): 75–98.

Merezhkovskii, D. S. "Vse protiv vsekh." *Zolotoe runo* 1 (1906): 90–97.

Merezhkovskii, D. S. "Zheltolitsye pozitivisty." *Vestnik inostrannoi literatury* 3 (1895): 71–84.

Mérejkowsky, D., Z. Hippius, and Dm. Philosophoff. *Le tsar et la révolution*. Paris: Société du Mercure de France, 1907.

Mikhailovskii, N. M. "Literatura i zhizn'." *Russkoe bogatstvo* 8 (1902): 76–99.

Mikhailovskii, N. M. "Literatura i zhizn'." *Russkoe bogatstvo* 9 (1902): 44–69.

Miller, I. A., D. Sdvizhkov, and I. Schierle, eds. *"Poniatiia o Rossii": k istoricheskoi semantike imperskogo perioda*, vol. 2. Moscow: NLO, 2012.

Miller, Orest, and Nikolai Strakhov, eds. *Biografiia, pis'ma i zametki iz zapisnoi knizhki F. M. Dostoevskogo*. St. Petersburg: Tipografiia A. S. Suvorina, 1883.

Miller, Renata Kobetts. "Nineteenth-Century Theatrical Adaptations of Novels: The Paradox of Ephemerality." In *The Oxford Handbook of Adaptation Studies*, edited by Thomas Leitch, 53–70. Oxford: Oxford University Press, 2017.

Miller, Robin Feuer. *Dostoevsky and* The Idiot: *Author, Narrator and Reader*. Cam-bridge, MA: Harvard University Press, 1981.

Miller, Robin Feuer. *Dostoevsky's Unfinished Journey*. New Haven, CT: Yale Uni-versity Press, 2007.

Miller, Robin Feuer. "Frank's Dostoevsky." *Slavic and East European Journal* 47, no. 3 (Autumn 2003): 471–77.

Mirovich, N. *Rytsar' bednyi. Dramaticheskie stseny v 5 deistviiakh v 6 kartinakh*. Soch. N. Stênson (Peredelano iz romana F. M. Dostoevskogo). 1899. SPbGTB. ORiRK. Access number: 69562, rukopisnyi tekst, M 640.

Mogilner, Marina. *Homo Imperii: A History of Physical Anthropology in Russia*. Lincoln: University of Nebraska Press, 2013.

Mondry, Henrietta. "*Petersburg* and Contemporary Racial Thought." In *A Reader's Guide to Andrei Bely's* Petersburg, edited by Leonid Livak, 124–37. Madison: University of Wisconsin Press, 2019.

Mondry, Henrietta. *Vasily Rozanov and the Body of Russian Literature*. Bloomington, IN: Slavica, 2010.

Morson, Gary Saul. "Dostoevsky's Anti-Semitism and the Critics: A Review Article." *Slavic and East European Journal* 27, no. 3 (Autumn 1983): 302–17.

Morson, Gary Saul. "Conclusion: Reading Dostoevsky." In *The Cambridge Companion to Dostoevskii*, edited by W. J. Leatherbarrow, 212–34. Cambridge: Cambridge University Press, 2002.

Mostovskaia, N. N. "Dostoevskii v dnevnikakh S. I. Smirnovoi (Sazonovoi)." In *Dostoevskii. Materialy i issledovaniia*, vol. 4, edited by G. M. Fridlender, 271–78. Leningrad: Nauka, 1980.

Murav, Harriet. "The Predatory Jew and Russian Vitalism: Dostoevsky, Rozanov, and Babel." In *Ritual Murder in Russia, Eastern Europe, and Beyond*, edited by Eugene M. Avrutin et al., 151–71. Bloomington: Indiana University Press, 2017.

Nemirovich-Danchenko, V. I. *My Life in the Russian Theatre*, translated by John Cournos. New York: Theatre Arts, 1968.

Nemirovich-Danchenko, V. I. Ekzempliar 1; "Nikolai Stavrogin," otryvki iz romana F. M. Dostoevskogo "Besy" [pervyi variant teksta]; Instsenirovka [Vl. Iv. Nemirovicha-Danchenko.] [1913, okolo 17 avgusta]–[1913, sentiabria, 3]. Moskovskii khudozhestvennyi teatr, BRCh ~ 661; MM ~ 661.

Nemirovich-Danchenko, V. I. "Nikolai Stavrogin, otryvki iz romana F. M. Dostoevskogo 'Besy.'" Dnevnik repetitsii. Sezon 1913–1914 goda, 1913, avgust, 16–1913, oktiabria, 31. Muzei MKhAT. RCh~95, MM~95, F1 44/46.

Nemirovich-Danchenko, V. I. "Otkrytoe pis'mo M. Gor'komu." *Russkoe slovo* 221, October 26, 1913.

Nemirovich-Danchenko, V. I. *Tvorcheskoe nasledie v chetyrekh tomakh*, vol. 2. Moscow: Izd. MAT, 2003.

Nikoliukin, A. N. *Rozanov*. Moscow: Molodaia gvardiia, 2018.

Ninov, A. "Rozhdenie teatra Dostoevskogo." In *Dostoevskii i teatr: sbornik statei*, edited by A. A. Ninov. Leningrad, 1983.

Nir, M. "Beseda s M. Gor'kim." *Teatr* 1459 (1914): 7–8.

Novgorodtsev, P. I. "Foreword to the Russian Edition." In Poole, *Problems of Idealism*, 81–84.

Novgorodtsev, P. I., ed. *Problemy idealizma: sbornik statei*. Moscow: Izd. Moskovskogo psikhologicheskogo obshchestva, 1903.

Novyi. "Teatr i muzyka." *Russkoe slovo* 282 (October 13, 1899).

Obatnin, G. V., ed. "Neopublikovannye materialy Viach. Ivanova po povodu polemiki o 'misticheskom anarkhizme.'" In *Litsa. Biograficheskii al'manakh*, vol. 3, edited by A. V. Lavrov, 466–77. Moscow: Feniks, 1993.

Obituary [of F. M. Dostoevsky]. *Peterburgskaia Gazeta*, no. 25, January 30, 1881.

Obolenskii, L. E. [N. N.]. "Literaturnye tipy." *Svet* 9 (1879): 96–105.

Olikov, M. "Teatr i muzyka." *Russkii listok* 280 (October 13, 1899).

Orlenev, P. N. *Zhizn' i tvorchestvo russkogo aktera Pavla Orleneva opisannye im samim*. Moscow: Academia, 1931.

Ornatskaia, T. I., and G. V. Stepanova. "Romany Dostoevskogo i dramaticheskaia tsenzura (60-e gody XIX v.–nachalo XX v.)." In *Dostoevskii. Materialy i issledovaniia*, vol. 1, edited by G. M. Fridlender, 268–84. Leningrad: Nauka, 1974.

Orshanskii, I. G. "Istoriia odnogo ideinogo prestupleniia. 'Prestuplenie i Nakazanie' F. M. Dostoevskogo." *Severnyi vestnik* (1896); 10: 15–34; 11: 48–70.

Orwin, Donna. "Achilles in *Crime and Punishment*." In *Dostoevsky Beyond Dostoevsky: Science, Religion, Philosophy*, edited by Svetlana Evdokimova and Vladimir Golstein, 367–78. Boston: Academic Studies, 2019.

Pakhmuss, Temira. "Dostoevskii v proizvedeniiakh Merezhkovskogo perioda emigratsii." *Novyi zhurnal*, kn. 184–185 (1991): 270–74.

Panova, Lada. *Russkii Egipet: Aleksandriiskaia poetika Mikhaila Kuzmina*, vol. 1. Moscow: Progress-Pleiada, 2006.

Paperno, Irina. *Chernyshevsky and the Age of Realism: A Study in the Semiotics of Behavior*. Stanford, CA: Stanford University Press, 1988.

Paperno, Irina. *Suicide as a Cultural Institution in Dostoevsky's Russia*. Ithaca, NY: Cornell University Press, 1997.

Pertsov, P. "Venetsianskaia shkola zhivopisi." *Novyi put'* 9 (1903): 11–54.

Petrovskaia, I., and V. Somina. *Teatral'nyi Peterburg: Nachalo XVIII veka–oktiabr' 1917 goda. Obozrenie-putevoditel'*. St. Petersburg: RIII, 1994.

Petrovskii, S. *Pamiati Imperatora Aleksandra III*. Moscow: S. Petrovskii, 1894.

Pipes, Richard. *Struve: Liberal on the Left, 1870–1905*, vol. 1. Cambridge, MA: Harvard University Press, 1970.

Platonov, L. V. *Kniaz' Myshkin. Drama v 5 deistviiakh. (Peredelka romana F. M. Dostoevskogo "Idiot.")*. 1895. SPbGTB. ORiRK. Access number: 40567, rukopisnyi tekst, P 375.

Poole, Randall A. *The Moscow Psychological Society and the Neo-Idealist Development of Russian Liberalism, 1885–1922*. PhD dissertation, University of Notre Dame, 1996.

Poole, Randall A. "The Neo-Idealist Reception of Kant in the Moscow Philosophical Society." *Journal of the History of Ideas* 60, no. 2 (April 1999): 319–43.

Poole, Randall A., ed. and trans. *Problems of Idealism: Essays in Russian Social Philosophy*. New Haven, CT: Yale University Press, 2003.

Prokopov, T. F., ed. *Tainyi pravitel' Rossii: K. P. Pobedonostsev i ego korrespondenty*. Moscow: Russkaia kniga, 2001.

Prozaik. "Khronika teatra i iskusstva. Malyi teatr." *Teatr i iskusstvo* 41 (1899): 712.

Putnam, George F. *Russian Alternatives to Marxism*. Knoxville: University of Tennessee Press, 1977.

Pyman, Avril. *A History of Russian Symbolism*. Cambridge: Cambridge University Press, 1994.

Radishcheva, O. A., and E. A. Shingareva, eds. *Moskovskii khudozhestvennyi teatr v russkoi teatral'noi kritike, 1906–1918*. Moscow: Artist. Rezhisser. Teatr, 2007.

Rampton, Vanessa. *Liberal Ideas in Tsarist Russia: From Catherine the Great to the Russian Revolution*. Cambridge: Cambridge University Press, 2020.

Re. "Khronika." *Teatr i iskusstvo* 42 (1899): 734.

Renan, Ernest. *History of the People of Israel Till the Time of King David*. London: Chapman and Hall, 1888.

Reznichenko, A. I. "'Zhizn' i tvorchestvo F. M. Dostoevskogo' A. S. Glinka-Volzhskogo: iz istorii odnogo 'nesbyvshegosia sobytiia.'" In *F. M. Dostoevskii i kul'tura Serebrianogo veka: traditsii, traktovki, transformatsii*, edited by Elena Takho-Godi et al., 249–66. Moscow: Vodolei, 2012.

Rice, James L. *Dostoevsky and the Healing Art: An Essay in Literary and Medical History*. Ann Arbor, MI: Ardis, 1985.

Rice, James L. "Dostoevsky's Endgame: The Projected Sequel to 'The Brothers Karamazov.'" *Russian History* 33, no. 1 (2006): 45–62.

Ricoeur, Paul. *Freud and Philosophy: An Essay on Interpretation*, translated by Denis Savage. New Haven, CT: Yale University Press, 1970.

Rogger, Hans. *Jewish Policies and Right-Wing Politics in Imperial Russia*. Berkeley: University of California Press, 1986.

Rozanov, V. V. "A. L. Volynskii. F. M. Dostoevskii." *Kriticheskoe obozrenie* 5 (1909): 37–42.

Rozanov, V. V. "Iz vostochnykh motivov." In *Sobranie sochineniia*, vol. 10, *Vo dvore iazychnikov*, edited by A. N. Nikoliukin (Moscow: Respublika, 1999), 177–86.

Rozanov, V. V. "Iz zagadok chelovecheskoi prirody." In *V mire neiasnogo i nereshennogo*. St. Petersburg: Tipografiia M. Merkusheva, 1901.

Rozanov, V. V. "Kontsy i nachala, 'bozhestvennoe' i 'demonicheskoe,' bogi i demony (Po povodu glavnogo siuzheta Lermontova)." *Mir iskusstva* 8 (1902): 122–37.

Rozanov, V. V. "Legenda o Velikom inkvizitore F. M. Dostoevskogo." *Russkii vestnik* 1–4 (1891).

Rozanov, V. V. *Legenda o velikom inkvizitore F. M. Dostoevskogo. Opyt kriticheskogo kommentariia*. St. Petersburg: Tipo-litografiia i notopechatnia S. M. Nikolaeva, 1894.

Rozanov, V. V. "Malen'kaia istoricheskaia popravka." In Nikoliukin, *Ss*, vol. 10, 144–51.

Rozanov, V. V. "Mesto khristianstva v istorii." In *Religiia i kul'tura*. St. Petersburg: Tipografiia M. Merkusheva, 1901.

Rozanov, V. V. *Mimoletnoe. 1915 god*. In Nikoliukin, *Sobranie sochineniia*, vol. 2, *Mimoletnoe* (1994).

Rozanov, V. V. "Na lektsii o Dostoevskom." In *Vlastitel' dum: F. M. Dostoevskii v russkoi kritike kontsa XIX–nachala XX veka*, edited by N. Ashimbaeva. St. Petersburg: Khudozhestvennaia literatura, 1997.

Rozanov, V. V. "Novaia rabota o Tolstom i Dostoevskom." In Nikoliukin, *Sobranie sochineniia*, vol. 27, *Iudaizm, Stat'i i ocherki, 1898–1901* (2009), 487–94.

Rozanov, V. V. "O drevne-egipetskoi krasote." *Mir iskusstva* 16–17 (1899): 29–32.

Rozanov, V. V. "Pis'mo v redaktsiiu." *Mir iskusstva* 15–16 (1900): 64.

Rozanov, V. V. "Poslesloviia k Kommentariiu 'Legendy o velikom inkvizitore' F. M. Dostoevskogo." *Zolotoe runo* 11–12 (1906): 97–101.

Rozanov, V. V. "Seriia nedorazumenii." *Novoe vremia* 8970, February 16, 1901.

Rozanov, V. V. "Sredi inoiazychnykh. (D. S. Merezhkovskii)." *Mir iskusstva* 7–8 (1903): 69–86.

Rozanov, V. V. *Sobranie sochinenii,* edited by A. N. Nikoliukin. Moscow: Respublika, 1994–2010.

Rozanov, V. V. *Sumerki prosveshcheniia: sbornik statei po voprosam obrazovaniia.* St. Petersburg: Tipografiia M. Merkusheva, 1899.

Rozanov, V. V. "Tema nashego vremeni." In Nikoliukin, *Sobranie sochineniia,* vol. 10, *Vo dvore iazychnikov* (1999), 167–71.

Rozanov, V. V. "Zametka o Merezhkovskom." In Nikoliukin, *Sobranie sochineniia,* vol.7, *Legenda o velikom inkvizitore* (1996), 446–47.

Rozanov, V. V. "Zvezdy." *Mir iskusstva* 7–8 (1901): 69–78.

Rosenshield, Gary. *The Ridiculous Jew: The Exploitation and Transformation of a Stereotype in Gogol, Turgenev, and Dostoevsky.* Stanford, CA: Stanford University Press, 2008.

Rosenthal, Bernice Glatzer. "The Transmutation of Symbolist Ethos: Mystical Anarchism and the Revolution of 1905." *Slavic Review* 36, no. 4 (December 1977): 608–27.

Rosenthal, Bernice Glatzer. "From Decadence to Religion: Ivanov and Merezhkovskij." In *Cultura e memoria: Atti del terzo Simposio Internazionale dedicato a Vjačeslav Ivanov,* edited by Fausto Malcovati, 141–50. Florence, 1988.

Rzhevsky, Nicholas. *The Modern Russian Theater: A Literary and Cultural History.* Armonk, NY: M. E. Sharpe, 2009.

S. "Obshchestvo Iskusstva i Literatury." *Artist* 18 (December 1891): 126–28.

Sakharov, V. I. "Dostoevskii, simvolisty i Aleksandr Blok." In *Dostoevskii: materialy i issledovaniia,* vol. 6, edited by G. M. Fridlender, 168–73. Leningrad: Nauka, 1985.

Sedgwick, Eve Kosofsky. "Paranoid Reading and Reparative Reading, or, You're So Paranoid, You Probably Think This Essay Is about You." In *Touching Feeling: Affect, Pedagogy, Performativity,* 123–51. Durham, NC: Duke University Press, 2002.

Seduro, Vladimir. *Dostoevsky in Russian and World Theatre.* North Quincy, MA: Christopher Publishing, 1977.

Semenova, Svetlana. *Nikolai Fedorov: Tvorchestvo zhizni.* Moscow: Sovetskii pisatel', 1990.

Sh., L. [Lev Shestov]. "Dostoevskii i Nitshe. (Filosofiia tragedii.). Predislovie." *Mir iskusstva* 2 (1902): 69–79.

Sh., L. [Lev Shestov]. "Pokhvala gluposti." In Chulkov, *Fakely,* kn. 2, 137–62.

Sh., V. "Besy." *Novoe vremia,* October 1, 1907.

Shklovsky, Viktor. *Za i protiv. Zametki o Dostoevskom.* Moscow: Sovetskii pisatel', 1957.

Skeptik. "Vslukh." *Grazhdanin* 86 (November 7, 1899): 7.

Skvortsova, N. V. "Aleksandr Blok v stat'e Andreiia Belogo 'Khimery.'" In *Blokovskii sbornik,* vyp. 657, edited by Z. G. Mints, 88–95. Tartu: Uchenye zapiski Tartuskogo gosudarstvennogo universiteta, 1985.

Slonim, Marc. *Russian Theater: From the Empire to the Soviets.* Cleveland, OH: World, 1961.

Smirnov, I. I. *Besy (Nikolai Stavrogin). Stseny iz romana F. M. Dostoevskogo v 6 kartinakh.* 1908. SPbGTB. ORiRK. Access number: 35302; litograficheskii tekst: S 506.

Smirnov, V. B. *F. M. Dostoevskii i russkaia demokraticheskaia zhurnalistika 70–80–kh godov.* Volgograd: Izdatel'stvo Volgogradskogo gos. universiteta, 1996.

Sobolev, A. L. "Merezhkovskie v Parizhe (1906–1908)." *Litsa. Biograficheskii al'manakh,* vol. 1 (1992): 319–71.

Sokolov, P. "Vera (Psikhologicheskii etiud)." *Voprosy filosofii i psikhologii,* kn. 2-4, no. 62: 909–33; no. 63: 1158–94; no. 64: 1305–62 (1902).

Solov'ev, Vladimir. "Referat V. S. Solov'eva, chitannyi v zasedanii Moskovskogo Psikhologicheskogo Obshchestva, 19-ogo oktiabria 1891 goda." *Voprosy filosofii i psikhologii,* no. 56 (1901): 138–52.

Solov'ev, Vladimir. "Prilozhenie. Zametka v zashchitu Dostoevskogo ot obvineniia v 'novom' khristianstve." In *Tri rechi v pamiat' Dostoevskogo (1881–1883 gg.).* Moscow: V Universitetskoi tipografii na Strastnom bul'vare (M. Katkov), 1884.

Solov'ev, Vladimir. "Russkii natsional'nyi ideal (Po povodu stat'i N. Ia Grota v 'Voprosakh Filosofii i Psikhologii')." In *Sobranie sochinenii,* vol. 5, 379–87. St. Petersburg: Obshchestvennaia pol'za, 1901.

Solov'ev, Vladimir. *Tri rechi v pamiat' Dostoevskogo (1881–1883 gg.).* Moscow: V Universitetskoi tipografii na Strastnom bul'vare (M. Katkov), 1884.

Solov'eva, I. N. *Nemirovich-Danchenko.* Moscow: Iskusstvo, 1979.

Solov'eva, I. N. "Nikolai Stavrogin." In *Moskovskii khudozhestvennyi teatr 100 let,* vol. 1, edited by I. N. Solov'eva and O. V. Egoshina. Moscow: Izd. MKhT, 1998.

Solus [K. I. Arabazhin]. "Moskovskii khudozhestvennyi teatr. 'Nikolai Stavrogin,' Otryvki iz romana F. M. Dostoevskogo 'Besy.'" *Birzhevye vedomosti,* April 8, 1914.

Stènson, N. *Rytsar' bednyi. Dramaticheskie stseny v 5 deistviiakh v 6 kartinakh.* Soch. N. Stènson (Peredelano iz romana F. M. Dostoevskogo). 1893. SPbGTB. ORiRK. Access number: 45455, rukopisnyi tekst, S 887.

Stepan, Nancy Leys. "Race and Gender: The Role of Analogy in Science." In *The Anatomy of Racism,* edited by David Theo Goldberg, 38–57. Minneapolis: University of Minnesota Press, 1990.

Stoler, Ann Laura. "Racial Histories and Their Regimes of Truth." *Political Power and Social Theory* 11 (1997): 183–206.

Stuelke, Patricia. *The Ruse of Repair: US Neoliberal Empire and the Turn from Critique.* Durham, NC: Duke University Press, 2021.

Sutugin, Sergei. *Brat'ia Karamazovy: Drama v 5 d. i 8 kart.* St. Petersburg: Izdanie S. Rassokhina, 1910.

Sutugin, Sergei. "Mysli o teatre." *Teatr i iskusstvo* 3 (1902): 51–52; 4 (1902): 75–78; 5 (1902): 99–101.

Suvorin, A. S. *Dnevnik A. S. Suvorina.* Moscow: Izd. L. D. Frenkel', 1923.

Suvorin, A. S. "O pokoinom." In *F. M. Dostoevskii v vospominaniiakh sovremennikov,* vol. 2, edited by K. Tiun'kin and M. Tiun'kina, 465–73. Moscow: Khudozhestvennaia literatura, 1990.

Suvorin, A. S. *V ozhidanii veka XX. Malen'kie pis'ma, 1889–1903 gg.* Moscow: Algoritm, 2005.

Suvorov, I. A. "Dekoratsiia epiloga." *Teatr i iskusstvo* 42 (1899): 734.

Swift, E. Anthony. "Fighting the Germs of Disorder: The Censorship of Russian Popular Theater, 1888–1917." *Russian History* 18, no. 1 (Spring 1991): 1–49.

Swift, E. Anthony. *Popular Theater and Society in Tsarist Russia*. Berkeley: University of California Press, 2002.

Swift, E. Anthony. "Russia." In *The Frightful Stage: Political Censorship of the Theater in Nineteenth-Century Europe*, edited by Robert Justin Goldstein, 130–61. New York: Berghahn, 2009.

Tal'nikov, D. [D. L. Shpital'nikov]. "Besovskoe navazhdenie." *Sovremennyi mir* 11 (1913): 202–14.

"Teatr. Tekushchii repertuar." *Severnyi vestnik* 3 (1895): 40–48.

"Teatr i muzyka." *Sankt-peterburgskaia viedomosti* 304 (November 6/18, 1899).

"Teatr i muzyka. Instsenirovannye 'Besy.' (Beseda s Vl. I. Nemirovichem-Danchenko)." *Russkoe slovo*, August 17, 1913 (O.S.).

Terras, Victor. *Reading Dostoevsky*. Madison: University of Wisconsin Press, 1998.

"The Muscovite Genius." *New York Times*, December 6, 1902.

Thurston, Gary. *The Popular Theatre Movement in Russia, 1862–1919*. Evanston, IL: Northwestern University Press, 1998.

Tihanov, Galin. *The Birth and Death of Literary Theory: Regimes of Relevance in Russia and Beyond*. Stanford, CA: Stanford University Press, 2019.

Tolz, Vera. "Constructing Race, Ethnicity, and Nationhood in Imperial Russia: Issues and Misconceptions." In *Ideologies of Race: Imperial Russia and the Soviet Union in Global Context*, edited by David Rainbow, 29–58. Montreal: McGill-Queens University Press, 2019.

Tolz [Tol'ts], Vera. "Diskursy o *rase*: imperskaia Rossiia i Zapad v sravnenii." In *"Poniatiia o Rossii"*, vol. 2, edited by I. A. Miller et al., 146–93.

Trofimov, Zhores, ed. *V. N. Andreev-Burlak: pamiat' i nasledie*. Ul'ianovsk: Simbirskaia kniga, 1995.

Trutovskii, K. A. "Vospominaniia o Fedore Mikhailoviche Dostoevskom. Materialy dlia kharakteristiki russkikh pisatelei." *Russkoe obozrenie* 1 (1893): 212–17.

Tsebrikova, M. "Dvoistvennoe tvorchestvo." *Slovo* 2 (1881): 1–30.

Ure, Adam. *Vasilii Rozanov and the Creation: The Edenic Vision and the Rejection of Eschatology*. London: Continuum, 2011.

V. L. "Khronika teatra i isskustva." *Teatr i iskusstvo* 41 (1899): 711.

Varneke, B. V. *History of the Russian Theatre*, translated by Boris Brasol. New York: Hafner, 1971.

Vassena, Raffaella. "Populiarnyi Dostoevskii: nachalo massovogo rasprostraneniia tvorcheskogo naslediia, 1881–1906." *Russian Literature* 111–112 (2020): 1–34.

Vengerov, S. "Dostoevskii i prichiny ego populiarnosti v poslednie gody." In *Otklik. Literaturnyi sbornik. V pol'zu studentov i slushatel'nits vysshikh zhenskikh kursov goroda SPb*, 277–95. St. Petersburg: Tipografiia A. S. Suvorina, 1881.

Verner, Andrew M. *The Crisis of Russian Autocracy: Nicholas II and the 1905 Revolution*. Princeton, NJ: Princeton University Press, 1990.

"Vesti otovsiudu." *Zolotoe runo* 11–12 (1906): 149.

Viktorov, D. V. "Pamiati N. Ia. Grota kak professora." In *Nikolai Iakovlevich Grot: v ocherkakh, vospominaniiakh i pis'makh tovarishchei i uchenikov, druzei i pochitatelei*, 175–85. St. Petersburg: Tipografiia Ministerstva Putei Soobshcheniia, 1911.

Vita Brevis. "Idiot." *Russkii listok* 280 (October 13, 1899).

Vitiugova, I. A. "I. L. Leont'ev-Shcheglov i F. M. Dostoevskii." In *Dostoevskii. Materialy i issledovaniia*, vol. 11, edited by G. M. Fridlender, 271–90. St. Petersburg: Nauka, 1994.

Volgin, I. L. "Dostoevskii i pravitel'stvennaia politika v oblasti prosveshcheniia (1881–1917)." In *Dostoevskii: Materialy i issledovaniia*, vol. 4, edited by G. M. Fridlender, 192–206. Leningrad: Nauka, 1980.

Volgin, I. L. *Poslednii god Dostoevskogo*. Moscow: Sovetskii pisatel', 1986.

Volynskii, A. L. *Bor'ba za idealizm*. St. Petersburg: Tipografiia M. Merkusheva, 1900.

Volynskii, A. L. *Kniga velikogo gneva*. St. Petersburg: Trud, 1904.

Volynskii, A. L. "O simvolizme i simvolistakh. (Polemicheskaia zametka)." In *Bor'ba za idealizm*, 477–87.

Volynskii, A. L. "Sovremennaia russkaia belletristika." In *Kniga velikogo gneva*, 167–99.

Volynskii, A. L. "Tragediia krasoty. 'Idiot.'" In *Dostoevskii*, 24–71. St. Petersburg: Obshchestvennaia pol'za, 1909.

Volynskii, A. L. *Tsarstvo Karamazovykh. N. S. Leskov. Zametki*. St. Petersburg: Tipografiia M. M. Stasiulevicha, 1901.

Volzhskii [A. S. Glinka]. "Avtobiograficheskie zapiski." In *Ss v trekh knigakh*, kn. 1, edited by Anna Reznichenko, 726–34. Moscow: Modest Kolerov, 2005.

Volzhskii [A. S. Glinka]. *Dva ocherka ob Uspenskom i Dostoevskom*. St. Petersburg: Tipografiia M. M. Stasiulevicha, 1902.

Volzhskii [A. S. Glinka]. "Literaturnyi otdel." *Kriticheskoe obozrenie* 1 (1907): 26–29.

Volzhskii [A. S. Glinka]. "Religiozno-nravstvennaia problema u Dostoevskogo." *Mir Bozhii* 6: 161–78; 7: 109–32; 8: 137–60 (1905).

Volzhskii [A. S. Glinka]. "Torzhestvuiushchii amoralizm (Po povodu 'Russkogo Fausta' A. Lunacharskogo)." *Voprosy filosofii i psikhologii*, kn. 4, no. 64 (1902): 889–905.

V—n, A. "Review of *Istoriko-kriticheskii kommentarii* . . ." *Vestnik Evropy* 5 (1885): 408–10.

Ward, Bruce K. "Dostoevsky and the Hermeneutics of Suspicion." *Literature and Theology* 11, no. 3 (September 1997): 270–83.

Weiner, Adam. *By Authors Possessed: The Demonic Novel in Russia*. Evanston, IL: Northwestern University Press, 1998.

West, James. *Russian Symbolism: A Study of Viacheslav Ivanov and the Russian Symbolist Aesthetic*. London: Methuen, 1970.

Williams, Rowan, ed. *Sergii Bulgakov: Towards a Russian Political Theology*. Edinburgh: T&T Clark, 1999.

Worrall, Nick. *The Moscow Art Theatre*. London: Routledge, 1996.

Wortman, Richard. *Scenarios of Power: Myth and Ceremony in Russian Monarchy from Peter the Great to the Abdication of Nicholas II*. Princeton, NJ: Princeton University Press, 2006.

Z., S. "Filosofskie vozzreniia Vladimira Solov'eva. Otchet o lektsii prof. S. N. Bulgakova v g. Kieve i stenograficheskaia zapis' prenii." *Novyi put'* 3 (1904): 71–104.

Z., S. "Zapiski o filosofskikh preniiakh. (Mezhdu N. A. Berdiaevym i M. B. Ratnerom)." *Novyi put'* 3 (1904): 212–42.

Zabuzhko, Oksana. "No Guilty People in the World? Reading Russian Literature after Bucha." *Times Literary Supplement*, April 22, 2022.

Zakharov, Vladimir. "The Dostoevsky Syndrome," translated by Aura Young. In Apollonio and Fitzpatrick, *The New Russian Dostoevsky*, 9–24.

Zakharov, Vladimir. "Paradoksy priznaniia: problema 'traditsii Dostoevskogo' v kul'ture XX veka." In *Dostoevsky and the Twentieth Century: The Ljubljana Papers*, edited by Malcolm V. Jones, 19–35. Nottingham, UK: Astra, 1993.

"Zapiski religioznykh-filosofskikh sobranii v S.-Peterburge. Zasedanie XVI. (Okonchanie prenii o brake)." *Novyi put'* 10 (1903): 263–420.

Zelinskii, V., ed. "Predislovie." In *Istoriko-kriticheskii kommentarii k sochineniiam F. M. Dostoevskogo*, vol. 1. Moscow: Tip. T. Malinskogo, 1885.

Ziolkowski, Margaret. "Dostoevsky and the Kenotic Tradition." In *Dostoevsky and the Christian Tradition*, edited by George Pattison and Diane Oenning Thompson, 31–40. Cambridge: Cambridge University Press, 2001.

Zograf, N. G. *Malyi teatr v kontse XIX–nachale XX veka*. Moscow: Nauka, 1966.

Zwahlen, Regula M. "Sergei Bulgakov's Intellectual Journey, 1900–1922." In *The Oxford Handbook of Russian Religious Thought*, edited by Caryl Emerson, George Pattison, and Randall A. Poole. Oxford: Oxford University Press, 2020.

Zwahlen, Regula M. "Sergii Bulgakov's Reinvention of Theocracy for a Democratic Age." *Journal of Orthodox Christian Studies* 3, no. 2 (2020): 175–94.

Index

Page locators in *italics* indicate illustrations.

adaptation. *See* theater adaptations

Adolescent, The (Dostoevsky), 34

Aleksandrinka theater, 20, 27, 32, 35, 37, 164n65, 165n85

Aleksandrov, V. *See* Krylov, Viktor

Alexander III, 22–23, 25–26

anarchism, 81, 83, 86. *See also* mystical anarchism

Andreev, Leonid, 96, 114, 134; *Beloved Specters* (play), 149–51, 153–55

antisemitism: Dostoevsky's, 6, 12, 52; late-imperial Russian, 15, 25, 50–51, 69; Merezhkovsky's, 62–66, 69, 106, 131; Rozanov's, 50–51, 59–60. *See also* Semitism

apocalypticism, 28, 33, 35, 46, 65, 73, 112–13, 122, 155

Aryanism: Merezhkovsky on, 15, 49–50, 62–66, 68, 70, 116; Rozanov on, 52–53, 55, 59; terminology of, 49–52

asceticism, 45, 49–50, 53, 65, 67

atheism, 105, 108–9, 153, 175n55; in *The Brothers Karamazov*, 15, 77, 82, 87–89, 108, 119, 125, 175n55; in *Crime and Punishment*, 21, 30–31; in *Devils*, 88, 105, 127, 132, 143; in *The Idiot*, 21, 29, 35, 37

author/character relationship: character as creator, 118–21, 123–25; character as mouthpiece, 81–82, 88, 105–6, 147, 179n6, 187n65; idealists on, 73–75, 79, 93, 95–96

author/critic relationship: as continuing legacy, 106–8, 111, 117, 125, 140; critic's primacy, 100–101, 104, 110, 119, 121, 124–25, 150; "overcoming" of author, 111–14

Bakhtin, Mikhail, 6–7, 74, 95–96, 111

Bal'mont, Konstantin, 3, 73–74, 111, 147

Belyi, Andrei, 16, 54, 99, 111–14, 121–22, 124, 153

Benois, Alexander, 139–40

Berdiaev, Nikolai: as idealist, 75, 77–79, 85, 135, 177n81; influence of, 2, 46, 74, 111; on Ivan Karamazov, 15, 85–88, 90–91, 123; *New Path/Vital Questions* editorship, 63, 96–97, 122; Russian liberalism and, 85, 93–94, 97

Bible. *See* New Testament; Old Testament

biographical criticism. *See* criticism

Blok, Aleksandr, 99, 113

Bloody Sunday, 1–2, 98

Briusov, Valery, 97, 99, 103, 114–15, 122, 124

Brothers Karamazov, The (Dostoevsky): atheism in, 15, 77, 82, 87–89, 108, 119, 125, 175n55; Bulgakov on, 15, 74–77, 79–80, 83–88, 90–92, 94; Dostoevsky on, 26, 81, 89–90; early reception of, 10, 27, 77–78, 80, 82; faith/Orthodoxy in, 7–8, 15, 25, 40, 79, 87–88, 106–8, 123, 147; idealists' identification with Ivan, 15, 75–78, 80–83, 86–97; Merezhkovsky on, 106–8, 149, 151–53; Moscow Art Theater's adaptation of, 16–17, 22–23, 126, 134–35, 138, 140–42, 151, 161n5, 185n17; Rozanov on, 52, 54, 70, 74, 78, 92, 96, 100, 112; Symbolists on, 73, 115–21, 125, 137; writing/publishing of, 11, 46–47, 81–82, 101

Buddhism, 69, 170n66